BEing Jesus' WALKing and TALKing Disciple

How the Holy Spirit will GROW
your daily discipleship
so you will GO make disciples

BEing Jesus' WALKing and TALKing Disciple

How the Holy Spirit will GROW
your daily discipleship
so you will GO make disciples

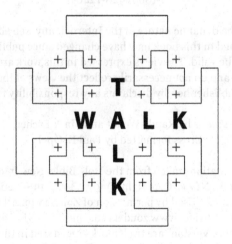

Randy Michael Wendt

WESTBOW
P R E S S
A DIVISION OF THOMAS NELSON

WestBow Press books may be ordered through booksellers or by contacting:

WestBow Press
A Division of Thomas Nelson
1663 Liberty Drive
Bloomington, IN 47403
www.westbowpress.com
1-(866) 928-1240

Photos by Randy Wendt and Mark Escher;
Cross formatted by Paul E. Opel

ISBN: 978-1-4497-9637-2 (sc)
ISBN: 978-1-4497-9638-9 (hc)
ISBN: 978-1-4497-9636-5 (e)

Library of Congress Control Number: 2013909893

Printed in the United States of America.

WestBow Press rev. date: 12/23/2013

Table of Contents

Preface

God begins His walk with us at our birth. From the time we are conceived in our mother's womb, God knows us and calls us by name. "This is what the Lord says—he who made you, who formed you in the womb..." (Isaiah 44:2a) He already has a design and plan for each of us. His desire is to see His perfect plan for us happen! "But now, this is what the Lord says—he who created you, O Jacob, he who formed you, O Israel: 'Fear not, for I have redeemed you; I have summoned you by name; you are mine. When you pass through the waters, I will be with you; and when you pass through the rivers, they will not sweep over you. When you walk through the fire, you will not be burned; the flames will not set you ablaze." (Isaiah 43:1-2)

What can stand in the way? We can! God has given us a free choice within an understanding of what is right and wrong. We can choose to walk with Him or not walk with Him. We can choose to follow Him or fall far away from Him. Adam and Eve made that choice, listening to the Devil's tempting voice through the serpent, and the rest is his-story.

God was not content to order a recall on His creation. Nor was He content to throw Adam and Eve back on His potter's wheel and reshape a new man and woman from the dust He originally used. No, He knew what to do and when to do it!

God sent His Son, our Savior Jesus, to take upon Himself the punishment for our sins. As a result, we would no longer be separated from God. God did it all and continues to do it all so that we can daily WALK with Him.

God gives us this costliest of all gifts for free. We can receive or reject it, realizing that there is nothing we can do to earn it. God has done it all for us through our Savior Jesus. Through our baptism, the Holy Spirit creates a saving faith in each of us. But His work doesn't stop there.

God gives us the Holy Spirit, not only creating faith to receive His gift, but also the constant companionship we need to continue that WALK He began with us in and through our baptism. Through our baptism, we have been crucified with our Savior Jesus in order that we might rise to newness of life...and WALK in that new life every day! He also gives us many life experiences that help shape our TALK about Him and for Him!

God so desires a daily WALK with His children that He gives us everything we need to journey with us for as long as we remain in these temporary tents. The joy of God's WALK with us doesn't end at our death. God through our Savior Jesus has gone ahead and prepared a permanent dwelling for each of us. We will WALK from death into life at the end of our day. Until then, the daily reminder of our baptism encourages the Holy Spirit to drown the old man with all its' sinfully self-centered ways and desires so that the new man can emerge. We are clothed in our Savior Jesus and empowered by His Holy Spirit to WALK, to bear fruit, to perform good works, and to tell others the story that has unfolded in our life...and can, by God's grace and mercy alone, unfold in theirs!

All that God does in, with, and through us becomes our shared TALKing points. Everyone loves a good story. We all desire to hear some good news, don't we? God talks to us through His Word. The Bible remains a marvelous and miraculous collection of divinely-revealed desires for His redeemed and restored daughters and sons. His own Holy Spirit speaks His words aloud through His WALKing disciples for a purpose—to make other daily WALKing disciples. Their life, in turn, with Him becomes a TALKing one from their shared perspective.

God has laid out the roadmap for the journey of your life, both this side of heaven on earth and the life we will WALK one day, face to face, with God in heaven. Aren't you ready to WALK that WALK with Him today? Right now? When you only know for certain, you have this day?

All that you discover, all that you encounter becomes the stuff of a TALKing disciple's life and word witness. Don't you have one life changing story to share with those the Holy Spirit will bring to you? Don't you have a daily disciple's story of transformation He will encourage and prompt you to share with someone's eager ears listening?

From the time I began preparing this book, I've had several new stops along the way. They were stops I didn't anticipate sharing with you. By the time you finish this book, my prayer is that you, too, will have a renewed WALK and TALK as Jesus daily disciple, too!

May the companionship of God's own Holy Spirit comfort and engage you as you WALK and TALK with Jesus, who desires to bear much fruit through you!

Introduction

You have come to know God as your Father, Savior, and Comforter. Your WALK with God began and continues while the devil will roll out every obstacle in his arsenal to thwart you!

I invite you to take the time to read all the Scriptures that are cited. Let these key verses light up like neon in your mind's eye. Reread paragraphs so you understand what's being discussed before moving on. Unlike a live lecture, you can always go back as many times as necessary to make sure you've grasped the concept for your own life application.

You may be a note taker. You may be a highlighter. You may be one who underlines. You may read through a book the first time in chunks, coming back for a second tour of details. Pray for God's own Holy Spirit to enlighten your heart and mind. Pray that God's own Holy Spirit will open all your senses to the message He wants you to receive from Him for this day. Come back often and reread a section or chapter to see if it provides the necessary direction at the mile marker you seek on this day of your WALK and TALK with God!

I love index cards! Ask anyone who knows me or who's participated in a course I teach! I've always brought a small pocket full of index cards containing scriptures I've prospected or revelations or teachings God's own Holy Spirit has chosen to give me for the day. I encourage you to do the same. Jot down ideas and date them. Keep one card per idea or scripture passage. Reflect on God's Word with the words He reveals to you. Invite God to speak to you through His Word in the version you've claimed as your own!

Grab an envelope and keep all your index cards from the revelations and teachings you've received from this book. Consider the envelope like a slow cooker. Let them stew with you as they simmer. Pull them out and savor them. See what God will continue to reveal to you about His daily WALK and TALK with you!

Consider stopping along the way within and between chapters by completing the "road marker" exercises. Purely optional, they will help you learn more about yourself and your WALK and TALK in light of what God has and will reveal to you on the daily journey.

If you're sharing this book in a small group study, share your responses with others. It's such a blessing to be on the journey together. Pray God will enlighten your path with fellow travelers like the two on the road to Emmaus. Ask God for the holy heartburn He would desire to give you and keep rekindling every time He reveals His Word to you for your WALK! Jot down so you don't forget His TALK with you and the dialogue than ensues. Weeks later, you'll appreciate these TALK points. You'll discover where the Lord has brought you from. You'll discover where you're heading to on your daily discipleship with Him!

PART ONE:

WALKing as Jesus' Disciple

- "Whoever claims to live in him must WALK as Jesus did."

    1 John 2:6

- "I know, O Lord, that a man's life is not his own; It is not for man to direct his steps."

    Jeremiah 10:23

- "I guide you in the way of wisdom and lead you along straight paths. When you walk, your steps will not be hampered; when you run, you will not stumble; Hold on to instruction, do not let it go; guard it well, for it is your life."

    Proverbs 4:11-13

- "But we have this treasure in jars of clay to show that this all-surpassing power is from God and not from us."

    2 Corinthians 4:7

- And God is able to make all grace abound to you, so that in all things at all times, having all that you need, you will abound in every good work."

    2 Corinthians 9:8

- So then, just as you received Christ Jesus as Lord, continue to live in him, rooted and built up in him, strengthened in the faith as you were taught, and overflowing with thankfulness."

Colossians 2:6-7

Chapter One

Who walks with God in the Bible?

The Bible tells the stories of those who have walked with God throughout its' historical pages. Their stories inspire us to learn more about the nature of God and how He chooses to create and maintain a distinctly unique relationship with each of us. No doubt some similarities exist. They can help us paint the picture of an almighty, all-knowing God who desires to walk with each of us as we make time for Him.

God had such a relationship with His first created human beings, Adam and Eve. Genesis 3:8 describes Adam and Eve's fellowship with God, "Then the man and his wife heard the sound of the Lord God as he was walking in the garden in the cool of the day, and they hid from the Lord God among the trees of the garden." God didn't desire to create and abandon. God wished to be involved in the lives of His children through a daily relationship with them. It's the same case with us, thousands of years later. God never changes. God's desire to be our Creator and Sustainer never changes either despite our fall into sin.

As we read and reflect through the pages that follow, we see by

Genesis 6 that the man and the world had become so evil and wicked, that God grieved! God grieved that man and animals and the earth were impacted by sin. God was no longer content to leave things as they had become. He determined to destroy everything and everyone, except for Noah and his family. God's relationship with Noah, described in Genesis 6:9, was of one who walked with God. God would establish a covenant with the only righteous ones left by preserving their lives in an ark, along with pairs of every animal. As they exited the ark after the great flood, God promised never again to destroy the earth by flood waters. Noah's walk with God continued as He blessed and multiplied life.

Beyond an unfinished tower in Babel, God calls Abram in order to make a substantial nation from him and Sarai (Genesis 12). Off they go, with all their possessions, at 75 years of age to continue on a walk with God to a land they knew not. Knowing God would remain faithful in His walk with them because God keeps His promises, the walk was not without bumps and disappointments. Abram sought to get ahead of God in the timing of offspring (Genesis 16), which caused problems down the road for them all.

What happens to us when we seem to get in the way and meddle with God's plans for us? Do we run out of patience, thinking we know what's best? In the end, when the dust settles, do we regret our tinkering? Like with us, God hangs in there with Abram and Sarai despite their taking things into their own hands. God shows His faithfulness to them, revealing His plan for them and the direction their walk with Him will take in the coming days (Genesis 17). Over time and circumstances, including a transformation of person and name, Abraham and Sarah see the fruit of their faith, "Now the Lord was gracious to Sarah as he had said, and the Lord did for Sarah what he had promised. Sarah became pregnant and bore a son to Abraham in his old age, at the very time God had promised him." (Genesis 21:1-2)

God not only delivers His promises to those who walk with Him, but He also is known to test them along the way. Such a test Abraham faced. Why wouldn't Abraham think God was crazy? Take and sacrifice your only son? The son of your old age and a barren wife?

[Editorial note: If you see text in Italics, you've come upon an interactive opportunity called a Road Marker (RM). I hope you choose to stop and engage in the inner discussion. You may also choose to document your responses.]

> *ROAD MARKER (RM): What cries and complaints flood your mind and escape your mouth as God appears to be testing you? Would you have spoken so?*

Not intending to have Abraham kill his son, God wanted to know how much faith Abraham had in God and the stretchability of his faith.

> RM: *Recall the times in your walk with God where you felt God testing your faith to see how stretchable it can be? How have you benefited from such an experience?*

Consider how Abraham and God walked even closer together as a result of this test. God speaks through an angel of the Lord by reiterating His promise and covenant with Abraham and the generations that would follow.

> RM: *How has God reassured you of His promises to you at the end of His testing you? How is it a sure sign of the walking nature of God with His children?*

God continues to walk with His people through the lives of Isaac and his son Jacob and the sons of Jacob as you journey through the pages of Genesis further.

> RM: *Skim over these chapters and see where you can find references to the walk God takes with His people. See what additional insights you can discover for your daily discipleship with Jesus!*

God fulfills His promises to make a strong nation of Israel in the days following Jacob's migration into Egypt. God used the misdeeds of Joseph's brothers to preserve his life. Joseph uses his visionary powers from God to preserve life during years of plenty and years of famine. Hear his testimony to his brothers. How would you have felt and spoke in the same way Joseph did? "And now, do not be distressed and do not be angry with yourselves for selling me here, because it was to save lives that God sent me ahead of you. For two years now there has been famine in the land, and for the next five years there will not be plowing and reaping. But God sent me ahead of you to preserve for you a remnant on earth to save your lives by a great deliverance." (Genesis 45:5-7).

> RM: *Consider a time during your daily discipleship where you couldn't understand what was happening and why? How much did you chalk it up to God's*

directing hand or your own sinful decisions? How did you feel anticipating "after the dust settled," all your why's might be answered?

Over the next centuries, the seventy who went down to Egypt would become the consummate nation God had intended, promised, and delivered! "Now Joseph and all his brothers and all that generation died, but the Israelites were fruitful and multiplied greatly and became exceedingly numerous, so that the land was filled with them." (Exodus 1:6-7). So much so, that a new king of Egypt, who knew nothing about Joseph, felt more than threatened by his homeland being filled to overflowing with non-Egyptians!

How would God change the course of His walk with His covenanted people? Fulfilling His promise, Israel became as many as the stars in the sky and the sands of the sea. But would that be it? Would they now languish in slavery and misery? "During that long period, the king of Egypt died. The Israelites groaned in their slavery and cried out, and their cry for help because of their slavery went up to God. God heard their groaning and he remembered his covenant with Abraham, with Isaac and with Jacob."(Exodus 2:23-24)

Why would God have allowed this to happen? What benefit would come out of such a situation of slavery? Why would God seem to be so slow in delivering His people and pursuing His promise of a Promised Land for His people?

> RM: *Where have there been times in your walk with God where you felt God led you to a barren desert with no sight or sound of Him in your life? Does God walk along with us only so far and then abandon us?*

Have you come to know otherwise as the children of Israel would come to know? God does hear our cry. God does hear our prayer. God does love and care and want to provide for us. (Isn't that what Jesus meant by teaching us to pray? Read Matthew 6:9-13.)

Do we have the patience and perseverance to wait upon God as we walk with Him and He walks with us? It's necessary, you know! God doesn't see things the way we see them. " 'For my thoughts are not your thoughts, neither are your ways my ways,' declares the Lord. 'As the heavens are higher than the earth, so are my ways higher than your ways and my thoughts than your thoughts.'" (Isaiah 55:8-9).

We read that God's sense of time isn't our sense of time in 2 Peter 3:8, "But do not forget this one thing, dear friends: With the Lord a day is like a thousand years and a thousand years are like a day." That's why God has to be leading us in our walk with Him and not the other way around. Forty years later, Moses would see the plight of God's people right before his eyes. He, too, like Abram, would try to do something about it rather than wait for God's actions. As a result of killing the Egyptian taskmaster, Moses fled Egypt and any possible punishment for his actions.

God's walk with Moses just didn't begin and end with him as a baby in the bulrushes! Years later, God would use the life circumstances of Moses to journey in a walk with God that would overwhelm most people! It surely overwhelmed Moses for all the excuses he came up with in his attempt to turn God down on His offer. Read for yourself the dialogue back and forth between God and Moses in Exodus 3:11-4:17.

Look at all the bantering back and forth between Moses and God. For every weak excuse Moses gave, God countered with a strong reason why God had faith enough in Moses to be used by Him! It even got to the point where God's anger was not just limited to a burning bush but against Moses himself!

God won out. He had worn Moses down with all the visible, viable resources only Almighty God could muster to equip Moses to walk down this road with Him!

> RM: *Have you been worn down by God during a particular bend or path on His walk with you? What can you learn from Moses experience here? Does it actually pay to go contrary to the will of God as God chooses to reveal it to you? (Just ask Jonah!) Through it all, God remains faithful to those who walk with Him, doesn't He?*

Through His words and actions, God works through Moses and his brother Aaron. The plagues come and go. God remains faithful through them all. The ultimate testing of Pharaoh becomes the foreshadowing of our own rescue from the slavery of sin on the night of the Passover (Exodus 12).

It was necessary to do exactly what God told them, wasn't it? If they took it upon themselves, not to slaughter the lamb, putting blood on both sides of the doorframe and remaining inside until morning, what would have been their fate? What God says to those who walk with Him, He doesn't suggest or strongly recommend. He says, "Obey!" (Exodus 12:24)

Wouldn't God deal with you in a similar way? If we debate, question, disagree, fail to follow, what will our outcome be?

What has it been? (Remember this point when long after they're on the road to the Promised Land, they disobey God and take more than they ought of God's provision for them for the day as He commanded! Exodus 16:20 reveals that those who disregarded God's instructions through Moses, keeping part of it until morning, found it was "full of maggots and began to smell."

Just like the Israelites, I find myself, and my walk with Him, more crooked when I take it upon myself to know and do what I think is best. Maybe that's why we ought to read, heed, and put into practice Proverbs 3:5-6, "Trust in the Lord with all your heart and lean not on your own understanding; in all your ways acknowledge him, and he will make your paths straight." What is God's promise for those that do so? He will make our paths straight!

> RM: *Recall the times you needed your crooked paths straightened out by God because you knew better. Just how crooked can they get? Why would we not look to the Almighty and All-knowing God first and trust His direction? Is it no wonder, in the end, that we often turn to Him to sort them out and get us back on track again?*

God is a highly detailed God, isn't He? He supplies us with all the expectations of how we ought to live, and love Him and our fellow man within the Ten Commandments. Reading the remainder of Exodus through Leviticus, we read page upon page, sentence upon sentence of the details of how things should be set up, how worship should be conducted, how we ought to treat each other. God stands ready to give us more than enough details for our welfare. Do we stand ready to follow every letter of every word He shares with us?

God is an exceptionally patient God, isn't He? Would you ever have the patience of God? Skimming through the Book of Numbers, we see the people complaining they can't do what God asks them to do. They're afraid they aren't strong enough to take possession of the land God told them to take. (Numbers 13:17-33) Would we blame Israel's response, second guessing and complaining before God, "If only? Why, God?" (Numbers 14:1-4)

So, why did God's children spend over 40 years to make a 10 day journey? Why did only two out of the original two million enter in to the promised land? Why would it have to do with disagreeing and disobeying with God? (Confirm your answer within Numbers 14:20-38)

> RM: *During a recent disagreement with God describe your thoughts and feelings within your dialogue with God. What was the outcome and how were you better or worse because of it?*

Those not daily walking with God would think God must not actually care. God only wants to take care of those who obey Him. God must only love those who love Him in return. Not true! Both the Old and New Testament give an account of the very nature of God in His dealings with sinful human beings like us. Here, as, we stop at Numbers 14:18, what can we learn about the loving nature and desire God has to be just? " 'The Lord is slow to anger, abounding in love and forgiving sin and rebellion. Yet he does not leave the guilty unpunished...' " God also reminds us through the words of His prophet Isaiah, " 'Let the wicked forsake his way and the evil man his thoughts. Let him turn to the Lord, and he will have mercy on him, and to our God, for he will freely pardon.' " (Isaiah 55:7)

> RM: *Recall how God has treated you in response to Numbers 14:18. Consider a time when you were bent on going your own direction in opposition to God. How did the opportunity for contrition (feeling sorry) and repentance (turning away from sin) finally arrive?*

God desires to save all people. Jesus wasn't sent to condemn the world and us in it, but to save us! (John 3:17) Peter may have been remembering God's pure nature spoken of in Numbers 14 when he writes in 2 Peter 3:9 about the patience of God, shown through His desire that no one should perish. Remember, God is not a God of recalls on His creation. He takes what He has and reshapes the clay as the Potter, not being angry and remembering our sins forever. (Isaiah 64:8-9) How would God's way of forgiving and forgetting our sins impact on how we would forgive and forget our sins and others?

What can we summarize about the nature of God as He walked with the children of Israel? Move along through the Book of Deuteronomy for Moses' take on it! Moses had been through it all, hadn't he? He knew God's commands. He knew God's love and desire, mercifully fulfilling all of His promises and covenant going back to Abraham. He knew God endured 40 years of their behavior. Yet, out of love God gave them (and gives us) all that's necessary to succeed.

Moses tells them and us in Deuteronomy 8:1-9 about the kind of God who walks with us: He leads us, He humbles us, He tests us, He feeds us, He speaks to us through His word, He clothes us, He disciplines us. And what is our response? Verse 6 says it all: Observe His commands, walk in His ways, and revere Him.

God would not have us starve in the wilderness, nor live on a diet of manna and quail forever! (Deuteronomy 8:7-9) We shall not lack anything good or valuable for our living and livelihood! And when we have finished eating and are satisfied, having settled down in fine houses with large herds and flocks, seeing all the silver and gold we have increased and multiplied, what would our God have us do?

"You may say to yourself, 'My power and the strength of my hands have produced this wealth for me.' But remember the Lord your God, for it is he who gives you the ability to produce wealth, and so confirms his covenant, which he swore to your forefathers, as it is today." (Deuteronomy 8:17-18) If you need any more convincing otherwise, read carefully God's promise in Deuteronomy 8:19-20 and take Him seriously!

Chapter Two

What does it mean to WALK?

Before our baptism into Christ Jesus, we didn't walk with Him or with God. How could we? God's Word tells us what our "life" was before God's mercy made us alive. Reading Ephesians 2:1-2 says it all! "As for you, you were dead in your transgressions and sins, in which you used to live when you followed the ways of this world and of the ruler of the kingdom of the air, the spirit who is now at work in those who are disobedient." Yes, there IS a Devil! Yes, the Devil IS at work in sinners!

> RM: *Think back to your days before walking with God. What kinds of thoughts did you have and where did they lead you? Were you self-centered, self-focused and looking out for yourself? Were you consciously focused on being a good person, doing good things for good people? But subconsciously, if they'd didn't do the same for you, would you stop being their do-gooder? If someone didn't do for you, would you continue to do for them?*

Being truthful with yourself, I'm certain you could sum up your life as walking apart from God, being centered in sIn with you at the center. Am I right? Did you catch the spelling of that word "sin"? I'll spell it again for you...s I n. Yes, you read it correctly!

With "I" am at the center of our life, we only care about ourselves and how we can benefit by others. We only love because we expect to receive love in return. Our nature is not to give; it's to get! We'll walk down our own path, our arms full with all the stuff we can muster to insure our own success. Ephesians 2:3 goes on to say, "All of us also lived among them at one time, gratifying the cravings of our sinful nature and following its desires and thoughts. Like the rest, we were by nature objects of wrath." No boundaries are necessary. No consequences are standing in the way.

Our sinful world would say there's no need for God in our lives. Paul points this out in 1 Corinthians 2:14, "The man without the Spirit does not accept the things that come from the Spirit of God, for they are foolishness to him, and he cannot understand them, because they are spiritually discerned." Without God and His own Holy Spirit to accept the things of God, we not only fail to understand them, we fail to see any value in them at all! Foolishness!

Our Lord Jesus points out that the world cannot accept God's Spirit because being in the darkness of sin, separated from the light of God's holiness, we cannot! "The world cannot accept him, because it neither sees him nor knows him. But you know him, for he lives with you and will be in you."(John 14:17)

Truly outside of the saving work of our Lord Jesus Christ, we are enemies of God! Our sinful nature and actions set us apart from the loving nature and grace of God as we read previously in Colossians 1:21. God doesn't want us to remain His enemies. God doesn't want us to remain separated from Him, whether on earth or one day in heaven. He wants to walk with us, and He made it all possible through His sinless Son, our Savior Jesus! "For God was pleased to have all his fullness dwell in him (Jesus), and through him (Jesus) to reconcile to himself (God the Father) all things, whether things on earth or things in heaven, by making peace through his (Jesus) blood, shed on the cross. (Colossians 1:19-20) (Parenthesis mine).

God doesn't speak empty words of promise to anyone who would listen to Him. He speaks words full of promises fulfilled and delivered upon through His Son our Savior Jesus Christ. God talks the talk and walks the walk as you've come to realize, "But God demonstrates his own love for us in this: While we were still sinners, Christ died for us."(Romans 5:8) He meets us on the road we're on and says, "Come follow Me! I've made it possible by My own sacrifice in your place! I'm the peace that you seek!"

Our Savior Jesus has made peace between us and God. "But now he has reconciled you by Christ's physical body through death to present you holy in his sight, without blemish and free from accusation"(Colossians 1:22). Why would our Savior Jesus do all these things if not to enable us to be in the presence of a loving God and Father who wants to walk daily with His child? To walk daily with you?

Come to understand the fullness of God the Father's love and mercy for you personally as you read Ephesians 2:4-5, "But because of his great love for us, God, who is rich in mercy, made us alive with Christ even when we were dead in transgressions— it is by grace you have been saved."

RM: *How do you walk? Do you walk according to your own way? Your own understanding of what it means to walk? (Proverbs 3:5-6) If it's not with God and God alone, then you'll only walk a crooked path that will stray miles and miles from Him! (Read God's testimony and promise to you concerning your walk with Him in Proverbs 4:11, 25-27)*

Throughout the Old Testament, God's covenant people lived and walked with Him. God became their teacher in all the ways of truth. They could look to God and trust in Him. They could pray and depend upon God. The Psalms speak volumes of the blessings afforded to those who would trust and depend upon God alone.

For example, Psalm 25 declares one's trust in God and one's desire to be shown His ways and taught His paths. Knowing that God is the only God of our salvation, we can wait upon Him and depend upon Him! "To you, O Lord, I lift up my soul; in you, I trust, O my God. Do not let me be put to shame, nor let my enemies triumph over me. Show me your ways, O Lord, teach me your paths; guide me in your truth and teach me, for you are my God my Savior, and my hope is in you all day long." (Psalm 25:1, 2, 4-5)

We learn from Isaiah 48:17, God knows what is best for us. He knows the direction we ought to take in our walk with Him. We see God desires to teach us!

As we read further in Psalm 25:8-9 and 12, God describes those who know they are in need of Him. They are sinners. They are humble. They fear and respect God. They know God will choose the way they are to be taught. They respond with the declaration of the goodness and uprightness the Lord demonstrates in all He does!

God would not seek to teach those who wouldn't want to learn from Him. Those who would learn from Him, in response then, would walk in His truth, wouldn't they? Often we may need to be united in our heart, our mind, our actions and reactions so that together they would reflect God's way and truth. We would pray and promise, "Teach me your way, O Lord, and I will walk in your truth; give me an undivided heart, that I may fear your name." (Psalm 86:11)

Our God is not a god of wood or stone! He lives! He hears! He answers! He has mercy! He also will physically intervene like no god of wood or stone can do! Along the walkway, our foot might slip! But, our God responds. Hear the testimony of God at work in us, as we read in Psalm 94:18, "When I said, 'My foot is slipping,' your love, O Lord, supported me."

> RM: *Recall how that has happened to you, perhaps more than once? What was God's response as you called out to Him? Did not His unfailing love support you? When anxiety swelled up to overwhelm you, crashing about you like so many tidal waves, did not His consolation bring you peace?*

God desires to keep us surrounded in His peace! "And the peace of God, which transcends all understanding, will guard your hearts and your minds in Christ Jesus." (Philippians 4:7) "You will keep in perfect peace him whose mind is steadfast, because he trusts in you." (Isaiah 26:3) It would be that perfect peace, as perfect as God is, and that steadfast peace, as steadfast as God is, which God would keep us because we would trust in Him!

All this comes about through our daily relationship with God, where we not only speak, but we also listen. God desires to speak with us daily and often. If we come before Him only to petition Him through our prayers, what does that say about our relationship with God?

God would have us listen and lean upon Him! Especially in the morning when we first rise to greet the new day He has begun to roll out for us! Our time of prayer is so vital in the morning hour. We must show Him our heart-felt and hand-folded dedication to Him in prayer. We learn to know it is the first priority on today's walk with Him! We do everything Psalm 143:8 tells us: "Let the morning bring me word of your unfailing love, for I have put my trust in you. Show me the way I should go, for to you I lift up my soul." (Psalm 143:8)

God would tell us, if we would only listen, of His loving kindness. God would tell us, if we would only listen, that we can lean upon Him. God would tell us, if we would only listen, how much we can trust IN Him.

God would cause us, if we would only allow Him, to know the way we ought to walk. God would cause, us if we would only allow Him, to lift up our inner self to Him, as we read above in Psalm 143:8. Won't you discover all those things and persons that would prevent such listening to God? Cast them away from your hearing. Call upon His own Holy Spirit for such a remedy in your walk with Him!

As the Holy Spirit has entered into our lives through our baptism, we are now to walk in the ways of that same Holy Spirit of God! We read about His salvation for us through baptism previously in Titus 3:5-7. God now clothes us with new clothes, resurrection clothes. We've left behind the grave clothes we once wore, as we were once dead in our sins. Now, He enables us through our baptism and faith in our Savior Jesus to become His sons and daughters. "You are all sons of God through faith in Christ Jesus, for all of you who were baptized into Christ have clothed yourselves with Christ." (Galatians 3:26-27)

Yes, there has been a change in our life. It's obvious to us, our family, our friends, our work associates! We no longer have a lifestyle that's far from God or the things of God. With God's own Holy Spirit actively at work in our lives, we can see where our fellowship is and who it's centered in. Our life witness becomes our word witness! Our WALK witness becomes our TALK witness.

As we allow Jesus the Way, the Truth, and the Life (John 14:6) to live through our lives, it's obvious He's talking the talk because He's walking the walk through us! Our fellowship in Jesus Christ through our baptism makes it all possible as we read in 1 John 1:6-7, "If we claim to have fellowship with him yet walk in the darkness, we lie and do not live by the truth. But if we walk in the light, as he is in the light, we have fellowship with one another, and the blood of Jesus, his Son, purifies us from all sin."

What is God's will for our lives and our walk with Him? We need to be actively WALKing according to His will and way. Our thinking needs to be renewed every day as God's Holy

Spirit transforms our mind. As we read in Romans 12:2, "Do not conform any longer to the pattern of this world, but be transformed by the renewing of your mind. Then you will be able to test and approve what God's will is—his good, pleasing and perfect will.

What is God's "good, pleasing and perfect will"? 1 Thessalonians 4:3 clearly tells us, "It is God's will that you should be sanctified…" We need to be made holy. How can sinners be made holy as God is? It's nothing that we can do, is it? Jesus tells us apart from Him we can do nothing. (John 15:5) That's why we need the daily power of the Holy Spirit at work through our baptism IN Christ Jesus to work its great transforming work in our lives daily!

Colossians 1:9-11 gives us the direction from God we seek as we turn to Him alone, receiving everything He knows we need. "For this reason, since the day we heard about you, we have not stopped praying for you and asking God to fill you with the knowledge of his will through all spiritual wisdom and understanding. And we pray this in order that you may live a life worthy of the Lord and may please him in every way: bearing fruit in every good work, growing in the knowledge of God, being strengthened with all power according to his glorious might so that you may have great endurance and patience".

> RM: *Put these words in the first person on an index card and carry them with you for a week. Each day pull out this card and remind yourself why He fills you with the knowledge of His will through spiritual wisdom and understanding. He does this for you*

so that you would walk worthy of His calling and please Him. He does this so that you would allow Him to bear the fruit He so desires to bear. He does this so that you will be daily strengthened with all God's own power, accomplishing all He asks you to do. He enables you not only to endure patiently whatever may be on your plate for the day, but He gives you His joy knowing you are truly walking IN God's will!

Through our baptism, we have new clothes given to us by God because we're a new creation in Christ Jesus through His resurrection power. (2 Corinthians 5:17) So, don't just sit there redressed in God's Easter finest! You have places to go, people to see, good works God would perform through you, lost folks whom God's Holy Spirit would speak to through you! Ephesians 4:24 gives you the directive to "put on the new self, created to be like God in true righteousness and holiness." It's a daily task He stands ready to perform through the Holy Spirit's working power.

We're all subject to the devil's roaring like a lion, "looking for someone to devour." (1Peter 5:8) The devil is trying to get us to put back on the old man and our corrupt nature (Ephesians 4:22). It becomes a war against the flesh. God gives us unique weapons that we can use in battle. We cling to His faithful Word and promise in 2 Corinthians 10:3-5, "For though we live in the world, we do not wage war as the world does. The weapons we fight with are not the weapons of the world. On the contrary, they have divine power to demolish strongholds. We demolish arguments and every pretension that sets itself up against the knowledge of God, and we take captive every thought to make it obedient to Christ."

Paul challenges us in Romans 6:12-13 not to let sin reign over you. Rather than offer yourselves to sin and the devil, offer yourselves to holiness and the One who can make you holy through His Spirit!

> RM: *Our daily walk needs to include thoughts to think about that align with the very nature of God. Examine yourself in light of Philippians 4:8, "...whatever is true, whatever is noble, whatever is right, whatever is pure, whatever is lovely, whatever is admirable— if anything is excellent or praiseworthy—think about such things." What things do you think upon and how do they equip you for His walk?*

Martin Luther points out our daily drowning of the old man involves our willing heart. The new man can emerge as we have God's own Holy Spirit within us. As Hebrews 10:22 would instruct us, He would cleanse our hearts and wash our bodies, through baptism, with the pure water of God and His Word.

Yes, there will be times when it appears we've failed to do all God has asked us to do. Yes, there will be times we run into temptation rather than run away from it. Yes, God will ask us to do things we think we're not capable accomplishing for ourselves or for Him! Our three-part WALKing attitude needs to respond as Paul encourages us in Philippians 3:12-14, "Not that I have already obtained all this, or have already been made perfect, but I press on to take hold of that for which Christ Jesus took hold of me. Brothers, I do not consider myself yet to have taken hold of it. But one thing I do: Forgetting what is behind and straining toward what is ahead, I press on toward the goal to win the prize for which God has called me heavenward in Christ Jesus."

First, forget the past, especially those things forgiven and forgotten by God! "As far as the east is from the west, so far has he removed our transgressions from us." (Psalm 103:12) Don't let the devil try to take you back to a point in your life where your sins have been forgotten by God. Don't try to dredge up what's no longer there!

Second, stretch forward to what God places ahead of you, whether an opportunity or a responsibility! That's what Paul is talking about when he says to strain forward.

Third, you will press on toward the goal our Lord Jesus has set before you.

What is His calling for you? Where will He take you through His calling? How will you know it's His calling, having arrived and eventually completed it? Yes, God surely wants us to be walking with Him every day, and in every way He alone can enable us, doesn't He?

God doesn't desire that some would only drop in on Sunday's. I'm speaking of the Sunday WALKers; those who walk in to church on a Sunday morning, stay for an hour or so, and walk back out. They're content to have done the right thing, given God His due, and now are ready to get on with the rest of the week alone!

The sad thing is some can't help but know any other way. They're the product of a generation or more who've done the same thing and led by example. Generations of Sunday only disciples, who only hear God's Word once a week; who only pray along with the worship leader and fellow worshippers once a week; who feel satisfied with a few crumbs from God's table.

Our Lord Jesus would call these the lukewarm Christians. Neither cold nor hot in their relationship with God, they are content with what they have. They have no vision or desire for a walk other than this once a week one! Truthfully, God is not content with lukewarm relationships. He tells us, He would rather have us be cold towards Him, not even having a relationship with God, or on fire in a relationship with Him. We can confirm this by our Lord Jesus own words in Revelation 3:15-16, " 'I know your deeds, that you are neither cold nor hot. I wish you were either one or the other! So, because you are lukewarm—neither hot nor cold—I am about to spit you out of my mouth!' "

One of the greatest things about being in this WALKing relationship with God is that we are not walking alone. We are walking with other daily disciples of our Lord Jesus. He gathers us and gives us a place called the Church so that we will walk together with God and each other. He reminds us, we have a relationship worth His attention through us.

2 Thessalonians 1:3 points out our responsibility to thank God and to pray for other believers. We would pray that they might turn away from Sunday-only walking. We would pray that their love IN Christ Jesus towards God and each of us would also increase. As we become aware of their lukewarmness, we have a responsibility through God's own Holy Spirit to point out to

them what we have come to see and know and experience in our own daily discipleship. We are to pray that the same Holy Spirit would create an opportunity to share with the lukewarm Sunday walker what it means to have holy heartburn, like the Emmaus disciples did in Luke 24!

Philippians 4:9 talks about role modeling before each other what it means to daily WALK as our Lord's disciples. Paul writes, "Whatever you have learned or received or heard from me, or seen in me—put it into practice." God desires we grow in our relationships of love and trust with each other, as well as learning and encouraging each other.

> RM: As you read this passage, think about the daily walking disciples God has placed in your life. What have you learned from them? What have you received from them? What have you heard and seen in and through their lives that would encourage you, set an example, and hold you accountable for God's Holy Spirit to be actively at work in your walk? Knowing the walk is not enough. Paul urges us to PRACTICE! Practice these things not just on Sunday mornings for an hour. How about every day for the rest of your earthly life and His discipleship of you?

Have you thanked God and them for their companionship as they walk with you, and you with them? Be reminded God encourages a prayer-fueled relationship with fellow daily walkers.

"We always thank God for all of you, mentioning you in our prayers." (1 Thessalonians 1:2) "Brothers, pray for us."

(1 Thessalonians 5:25) "With this in mind, we constantly pray for you, that our God may count you worthy of his calling and that by his power, he may fulfill every good purpose of yours and every act prompted by your faith." (2 Thessalonians 1:11)

What would God seek to accomplish through His walk with us? How can we encourage and be encouraged in our walk with God and each other as we lift each other up in prayer?

Peter encourages us with words that would drive us on God's walkway as we come to know them in 1 Peter 3:8, "Finally, all of you, live in harmony with one another; be sympathetic, love as brothers, be compassionate and humble." We don't pick and choose our fellow walking disciples. God has done that already through the church you've become a part of.

How ought you all to grow and go? Be like-minded, he says. How difficult can that become when we each walk a road that may have had different stops, different lengths, different struggles, different joys, and different sorrows? True, there will be differences. Doesn't God call us together in like-mindedness because we all have, as Ephesians 4:5 testifies, one Lord, one faith, and one baptism?

Yes, God gives us each other, our community of faith as the Body of Christ, to be joined and held together, each one supporting the other so that we all would grow, individually and together. God enables each of us to be built up in His love. Ephesians 4:16 describes the Holy Spirit at work in and through each member of the body of Christ, "From him the whole body, joined and held together by every supporting ligament, grows and builds itself up in love, as each part does its work."

Those last six words are crucial to our growth in love and harmony, aren't they?

It only stands to reason then that Peter goes on to say in the rest of 1 Peter 3:8 to be sympathetic, love one another, compassionate and humble before each other in our Lord Jesus...all characteristics He lived as our example!

> *RM: Take a prayerful look at what Hebrews 10:24-25 has to say, as a community of daily walking disciples of our Lord Jesus! "And let us consider how we may spur one another on toward love and good deeds. Let us not give up meeting together, as some are in the habit of doing, but let us encourage one another—and all the more as you see the Day approaching." How can we encourage each other, in such a way and walk as God enables us? In what ways can God enable us to be more loving, to do more good in His name? How can we encourage each other more and more, knowing that our days become closer and closer to our Lord Jesus imminent return?*

As you've come to see, God's Word is not silent about walking. Nor does God choose to say a few words here or there about the walk He invites us to take with Him. He chooses to inform, instruct, and inspire us, doesn't He?

God informs us that He desires to walk with you. Reread this chapter and write out all the quoted verses that inform you of God's desire to walk with you. Write them each out on an index card so you can have before you, at your finger tips, just a few words from Him. (I would challenge you, consult a concordance to locate additional references to walk, walked, walking and see where God speaks further!) Let God instruct you in such a way that you will be obedient to His will for your walk.

God inspires us with all the delivered promises we find in His Word. Much like the whole Word of God is that lamp (Psalm 119:105) to show us His walkway, so we can give Him all thanks and praise that He has enabled us to continue our walk with Him beyond the pathways on earth. He stands ready to call us home to be with Him and walk with Him throughout eternity.

Chapter Three

Whose direction do I take?

In the first chapter, we reviewed the lives of people in the Bible who walked with God and of whom God walked with them. While we covered their lives, we really didn't cover the tenets of God's walking with us. Why would God choose to walk with us? How does He choose to walk with us? What expectations does God have in our walk with us? What direction does God want us to take? And then the question posed in this chapter, "Whose direction do I take?"

Before talking about the WALK Jesus enables us to take this side of the cross, I'd like to walk back with you through a couple of Old Testament tenets. Let's prospect a bit through God's Old Testament to see the foundation laid by God Himself as He walked then and continues to walk with His children.

In Genesis 5, we have a long list of the people and the length of lives they "lived" and subsequently "died." It's interesting to note that an important exception is made for a man named Enoch. Perhaps you may recall that easy to remember and recite Bible verse from your Sunday School days? It's repeated twice in Genesis 5:22 and 24 saying how Enoch walked with

God. Why the exception here? Why didn't God continue his litany by saying, "Enoch lived....Enoch died"? There must have been something different, something outstanding about Enoch. No one else is cited in this chapter as having WALKED with God! Such a special relationship Enoch had with God.

Hebrews 11:5-6 describes the faith God rewarded as one "who earnestly sought God." Could we say that our life was a WALK with God? In other words, there can be more than merely living with God. Living would describe a state of being while WALKING would describe a state of action and activity. Which would you rather be? Someone who lived with God or someone who WALKED with God?

Up to this point as well, God never really described HOW one could WALK with Him. But, God did not choose to remain silent. He spent many words through many Old Testament writers to answer all those questions I posed a few moments ago at the start of this chapter! Let's take God's Word for it and be clear in our mind and heart how WALKING with God can all come together for us!

First, God describes His desire to walk with us! Leviticus 26:12 establishes a promise that He makes and keeps for all eternity, "I will walk among you and be your God, and you will be my people." God asks them to make a sanctuary where He will live. (Exodus 25:8) Micah 4:5 reminds us, "We will walk in the name of the Lord our God for ever and ever." He not only wants to be our God but He wants to walk among us! More than just living with us, isn't it? God will not just point out a destination for His people; he will lead them safely there.

Second, God wants us to walk in His way so that we will be prosperous. In Deuteronomy 5:33, God wants us to know, "Walk in all the way that the Lord your God has commanded you, so that you may live and prosper and prolong your days in the land that you will possess." (Much like His commandment to us to honor our father and mother, that our days will be long... See Paul's commentary in Ephesians 6:2-3 for a refresher!) In addition, Proverbs 6:22 encourages those who walk with God to keep our father's commands and not to forsake our mother's teaching...as they both will guide us!

Third, God wants us to KNOW His ways and commandments. We ought to take every opportunity to learn them including the times when we're walking. I believe Deuteronomy 6:6-7 (and 11:19) make a good case for owning and using an Audio Bible during those long commutes in traffic or during an otherwise boring trip! "These commandments that I give you today are to be upon your hearts. Impress them on your children. Talk about them when you sit at home and when you walk along the road, when you lie down and when you get up." (Deuteronomy 6:6-7) What better way than to hear and learn how God wants to bless us on our WALK with Him? Can you see how a determined use of index cards while prospecting in the Bible can benefit you?

Fourth, God does not invite us to pick and choose what we will follow or not follow in our walk with Him! It's got to be all, as we read in Deuteronomy 10:12-13, "...what does the Lord your God ask of you but to fear the Lord your God, to walk in all his ways, to love him, to serve the Lord you God with all your heart and with all your soul, and to observe the Lord's commands and decrees that I am giving you today for your own good?" as well as Joshua 22:5, "But be very careful to keep the commandment and the law that Moses the servant of the Lord gave you; to love the Lord your God, to walk in all his ways, to obey his commands, to hold fast to him and to serve him with all your heart and all your soul."

Walking with God means WALKING in ALL His WAYS! God does not want a half hearted response to Him! Remember those who are lukewarm children? There's no choice we make. There's no alternate walkway we can take. God is emphatic! God speaks clearly His will for our walk with Him! Are we listening as we hear a voice behind us saying, "THIS is the way, my child! Now, WALK in it!" (Isaiah 30:21)?

Fifth, God wants us to declare we will walk with Him. He wants a solemn oath, a pledge we'll walk with no other god as He reminds us in His first commandment! We must not simply know or be aware of what He expects from us. By His power and Spirit, we must WALK in His ways with Him as Deuteronomy 26:17 challenges us, "You have declared this day that the Lord is your God and that you will walk in his ways, that you will keep his decrees, commands and laws, and that you will obey him."

Sixth, God enables us to walk in His freedom according to Psalm 119:45, "I will walk about in freedom, for I have sought out your precepts." Proverbs 4:11-12 says of God's participation in our walk, "I guide you in the way of wisdom and lead you along straight paths. When you walk, your steps will not be hampered; when you run, you will not stumble. "Likewise, God will not withhold any good thing from us because as we walk with God, our walk is blameless. God bestows both His favor and honor on us, as we read in Psalm 84:11, "For the Lord God is a sun and shield; the Lord bestows both favor and honor; no good thing does he withhold from those whose walk is blameless."

Seventh, God does not intend for our walk to be permanently fixed here on earth. We have those famous, often recalled words from Psalm 23:4, that assure us even when we walk through our last moment towards death, He is with us to comfort us. Isaiah 57:2 also promises, "Those who walk uprightly enter into peace; they find rest as they lie in death." We can find that rest we need for our souls even before death as Jeremiah 6:16 reminds us, "...ask where the good way is, and walk in it, and you will find rest for your souls."

Two pillars within Old Testament scripture that we can wedge ourselves between are Isaiah 40:31, "But those who hope in the Lord will renew their strength. They will soar on wings like eagles; they will run and not grow weary, they will walk and not be faint," and Micah 6:8, "He has showed you, O man, what is good. And what does the Lord require of you? To act justly and to love mercy and to walk humbly with your God."

> *RM: Again, I would encourage you to write these out on an index card and keep them with you. Read and recall them so often that they become a part of your memory. Much like Mary pondered God's sayings to her in her heart, won't you consider doing the same with these two verses? Look them up in your own Bible and write them out and be blessed by them.*

> *RM: In Isaiah 40:31, those who walk with God are compared to eagles. How would you compare your*

life to that of an eagle? Recall times when your hope in God did renew the strength you needed, not just so you could go on, but so that you could soar! When have there been times when you grew weary in your walk with God? How did you know that calling upon Him would help you not grow faint from lack of God's eternal energy as you walk with Him?

RM: *I know you've heard these words from Micah 6:8 before. Have you pondered them in your heart however? You know! God has shown you what is that good thing that He requires of you if you're going to be His child and walk with Him! Does justice prevail through your heart, mind, words, and actions? Do you love the unconditional and undeserved mercy of God? As He has shown it to you do you show it to others? Are you humble? Is your humility sincerely grounded in the silence of doing God's good works towards all people without expecting or receiving anything else in return?*

Aren't those powerful tenets from God's Word? Can you see the eternalness of them? Can you value the relationship God's Old Testament people had with God while they awaited the fulfillment of their salvation from sin through God's Son, our Savior Jesus? Those of us this side of the Cross of Christ can be thankful indeed that we live in all the promises of God fulfilled through our Lord and Savior Jesus Christ.

For us, Jesus makes the WALK possible, powerful, fruitful and memorable for each of us! Let's take the bridge into the New Testament to see how our Savior and Lord Jesus DID make such a WALK with Him ALL those things!

Jesus makes the WALK possible through our baptism. I've spoken a lot about baptism so far. Why? Because baptism is a powerful gift from God. Because baptism isn't what we do as a result of our faith...baptism is a means by which God imparts His grace to us. Only HE could die on the cross for us. Only HE can save us from our sins. Only HE can give us the free gift of forgiveness and eternal life through baptism. Let's be reminded again of a few key Scripture passages from God's Word that point this out.

- John 3:5-6, "Jesus answered, 'I tell you the truth, no one can enter the kingdom of God unless he is born of water and the Spirit. Flesh gives birth to flesh, but the Spirit gives birth to spirit." What does baptism do for us? It gives us the new birth we need, birth by the Holy Spirit of God, who is at work in and through baptism.

- Mark 16:16 promises, "Whoever believes and is baptized will be saved, but whoever does not believe will be condemned." As a person is able, he or she should be baptized. If they are unable, like the thief on the cross, to be baptized, their faith in Jesus will be enough.

- Titus 3:5 reminds us, "He saved us, not because of righteous things we had done, but because of his mercy. He saved us through the washing of rebirth and renewal by the Holy Spirit." GOD saved us by the work of the Holy Spirit. It's HIS Holy Spirit who washes and renews us by the water of baptism.

- I Corinthians 6:11 states clearly three things that God's own Holy Spirit has done for us, "But you were washed, you were sanctified, you were justified in the name of

the Lord Jesus Christ and by the Spirit of our God."
We may not understand how God works through our
baptism. That's where faith believes for us. We trust in
the truth God speaks about what He does for each of
us in baptism!

- Ephesians 4:4-5 describes, "There is one body and
  one Spirit—just as you were called to one hope when
  you were called—one Lord, one faith, one baptism."
  Baptism unites us to Jesus through His death and
  resurrection. Baptism also binds all God's faith-filled
  into that one Body of Christ.

- Ephesians 5:26 describes the desire of our Savior and
  Lord Jesus for His children to have His baptism within
  the body of Christ, His church, "to make her holy,
  cleansing her by the washing with water through the
  word." It's the means by which He shows the love He
  had to give up His life for the church. We are cleansed
  by baptism's washing with water through the very
  Word and command of God. The power of the Word of
  God and the water of God's baptism are those means
  God Himself has chosen. God gives us these means to
  receive His gift of forgiveness and eternal life.

- Galatians 3:26-27 speak of our sonship in Christ
  Jesus, "You are all sons of God through faith in Christ
  Jesus, for all of you who were baptized into Christ
  have clothed yourselves with Christ." How do you see
  yourself as clothed with our Savior and Lord Jesus
  through baptism? In what ways are you different from
  one not baptized?

Jesus makes the WALK powerful through His presence. His presence, like that of God the Father and the Holy Spirit is all wrapped up in His Name! As God described Himself to Moses, His covenanted people, Pharaoh and Egypt, and the many nations and peoples following them, God chose the name, "I AM WHO I AM." (Exodus 3:14)

Just as the Old Testament saints walked with "I AM" so did Jesus, the Son of God. He continued that identification and that walk with His New Testament saints by identifying Himself as I AM. His power and presence in our lives and in our walk with Him can be described by all the attributes of His own "I AM's." The Gospel of John teaches us as we read the passages in John 6:35, 48, 51; 8:12; 10:7, 9, 11, 14; 11:25; 14:6; 15:1, 5.

I AM the Bread of Life. (John 6:35, 48, 51) Jesus demonstrates His power as the living Word. He satisfies our soul's hunger for God Himself, His promises, His forgiveness, His gift of eternal life. In Jesus alone, we have found this living bread from heaven. Jesus came down to enliven us and sustain us for the walk He calls us to take as we follow Him. He reminds us as well of that other sacrament He instituted, the Lord's Supper. It has the power of eternal life extended to all who would believe and eat His body and drink His blood. (John 6:53-58)

I AM the Light of the World. (John 8:12) Jesus demonstrates His power as the light of this world. Those who walk with Him no longer walk in darkness. We no longer have to live in doubt whether we will ever be good enough or do enough good works to satisfy God. We can't! He CAN! We need look no where else or to no one else. He is the only way through which we can enter into the presence and pleasure of God our Father (John 14:6)

I AM the Gate. (John 10:9) Jesus demonstrates His power as being the only gate we can enter through for salvation. He provides our sustenance on the journey we walk with Him. He would protect us from the thief who would want to come through the gate to steal and kill and destroy us.

I AM the Good Shepherd. (John 10:11, 14) Jesus demonstrates His power through the unconditional love He has for each of us...as if we were the only one He loved and cared for; the only one He came and died for! He demonstrates that powerful love He has for us by doing that! He laid down His life for us, those whom He knows and who know Him by name!

I AM the Resurrection and the Life. (John 11:25) Jesus demonstrates His power over death. We all will die physically. We don't have to die spiritually. He has made it possible for us to never die spiritually (verse 26). As Jesus asks Martha, so He asks us, "Do you believe?"

I AM the Way, and the Truth, and the Life. (John 14:6) Jesus demonstrates the power He alone has been given by God the Father. There can be only one way, truth, and life. He is that One! He is all and offers all to any and all who would receive Him and what He has done for each of us. We have these gifts of His all wrapped up with a bow and a gift tag. Guess whose name is on the gift tag? Yours! Mine! John 3:16 reminds us that God so loved the whole world. Jesus gift is for everyone who would receive it! How have you come to know the power of His way, truth, and life? Who do you know who still needs to receive His gift?

I AM the Vine. (John 15:1, 5) Jesus demonstrates His power to reconnect us to God our Father. We are no longer out there either unattached or dying on some dead vine. NO! We are connected as branches to Jesus the Vine. We are drawing upon His power daily for our daily walk with Him. As we abide in Him and He abides in us, we have a purpose and a meaning for our walk together...we are to bear much fruit that proves we are His disciples and gives glory to God the Father (verse 8). More on this shortly!

> RM: *Within your daily walk as His daily disciple, how much have you called upon God, our Father, our Lord Jesus and the Holy Spirit to demonstrate their power in and through your life? Which of Jesus' I AM's can you recognize at work in your daily discipleship? Describe how He has been at work in you as His "disciple under construction" as that I AM?*

The same creative and sustaining power of God the Father, maker of heaven and earth, who spoke a word and it was done....can be seen in our lives through God the Son, the redeemer of the world, who became the living Word for us... and through God the Holy Spirit, the one who brings us into our faith relationship with the triune God, keeps us and grows us in that relationship and daily walk with Him, and sends us forth to go into all the world to make disciples.

Jesus makes the WALK fruitful through His work in us. How do we see His fruitful work in and through us? We see it as we remain connected to Jesus the vine as His branches! Let's go back to John 15 for a more in depth study and understanding of how Jesus makes this aspect of our daily WALK with Him so fruitful!

This section of John's Gospel (John 13-17) are power-filled chapters of Jesus' last teaching to His twelve before His betrayal, trial, and death on the cross for each of us. Beyond this night, Jesus would not have the opportunity to teach any more let alone have such intimate access as servant and savior to those He lived and taught for these last three years. Every daily disciple of our Lord and Savior Jesus NEEDS to be grounded in these chapters. Their significance is beyond our temporal understanding. I cannot underscore enough their power and importance for our daily walk with God, Father, Son and Holy Spirit!

Open your Bible to John 13 and follow along with me for a few moments, won't you? The last Passover has come. Jesus has come through time and eternity for this night. He would become the very Passover lamb for each of us. His very blood shed and poured over us, so that the second eternal death would pass over us. But before that all would come to pass, Jesus would show us one aspect of His desire to be our servant, beyond His death for us! He would wash the feet of His disciples and ask them to do the same (John 13:4-17).

As He had taught the greatest of God's commandments previously, Jesus tells us by His own example, " 'A new command I give you: Love one another. As I have loved you, so you must love one another." (John 13:34) This aspect of our WALK can become a silent witness, testifying to whose we are in verse 35, "By this all men will know that you are my disciples, if you love one another.'"

RM: *In what ways does this command of Jesus become a real challenge within your daily discipleship? How have there been times the Holy Spirit seems to have sent fellow disciples into your life that are difficult to love? How has He been able to resolve such obstacles so His love prevails? How have you shared those occurances as opportunities to reflect His discipleship of you?*

John 14 is a frank discussion of how Jesus is the only way to the Father; He is the only way, truth, and life. (John 14:6-14) Jesus takes this last hour introducing the role of the Holy Spirit in the lives of all His daily disciples. (John 14:16-17, 26) They wouldn't fully understand or appreciate what Jesus is offering them until after the Ascension. But that same power of the Holy Spirit to teach all things and bring to memory what Jesus has taught us is still present in our daily walk with Him!

Now we come to John 15:1-17 where Jesus uses a last illustration and His last I AM to describe His power at work! Here's where I'd like to stop and prospect with you for a few moments.

Through our baptism, we have entered into a relationship with our Savior and Lord Jesus that is intimate indeed. We become and remain a living, feeding, fruit bearing branch attached to His Vine! As He spoke earlier, He and the Father are One in a relationship where the Father is the vinedresser, the One who cares and tends for the Vine.

RM: *Describe the aspects of your spiritual life that show God's branches attached to Jesus, the Vine. How are some healthier and stronger than others? What makes the difference?*

The Father is also responsible for pruning, or cutting away, any branch that does not bear fruit. I reckon this to God's testing us, as we're told in 1 Thessalonians 2:4b, "We are not trying to please men but God, who tests our hearts." Why, through pruning, would God test us? How might we benefit having our faith and dependency upon Him stretched beyond our accustomed limits? Reading James 1:2-3, we would be challenged to match our responsiveness to James, "Consider it pure joy, my brothers, whenever you face trials of many kinds, because you know that the testing of your faith develops perseverance."

> RM: *How are you looking for the fruit of perseverance to be borne through your branch connected and pruned by God? How does it seem challenging for you to consider God's pruning through testing as PURE JOY? How does it get any easier or desirable in your daily discipleship?*

Don't mistakenly accuse God of tempting us when you really would mean testing us. There is a difference! God never tempts us because temptation could and often does lead to sin. God would not do that. It's not in His nature! We read further on in James 1:13-15, "When tempted, no one should say, 'God is tempting me.' For God cannot be tempted by evil, nor does he tempt any one; but each one is tempted when, by his own evil desire, he is dragged away and enticed. Then, after desire has conceived, it gives birth to sin; and sin, when it is full-grown, gives birth to death."

Haven't you been able to trace back the development of sin in your life? How does it go back, like links of a chain, from desire conceived from an enticement dangling in front of you? Remember your sinful nature wanting to bear sinful fruit? The more you let it go, the more you let it grow!

It's also out of love for us that God the vinedresser may, from time to time, discipline us. How often in your daily walk with God have you questioned whether this was a time of testing or discipline? You may ask, "Why me, God? What have I done to deserve this?"

> RM: *Describe the last time you've asked the "WHY" questions of God. (If not you, than recall a fellow disciple discussing this with you.) WHAT was behind the WHY's? WHEN did you finally welcome His discipline? HOW has it changed your accepting more and questioning less the perfect will of God for you?*

The writer to the Book of Hebrews paints a different picture of God's righteous and loving behavior towards us. Hebrews 12:5-6 tells us, " 'My son, do not make light of the Lord's discipline, and do not lose heart when he rebukes you, because the Lord disciplines those he loves, and he punishes everyone he accepts as a son.'" Just like a gardener pays attention and invests time and energy and resources into his work of tender care for his plant, so does God with you.

If God didn't love you, He wouldn't discipline you! You ought to be encouraged that God considers you His son (and daughter)! What's the purpose of God's pruning or discipline or testing in our daily walk with Him? Hebrews 12:10-11 point it out clearly, "Our fathers disciplined us for a little while as they thought best; but God disciplines us for our good, that we may share in his holiness. No discipline seems pleasant at the time, but painful. Later on, however, it produces a harvest of righteousness and peace for those who have been trained by it."

Have you ever read or considered this truth from God's Word before? How much of a difference should it make in your response to God's active work in your life through your walk together? He says God's discipline is not only for our good but also for our becoming holier.

> RM: *Ponder and respond with answers to these questions: How are we to become more and more like our Lord Jesus Christ? Why have we put on Christ through our baptism so that we might live and walk IN Christ? When will we know, as verse 11 says, that it will produce a harvest of God's righteousness and peace? Why wouldn't we want God at work in our lives in this way for this purpose and outcome?*

Isn't bearing fruit the expectation of any plant? Why is it any different in our daily discipleship with our Lord Jesus? It's not! John 15:4 sets the relationship and expectation between our Lord Jesus as the Vine and we, His disciples, as the branches, " 'Remain in me, and I will remain in you. No branch can bear fruit by itself; it must remain in the vine. Neither can you bear fruit unless you remain in me.' "

He even promises in verse 5 that we will bear much fruit; not just a little, but a lot! How can He make such a promise? He explains how it can happen in the latter part of that same verse.

We can't bear any fruit whatsoever on our own. He must bear it through us! Jesus does it ALL!

> RM: *Where would you sincerely invite God the Father to test and stretch your faith? What direction and location would you want God the Father to take you in your walk with Him? What area of your life would you pray that your Lord Jesus would become Lord over? Where would you ask the Holy Spirit to bring more of His holiness in your daily walk?*

As if we didn't hear Jesus right the first time, He reminds us again in verse 16 the relationship we have entered into with Him, " 'You did not choose me, but I chose you and appointed you to go and bear fruit—fruit that will last.' " It's not our choice! We have not decided to follow Jesus. We have not chosen Jesus over against any other god or the devil. NO! Jesus, who is the Way, the Truth, and the Life, says HE has chosen us! Chosen us for what purpose? To GO, bear fruit that lasts!

What kind of fruit can this be? I believe there is a distinct direction that Jesus asks us to allow the Holy Spirit to take in and through our lives! Our bearing fruit is GOING and proving we are His disciples to the glory of God the Father as Jesus tells us in John 15:8, " 'This is to my Father's glory, that you bear much fruit, showing yourselves to be my disciples.' " What else would God want us to be occupying our time if not for GOING and MAKING disciples? Isn't that what He calls and asks us to do in Matthew 28:19, when Jesus doesn't ask us, but tells us, " 'Therefore go and make disciples of all nations, baptizing them in the name of the Father and of the Son and of the Holy Spirit' "?

Talk about fruit that lasts! Talk about proving we're His disciples by allowing the Holy Spirit to speak through us! To the lost and the Dechurched (those who have chosen to leave Christ's fellowship through a local church)! We are now Jesus friends in order that we might take Him and His message to our friends, are we not? Hear these words of Jesus in John 15:14-15, " 'You are my friends if you do what I command. I no longer call you servants, because a servant does not know his master's business. Instead, I have called you friends, for everything that I learned from my Father I have made known to you.' "

> RM: *How has Jesus shown you are no longer His servant but His friend? How have you been led to describe Jesus as your friend to others, whether lost or found?*

Yes, we will have opposition! Do you think the devil would be happy by our actively being our Lord Jesus disciple in order that His Holy Spirit would have the opportunity to make disciples through us? I don't think so! Jesus had to lay that out for His daily WALKing and TALKing disciples, you and me, as well (Please, take time to read it all in John 15:18-27)!

So, yes, we NEED the Holy Spirit to fulfill many things through us as Jesus outlines them for us in John 16. The Holy Spirit convicts us, the world and the Lost of our sin. (John 16:8-9) The Holy Spirit will guide us and them into all truth even as Jesus is the Way, the Truth, and the Life, as Jesus describes His promise in John 16:13, " 'But when he, the Spirit of truth, comes, he will guide you into all truth. He will not speak on his own; he will speak only what he hears, and he will tell you what is yet to come.' "

The Holy Spirit will bring us to faith through our baptism, as we've said before, in order that we might GROW in our faith and GO in that faith. The Holy Spirit enables us to share Jesus with those ready to listen and respond to His free gift of eternal life.

John 17 gives us a glimpse into the mind of our Savior and Lord Jesus as He awaited betrayal. He knew He was finished teaching and now needed to be praying! Praying for Himself, giving thanks to God that He has been used by God according to God's plan and purpose for each of us. (John 17:1-5) Jesus turns His attentive prayer on behalf of these disciples He has traveled with and taught. He asks for the Father's protective hand to be upon them as they continue the work Jesus has begun.

He knows they will be hated by the world. (John 17:6-19) God's sanctifying power can keep them holy even as God is holy. They will go out into the world as Jesus will command them. They will accomplish marvelous things, bearing much fruit, proving to be Jesus disciples and giving glory to God the Father.

Our Lord Jesus also knows to be IN prayer for us! Yes, you and me, the ones He refers to as those who will believe in me through their message, as He prays in John 17:20, " 'My prayer is not for them alone. I pray also for those who will believe in me through their message." Isn't that incredible? (Won't you read about the rest of Jesus' prayer for you in the remaining verses of John 17:21-26?)

> RM: *What is our response to Jesus' prayer? Why do you believe it's His desire to bear much fruit through*

us by His Holy Spirit? Why would He desire to create and keep us as His disciples while also making disciples through us? What could we be sharing about His story? How would we describe how we've come to know why He came and died? With God's Holy Spirit at work in such ways, how would we then GROW in our faith so that we would be enabled to GO in that faith to the Lost and the Dechurched?

Having served as a layperson and church worker at several locations, I understand that it's hard to ask disciples to make disciples if they are not disciples! Hard? Try impossible!

Why would anyone want to disturb the equilibrium of a relationship where the need for God is seldom if ever, discussed? Many Christians do a fantastic job hiding their Christianity. It's as if they take off their Christ clothes that were put on them in their baptism so that they don't have to be seen as a Christian. Or questioned as a Christian. Or give a witness to being a Christian. Sounds tough, I know! But you know if someone hadn't allowed the Holy Spirit to speak the Law that would show us our sins and our need for a Savior, and the Gospel, that would show us Jesus has done it all for us, just needing to receive His gift of grace...where would we be today?

While the second part of this book will focus in on our TALK as Jesus' disciples, I can't help but share a few paragraphs with you to whet your appetite and address this fundamental last point.

We cannot save anyone. We cannot win any soul for Jesus. We cannot do anything to bring anyone to Jesus. John 15:5 makes that abundantly clear! Hear our Lord's admonition to us, " 'I am the vine; you are the branches. If a man remains in me and I in him, he will bear much fruit; apart from me you can do nothing.' " Apart from Jesus, you can do nothing. No thing! Why would we want to push God's own Holy Spirit aside? Why would we want to do the work only the Holy Spirit is appointed by God, the Father to do?

The Holy Spirit IS appointed by God, the Father for this distinct purpose: the salvation and sanctification of our souls! Re-read John 14 and 16 for starters! It is abundantly clear, isn't it, that it's the Holy Spirit's job, not ours? Why would we want to take it on then?

There appears to be some confusion out there, and I can't help but point the finger at the author of confusion, the devil himself. The devil is all for twisting the truth of God's Word around. Does the devil want you and me to be out there GROWing in our faith and GOing forth sharing our faith? Of course, not!

The devil likes to deceive Christians into believing that they are better off NOT going and sharing their faith with anyone until they know it "backwards and forwards!" Nope, you ought not to be out there talking about Jesus because you don't know what question someone's going to ask you...that you can't answer! Whaat? If God calls some to be pastors, teachers, or evangelists (Ephesians 4:11), why do I think I'm one of those? I know I'm NOT! The lie of the devil, "I don't have to be Jesus witness" is seen in the truth of Jesus' words in Acts 1:8, " 'But you will receive power when the Holy Spirit comes on you; and you will be my witnesses in Jerusalem, and in all Judea and Samaria, and to the ends of the earth.' "

The devil would have us believe, "Jesus doesn't call me to be a fisher of men," when Jesus clearly invites us, " 'Come, follow me,' Jesus said, 'and I will make you fishers of men.' " (Matthew 4:19) Peter and Andrew understood so well that "at once they left their nets and followed him" (Matthew 4:20)!

> RM: *Recall times you fell victim to the devil's lies. How did the Holy Spirit reveal His truth to you? How have opportunities presented themselves to TALK His talk with those willing to listen? How did those demonstrations of the Holy Spirit at work in and through you encourage you?*

Picture St. Paul, formerly Saul that we spoke of previously in Chapter One. You've got a pretty clear picture of who he was, right? Versed in the Word of God? A polished public speaker? A convincing and convicting disciple and witness for Jesus Christ? Read his own words in this description he shares in 1 Corinthians 2:1-5:

"When I came to you, brothers, I did not come with eloquence or superior wisdom as I proclaimed to you the testimony about God. For I resolved to know nothing while I was with you except Jesus Christ and him crucified. I came to you in weakness and fear, and with much trembling. My message and my preaching were not with wise and persuasive words, but with a demonstration of the Spirit's power, so that your faith might not rest on men's wisdom, but on God's power."

> RM: *Could you see any of yourself described in Paul's words? How about proclaiming his testimony about God without eloquence or superior wisdom? How*

about coming before others with weakness, fear, and much trembling? How about sharing a message that didn't use wise and persuasive words? Take a moment to confess how Paul's humble description of himself was yours, too! Describe how the Holy Spirit was set free to accomplish His work through you?

How does God use us to make disciples? Paul leaves no room for doubt, discussion, or quite frankly disobedience! It's not ME! It's HE! He, being the Holy Spirit, will do it! 1 Corinthians 2:4b tells us, "with a demonstration of the Spirit's power." God's will is that all should come to faith in Jesus Christ. God wants everyone to receive the gift He's prepared, wrapped, and placed with their name on the tag. God doesn't want anyone to perish as we recall Jesus' words in John 3:16 but that all should come to repentance!

Within the powerful parable of the Lost Son, Jesus portrayed us as the prodigal and God as the father. Remember His words in Luke 15:24? " 'For this son of mine was dead and is alive again; he was lost and is found.' " Just as we were dead in our trespasses and sins, as Ephesians 2:1 points out, so we can be found alive in Him through our baptism. 1 Peter 3:21 also points this out. God, like the Lost Son's father, is waiting every night for the one lost sheep to come and receive the gift He's prepared for them, isn't He? (Luke 15:5-7)

Who's that lost, sinning sheep in need of repentance in your life? Who's the Zacchaeus God has placed in your life? Who needs salvation to come into their house, under their roof as Jesus said in Luke 19:9, " 'Today salvation has come to this house' "? Remember why Jesus came? " 'For the Son of Man came to seek and save what was lost.' " (Luke 19:10) Wasn't that you and me? Isn't that Our Father and His Son Jesus and His Holy Spirit at work seeking and saving?

RM: *You may be the only Bible this Lost or Dechurched person may ever read. Why would God have put you in their life? Or why would God have put them in your life? Recall such an occurrence as the opportunity God transformed an obstacle. What did God provide so that they could see God's promises fulfilled in and through you? How did they come to know about Jesus Christ through your life witness?*

Don't let another day go by without beginning to commit yourself to PRAY for them, both specifically and persistently!

- PRAY that God's own Holy Spirit will begin to get you (and them) ready for a divine appointment.

- PRAY that God would bring you two together. PRAY for opportunity eyes to see the opportunities to come together.

- PRAY that you would listen, just listen to what's happening in their life. PRAY that you would be attentive, taking care to hear what they're saying and not feel led to respond.

- PRAY that you can remain silent so that God's Holy Spirit can speak between the two of you according to His timetable.

- PRAY that they will open the door to learn more about your relationship with God. PRAY for the Holy Spirit to give you the words He knows you should say...much as Paul talked about earlier.

God walks with you daily for a purpose: to give you a life filled with blessings He has worked in and through your life. He doesn't want you to be tight lipped. He wants you to share these same blessings with others. What person in love with another person, ever fails to speak of their love and devotion to that person?

Why should it be any different within the demonstrated relationship your Savior Jesus Christ has with you? Take seriously to heart these words of Peter as Jesus is Lord in your heart, "But in your hearts set apart Christ as Lord. Always be prepared to give an answer to everyone who asks you to give the reason for the hope that you have. But do this with gentleness and respect."(1 Peter 3:15)

Would you pray that God's Holy Spirit will speak through you? Would you pray that God's Holy Spirit will set a divine appointment between you and your Lost or Dechurched person? You better believe the Holy Spirit will deliver upon this request. God WILL answer such specific and persistent prayers! You must be ready to do your part! Be ready to give an answer about the reason for your hope, our Lord and Savior Jesus, who lives in you! Let His Holy Spirit speak through you with gentleness and respect!

I know that this becomes easier and joyful as we WALK and TALK. We have God's stories to share with others. We have demonstrated occurrences where we see God at work and marvel with questions like, "How did that happen? Where did those words come from?" We will be used by God as we allow Him to use us! We will be used by God as we continue to WALK in Him. Paul gives us our daily discipleship directions within Colossians 2:6-7, "So then, just as you received Christ Jesus as Lord, continue to live in him, rooted and built up in him, strengthened in the faith as you were taught, and overflowing with thankfulness." Read on to Chapter Four in order to learn how the Holy Spirit can discipline us for such work in our daily discipleship with Him!

Chapter Four

What discipline does a disciple need?

When our Savior and Lord Jesus invited us through our baptism to become His daily disciple, we began a walk which He provides and enables by the Holy Spirit. As I've said previously, it's the role of the Holy Spirit not only to bring us to faith and keep us in faith but also to help us grow in that faith! We are described in 1 Corinthians 1:2, much like the church in Corinth, as "those sanctified in Christ Jesus and called to be holy, together with all those everywhere who call on the name of our Lord Jesus Christ—their Lord and ours"!

We are no longer alone walking in darkness. We are not even our own anymore! We have been bought with the blood of Christ so that His Holy Spirit can dwell in us. Have you come to understand, believe, and testify these words from 1 Corinthians 6:19-20?

"Do you not know that your body is a temple of the Holy Spirit, who is in you, whom you have received from God? You are not your own; you were bought at a price. Therefore honor God with your body." (1 Corinthians 6:19-20)

We are the temple of God! God promises us in 2 Corinthians 6:16b, "For we are the temple of the living God. As God has said: 'I will live with them and walk among them, and I will be their God, and they will be my people.'" This is referenced back to Leviticus 26:12, when Israel would be led to God's promised land the first time. It is also referenced back to Jeremiah 32:38, when Israel would be led back to God's promised land the second time.

> RM: *How about us? How have we failed to recognize our bodies as God's temple? How have we failed to allow God to lead us, not just once, but twice, or more? What did it take for us to recognize such failure? What can cause us to fall into such failure?*

The Holy Spirit doesn't dwell in us so that we might grow fat spiritually! Our Savior and Lord Jesus didn't die on the cross in our place so that we can be preserved in our faith, awaiting His eminent return.

As we've seen previously, Colossians 2:6-7 speaks quite matter of factly when God, speaking through Paul, gives us our walking instructions: As you have received Jesus the Lord, live in Him as one rooted and built up (like Jesus tells us in John 15)! Be established in your faith based on what you've been taught. Don't just be average or mediocre! Overflow with thanksgiving!

You have a spiritual body IN Jesus Christ, your Savior and Lord. You need to be built up in it! Jude reiterates this point of being built up in verses 20-21, "But you, dear friends, build yourselves up in your most holy faith and pray in the Holy

Spirit. Keep yourselves in God's love as you wait for the mercy of our Lord Jesus Christ to bring you to eternal life."

> RM: *How have we seen ourselves built up in our faith by the Holy Spirit? What do you believe Jude means when he tells us to be "praying in the Holy Spirit"? Jude doesn't reference this as speaking in tongues. What would such a prayer look or sound like? What aspects of our daily discipleship need His keeping "in God's love as we walk with Him until He brings us to eternal life"?*

Colossians 1:9-11 points us in the right direction, in the way God would have us walk as His daily disciples! "For this reason, since the day we heard about you, we have not stopped praying for you and asking God to fill you with the knowledge of his will through all spiritual wisdom and understanding. And we pray this in order that you may live a life worthy of the Lord and may please him in every way: bearing fruit in every good work, growing in the knowledge of God, being strengthened with all power according to his glorious might so that you may have great endurance and patience".

Let's tear this apart into doable components. As His daily disciples, we are not His people unto ourselves! We ought to have spiritual care and concern for others in the body of Christ. We ought to show such care and concern by our faithful and fervent praying. We ought to share those prayer needs we have, even ones that would reflect our corporate sinful nature and weakness so that we might live and walk in God's grace and forgiveness! We ought to please God in every way by bearing fruit, growing in the knowledge, and being strengthened with

His power. In the end, we would receive the endurance and patience He promises, wouldn't we?

> *RM: Look at the last thirty days of your daily discipleship with Jesus. Recall the opportunities you have been IN prayer, asking God to fill your fellow disciples with God's "spiritual wisdom and understanding." Describe how your life or the life of another disciple was "worthy of the Lord" and "pleasing him in every way"? Share how you've been strengthened with God's "great endurance and patience" through such fruit-filled activity of the Holy Spirit within you?*

We know from John 15, Jesus wants us to bear abundant fruit. He will enable us as we continue to grow more in the knowledge of God. We will be strengthened with all His power recognizing that though we may be weak, He can be strong IN us. How often have you testified with Paul's declaration in 2 Corinthians 12:10, "That is why, for Christ's sake, I delight in weaknesses, in insults, in hardships, in persecutions, in difficulties. For when I am weak, then I am strong." As a result, we would come to know and bear the fruit of endurance and patience. We would rejoice to see such fruit borne in and through our lives and actions, wouldn't we?

> RM: *Consider Paul's checklist of real life occurrences that were strength building ones. When were you subject to insults? Hardships? Persecutions? Difficulties? How did the Holy Spirit cause you to delight in them? How did you finally realize God's intention to become the strength you needed to respond to them the way He would respond?*

This perseverance is so necessary! This faith and confidence in the mighty power of God comes about as we see God Himself deliver upon the promises He makes to each of us. Don't become discouraged when it may not come as quickly or as packaged as we would like or think! We are reminded and reassured in Hebrews 10:35-36, "So do not throw away your confidence; it will be richly rewarded. You need to persevere so that when you have done the will of God, you will receive what he has promised."

> *RM: In retrospect, when have there been times you've thrown away the confidence God would give you? How can we give testimony to those the writer to the Hebrews goes on to describe in 10:39, "But we are not of those who shrink back and are destroyed, but of those who believe and are saved"?*

We are the clay; He is the potter as Isaiah 64:8 points out, "Yet, O Lord, you are our Father. We are the clay, you are the potter; we are all the work of your hand." It's not our place as clay to tell the potter how to form and shape us, as Isaiah 45:9 reminds us, " 'Does the clay say to the potter, 'What are you making?' " It's God's responsibility as our potter to shape and reshape us as He deems best. God revealed this to Jeremiah and to us in Jeremiah 18:4, 6, "But the pot he was shaping from the clay was marred in his hands; so the potter formed it into another pot, shaping as it seemed best to him.... 'O house of Israel, can I not do with you as this potter does?' declares the Lord. 'Like clay in the hand of the potter, so are you in my hand, O house of Israel.' "

> *RM: How can we trust Him to know what that is*
> *and how to do it? Are there certain aspects of our*
> *life we would feel more confident handing off to God*
> *to reshape? Why would this not be pleasing to Him?*

God would show us that the priceless treasure of Who He is can be found in each of us. 2 Corinthians 4:7 paints the proper prospective, "But we have this treasure in jars of clay to show that this all-surpassing power is from God and not from us." Think of all the treasure He has stored up in you and I! Aren't we truly fragile and ordinary jars of clay? Aren't we blessed that our Holy God would choose to dwell in us and exhibit His "all-surpassing" power in and through us?

We know our spiritual selves well enough to know that there are ups and downs, highs and lows, peaks and valleys...all we've encountered within our walk with God, no matter how long or far we've been walking together. We also know how lazy we can be when it comes to doing the work of walking with God. Work, you say? Yes, to do something well requires a passion to do it, practice doing it often, and patience to know it takes time, doesn't it?

> RM: *Ponder these questions won't you? Do you have*
> *a deep heart felt passion, the Holy Heartburn I spoke*
> *of previously, so that you would do all you could*
> *to sit like Mary and learn from Jesus? You need to*
> *learn how to function with this spiritual body, don't*
> *you? How are you going to learn unless you practice*
> *a spiritually disciplined life? How often will you fail*
> *or fall short? How often will temptation lead to sin*
> *and the need for God's forgiveness?*

What will the Holy Spirit desire you to receive so that you dedicate the necessary daily time for your daily discipleship? Discipline! (Interesting how the word describing the person of a "disciple" comes out of the trait of such a learner/follower who exhibits "discipline"!)

Proverbs 23:23 admonishes us to possess three things, "get wisdom, discipline and understanding." We would gain all these things from God, who stands ready to teach and equip us. We will come to appreciate the blessings God has in store for us as we become aware of them and live by them.

Proverbs 4:11-13 points this out: "I guide you in the way of wisdom and lead you along straight paths. When you walk, your steps will not be hampered; when you run, you will not stumble. Hold to instruction, do not let it go; guard it well, for it is your life." We need only look to God and the Holy Spirit, His designated instructor, for our spiritual growth and maintenance. He can choose to give us a passion for spiritual discipline so that with practice and patience we might grow closer in God's love and holiness!

What are spiritual disciplines? Why would the Holy Spirit use them? As the Holy Spirit chooses how to make us more holy, more Christ-like, He may choose to use any number of some fifty known spiritual disciplines as tools to accomplish His transforming, clay shaping work in our spiritual lives.

It's as if the Holy Spirit has a tool kit or a well equipped gym for His use. He chooses to use spiritual disciplines like varying forms and practices of prayer, fasting, reading God's Word, Sabbath rest and practice, worship, service, humility in varying degrees throughout our walk with God to lengthen it, strengthen it, deepen it, extend it...all with the goal that we may become perfect in Christ. (Colossians 1:28) This comes about through our receiving His passion, practice and patience as He would instruct us in all wisdom. Matthew 5:48, " 'Be perfect, therefore, as your heavenly Father is perfect.' " is linked to Colossians 1:28, "We proclaim him, admonishing and teaching everyone with all wisdom, so that we may present everyone perfect in Christ." The Holy Spirit's use of spiritual disciplines in our spiritual lives would make us perfect as our heavenly Father is perfect!

Why would the Holy Spirit use spiritual disciplines? 2 Corinthians 7:1 paints a pretty accurate picture of our need and His necessity to use them. "Since we have these promises, dear friends, let us purify ourselves from everything that contaminates body and spirit, perfecting holiness out of reverence for God." We need to be purified. We need to be sanctified. We need to daily drown the old man and his sinful desires. We need to know that the devil could use anything to attack our body, and spiritual spirit through temptation (More on that in Chapter Six!) Passion that only the Holy Spirit can instill in us bears fruit through disciplined, faithful practice He can give us as He perfects us in His holiness.

Remember it is God's desire that His children be holy as He is holy. 1 Thessalonians 4:3 states it is God's will that we be sanctified, made holy! Later in the same chapter, verses 7 and 8 admonish us that God calls us to live a holy life. "For God did not call us to be impure, but to live a holy life. Therefore, he who rejects this instruction does not reject man but God, who gives you his Holy Spirit." (1 Thessalonians 4:7-8) If we should reject such teaching and instruction, then we are rejecting God the Holy Spirit, who was given to us for such a purpose!

> RM: *How do these pretty strong words motivate and discipline you into such a holy life? How often are we unaware of sins we've committed against others unless someone points them out? Why would we benefit asking another daily disciple to see areas of our spiritual life requiring more of the Holy Spirit's disciplined work within us?*

We need to come to the realization that when it comes to becoming more holy, more sanctified, it's not ME; it's HE! What can the Holy Spirit accomplish? God has given us our spiritual bodies. God has shaped us out of the dust of the earth. The clay He holds as the Potter holds the light of Christ within us. It's the light of Christ, shown through our hearts, that gives us the knowledge and power of God to walk in a world of darkness. Such a power of God comes from God Himself, not us! We cannot save ourselves nor can we make ourselves holy as God is. Only HE can do it, and He desires to do it through us, jars of clay!

Yes, God is able, isn't He? 2 Corinthians 9:8 describes that all abounding grace God has given to you, your salvation, and doesn't just end with that! "And God is able to make all grace abound to you, so that in all things at all times, having all that you need, you will abound in every good work." Within our spiritual body, as God's Holy Spirit builds us up, He gives us all things at all times having everything we need when we need it.

While we may be tempted to think it's as much as we do that will bring about even more holiness, it actually needs to be less of ME; more of HE! We don't set out to be praying more, fasting more, reading God's Word more with the expectation that the more we put in, the more we get out! No, remember Jesus declaration to us in John 15:5? Apart from me, you can do nothing? We are not able; He is ALL able!

> RM: *Reading these two promises of God what further convincing do you need to keep trying to do it all on your own? Honestly spend time in reflective prayer upon the abounding grace God is able to provide for you. Note any obstacle you would believe God is unable to overturn or transform according to His perfect will for you! Rise from prayer recognizing GOD and GOD ALONE can accomplish whatever HE sets His mind to do through you...as long as you let Him!*

Jesus was able to take upon Himself our sins and die in our place a death that was acceptable to God the Father. Within that redeemed relationship with God, He gives us the Holy Spirit, who is able to sanctify us and make us more Christ like! Romans 8:32 points out, "He who did not spare his own Son, but gave him up for us all—how will he not also, along with him, graciously give us all things?"

We may not know what to do, what to pray for, what spiritual discipline is best for us at a particular point in our spiritual body building. The Holy Spirit knows! He makes us strong when we are weak! (2 Corinthians 12:10) We are assured in Romans 8:26, "In the same way, the Spirit helps us in our weakness. We do not know what we ought to pray for, but the Spirit himself intercedes for us with groans that words cannot express."

Just as, it's not us who benefits from the number of times we perform some spiritual discipline, we also do not perform spiritual disciplines in order to be seen by others. While physical body builders might go to be seen by others and show off what they have accomplished, it's not the same with spiritual body building! God will not reward us or build us up based on how much and how often we do "holy exercises!" Jesus warns us against that in Matthew 6:1, " 'Be careful not to do you acts of righteousness before men, to be seen by them. If you do, you will have no reward from your Father in heaven.'"

> RM: *When would there be times you would be tempted to boast and brag about how holy you are? While you may give God the credit, how does the focus remain on Him at work and not on you? Carefully consider and ponder this outcome if you feel led to "boast in the Lord!"*

We must not put the focus on outward signs or the Holy Spirit's use of spiritual disciplines in our spiritual lives and bodies. Rather don't let anyone see all the activity going on below ground, like in a plant or within your spiritual body. We don't need to be digging below the surface to evaluate the state of the root system. We don't need to be wondering just how connected our brother or sister in Christ is or compared to us. No, we ought to encourage and be encouraged by what's happening above ground, whether it is a fruit-filled branch or a daily disciple's disciplined display of fruit which only the Holy Spirit can grow! Do you think that's why God's Word says in several places that if we're going to boast, " 'let him who boasts boast in the Lord.' " (1 Corinthians 1:31)?

What, then, am I supposed to do? Discover through God's Word what four "I am's" you are as His Disciple. Two we've spoken of already, but it can't hurt to review again, can it? Remember, practice, persistence, and patience?

I am a branch. (John 15:5) In the previous chapter, we spent time talking about this dynamic depiction of a daily disciple's life and walk. What more can you learn from it if you pondered all these things from God in your heart, like Mary in Luke 2:19? There's something "freeing" to my soul and spirit and way of thinking when I am assured there is nothing I can do to be fruit bearing or become holy like Jesus! That means I can never run out of the necessary power. I can never do something wrong that would botch things up. All authority and power has been given to the Holy Spirit. All that He needs is the accessibility to me. I must surrender my total self to Him in order for the Holy Spirit to have the necessary space to work within my spiritual body and life.

The other message that Jesus repeatedly promises is that as we're connected to Him, and connected to the will of the Father, He will make all things possible for the Holy Spirit to accomplish His work. (John 15:7, 16 b) Our prayers need to be focused on such a Person and goal as the Holy Spirit, our Sanctifier, who would sanctify each of us!

I am a vessel. (2 Corinthians 4:7) Earlier in this chapter, we spoke about this categorization as clay. Have you pondered how your spiritual body becomes a vessel, holding God's treasure, and shaped totally by God's powerful hand? Perhaps our Lord Jesus knows we need to hear more than once just how things truly are, how powerful He truly is? How much are His grace and mercy truly a gift we cannot earn or create but only receive? Again, taking upon ourselves the yoke of our Savior and Lord Jesus (Matthew 11:30), don't we find it to be light in comparison to all He did for us? He wants the Holy Spirit to teach us His ways, ways of His holiness.

> RM: *What could we let go so that He would fill our hands with all that is necessary to carry His holiness? What direction would we be taking contrary to His way and walk towards holiness? Hasn't He shown us if He is able and capable of our salvation, isn't His Holy Spirit capable of transforming our vessel of clay into His vessel of holiness?*

I am a servant. (Romans 12:1-18) God desires us, as His servants, to present our bodies, both physical and spiritual, as living sacrifices that are holy and pleasing to Him. (Remember it pleases God that we know and walk in His ways as Joshua outlines in Joshua 22:5.) We ought not to think more highly of ourselves than we ought. Again, God gives us another admonition to take to heart within the practice of spiritual disciplines. We don't do them; HE does them for our personal holiness, not meant to be judged or compared to another disciple's! He puts us in one body with different gifts, which He gives in order to be used according to the grace God has given us (verses 3-8). Much like the fruit of the Spirit, which He bears through His Spirit as He enables us to walk in His Spirit (Galatians 5:22-23, 25), so we're reminded again of what a life of holiness ought to look like and play out in the daily WALKing and TALKing disciple (verses 9-18). As our Savior and Lord demonstrated His life as a servant, especially on the last night with His disciples, we ought to take to head and heart His words and heed them (Remind yourself by reading again John 13:14-17)!

> RM: *As servants side by side, how would the devil try to break up the understanding God would have us practice in how we think about ourselves and each other? How would we depend upon God to put self-seeking boastfulness aside? How would we invite others to be cheerful in diligently serving the Lord and not self?*

I am a witness. (Acts 4:20) I've saved this point for last because according to God's plan and desire, it would naturally follow. As I mentioned previously, how can we expect disciples to make disciples if THEY aren't daily disciples? We can't! It won't happen! But, now that you've come to understand what it means to be a daily disciple...and how God desires all men to be saved and come to the knowledge of the Truth, Jesus Christ (1 Timothy 2:4), you can respond more favorably to God's command to GO and make disciples (Matthew 28:19); to BE His witnesses (Acts 1:8b); and to be ready to GIVE a reason for the hope that is in you (1 Peter 3:15)!

Through your daily disciple's walk, through the Holy Spirit's transforming and sanctifying work in your life, you will have a testimony. You will have a witness. You will have God-inspired stories to share with all those who would listen...whom the Holy Spirit will send by His power (1 Corinthians 2:4-5) and with whom the Holy Spirit will give you His own words (1 Corinthians 2:13) to share in the stories! You will be enabled by the Holy Spirit's work in and through your life to say with Peter and John, "For we cannot help speaking about what we have seen and heard." (Acts 4:20)

> RM: *How would you chime in with the Samarian woman at the well, who was so overcome with her time with Jesus, she said to anyone who would listen, "Come, see a man who told me everything I ever did" (John 4:29)? What things would Jesus have revealed in your life that you would share with those who would listen?*

Chances are as the Holy Spirit is at work in such a divine appointment He would arrange, your responder would say like the townspeople of that Samaritan woman, "We no longer believe just because of what you said; now we have heard for ourselves, and we know that this man really is the Savior of the world." (John 4:42)

Do you mind if I invoke author's privilege and share with you some things that may not be found or ground in Scripture? Call them lessons from the Spiritual School of Hard Knocks? (Matthew 7:7-8)

There will be times on your daily discipleship walk when you receive a renewed and refreshed step to your walk. It won't be what you did or failed to do. It's what the Holy Spirit will continue to be doing as you respond to Him. Jesus often talks about faith that is lacking in His disciple's lives. He tries to reassure us in Matthew 17:20, " 'I tell you the truth, if you have faith as small as a mustard seed, you can say to this mountain, 'Move from here to there' and it will move. Nothing will be impossible for you.'"

> RM: *Why do we fail to see the power of the Holy Spirit IN us? Consider why we fail to believe God has that same kind of power ready to work in and through us! Why do we fail to understand that the amount of faith isn't as necessary as HAVING the faith to believe God will do what He says He will do?*

Remember Peter walking on the water as Jesus says, "Come!" (Matthew 14:29) He had enough faith, as long as his eyes were on Jesus. Peter came as far as arms length to Jesus on the water. And then, Peter took his eyes off of Jesus and tried walking on the water on his own. What happened? He cried out for Jesus to save him because he started to sink! And Jesus replies? "You have so little faith! Why did you doubt me?" (Matthew 14:31)

This was not the first time Peter got it into his head to try and do it all on his own. (Luke 5:1-11) He was a skilled and seasoned fisherman, who first met Jesus at the end of a time of teaching. Jesus asked Peter to go out on the lake and bring in the catch of fish waiting for him. Peter's so-so faith caused him to try and do what Jesus said, despite his excuse that he hadn't caught anything, the whole night having now ended! But they couldn't bring in all the fish Jesus enabled them to catch, could they? And Peter's reply? He knew that Jesus knew him for who he truly was...one who would do it all on his own! He was capable. He was successful. He was experienced. He didn't even need the Son of God to help him when it came to fishing. Or did he? If Peter recognized that he needed Jesus, could he change his ways? Could he encumber enough faith to believe? Would he take Jesus at His word and become that catcher of men? Remember he immediately left everything and followed Jesus?

> RM: *Look inside yourself and ask, "How much am I like Peter? What would cause me to respond the way Peter did?" Identify some tendencies the devil would be aware of and use as obstacles between yourself and Jesus.*

Get past Peter's faith enabling him to walk on the water. Move on month's later past Peter's vehement cursing and denial of Jesus, which Peter made again with his eyes off Jesus. (Luke 22:60-62)

You would think Peter would have learned something by now, don't you? Well, perhaps the third time's the charm? Now, after the resurrection, Jesus appears one morning unknown to Peter and the others. (John 21:1-14) Again, experienced Peter out on the lake, not having caught any fish all night, encounters a voice and scenario he should have recalled from Luke 5! Again, Jesus shows Peter and the others that if they would only keep their faith and actions in line with Jesus commands, they wouldn't be able to handle all the blessings that would come their way. It didn't pay to do it on their own. It didn't yield any kind of measurable results if they depended upon their own strength and understanding, did it?

> RM: *When you consider Proverbs 3:5-6, "Trust in the Lord with all your heart and lean not on your own understanding; in all your ways acknowledge him, and he will make your paths straight," what more ought you to be doing?*

We read that as Peter does what Jesus asks, they couldn't bring in the multitude of fish, AGAIN! Jesus' power is overwhelming and far exceeds our limited faith and ability! Peter can't face Jesus. Time to jump ship!

I wonder if these three times were the reason why Jesus asked Peter three times about his love for Jesus and his response to Jesus? Would Peter finally get his eyes off himself, his own abilities and limitations, and let God's Holy Spirit transform Peter into that trusting, faith believing, Jesus-following fisher of men? Would he let God's Holy Spirit have His way like Jesus originally asked him to be three years and many lessons and miracles before? (John 21:15-19) Jesus had enough faith in the Holy Spirit's power to transform lives, didn't He? Because two more times now, Jesus says to Peter, "Follow Me! You must follow Me!" (John 21:19, 22)

> RM: *What about you? Has God exceeded the three time rule with you? How does God continue to reshape you into a believing and receiving disciple who knows better not to question anymore? What stories could you share that would help others "get the picture" that Peter eventually did?*

How would Peter turn out? He would have enough faith, and eyes off himself and what he had, to say in Jesus name, "Walk!" to a crippled beggar. (Acts 3:6) Peter would be filled and responsive to the Holy Spirit and His divine appointment after he and John were seized and put in jail. (Acts 4:1-12) He had that reason for hope in him as well as the Holy Spirit given opportunity to let the Holy Spirit speak through Him...and, so He/he did! Acts 4:13 gives testimony to the Holy Spirit's power and authority by God to accomplish His work doesn't it? "How could these unschooled and ordinary men say these things? What courage?" What faith! Talk about BOLD! Peter's spirit became BOLDER by God's Holy Spirit when he testifies as I shared earlier, "We can't help speaking about what we've seen and heard!" (Acts 4:20)

Peter learned it was far better to move away from the shallow shoreline into the deep water where Jesus was calling him. How about you? Have you the demonstrated faith to find you in the deep water with Jesus?

> RM: *Don't you wish at this point that you could be transformed like Peter? Take some time out to reflect how you can you identify with Peter.*

I can! For too many years, I tried to be Jesus disciple ON MY OWN! I thought I had everything necessary to be His teacher, preacher, and passionate communicator. I may have had a few fruitful opportunities by the grace of God. But, believe me, God was not blessing my faith-unto-myself efforts! God could do SO MUCH MORE! Would I let Him?

I had my John 21 Tuesday when God's voice and Word finally got through to me! I had heard and seen it all before. I hadn't given Jesus my Lord the Lordship He rightfully should have in my teaching ministry. I was coming up with an empty net for all the times I went out fishing! How much more could He accomplish if HE was in charge, totally and completely? I would only come to know that by allowing Him total access within His teaching ministry. Yes, it was not right to call it "my" teaching ministry! If God was the giver and the equipper and the provider, then it had to ALL WAYS be HIS teaching ministry!

This book and all that has come slightly before and whatever after are a direct result of my John 21 Tuesday! Have you come to the point in your walk, in your daily discipleship with Him, that it's time to turn the walk over to Him and the Holy Spirit? Aren't you tired of coming up with an empty net? Aren't your tired of all the fruitless effort you've put out? Aren't you ready to let the Holy Spirit BE the Holy Spirit in your life and walk?

I am ashamed to say I, too, was like Peter up to the point of John 21. I have felt contrition; a heart felt sorry-ness for my sins of doubt. I confess that I tried to do it all on my own, trusting Jesus to be my Savior, but not my Lord. By the power of the Holy Spirit, I daily drown the old man that would want to be the old self-centered, self-seeking, self-driving, self-achieving Randy Michael Wendt. I pray by His grace and mercy that His Holy Spirit would bring about true, fruitful repentance, that would not point to me and my effort, but would give glory and praise to God alone who could accomplish His good work through me. As a result, my daily walk has been more a disciple's walk with His teacher rather than a disciple's walk trying to become his own teacher!

I wish to bring forth a fresh message from the Lord that would speak to me, as well as anyone else, who would be led by His Holy Spirit to read and listen. I pray your Holy Spirit generated, heart burning question becomes, "How am I to WALK and TALK in His Name?"

The Holy Spirit stands ready to teach you, as His very own daily disciple. School's in session! Won't you pray, "Show me, O Lord, Your message and Your teaching for my discipleship"?

He answered that prayer for me and gave me His Word and teaching faithfully in every chapter of this book. I've come to understand that it's not a dictation; it's a revelation! God answers my heartfelt petition to know His Word, His Will, and His Way for my discipleship and disciple-making. He also knows what He wants you to know.

BE encouraged by these words I would adopt from Paul found in Colossians 1:25-29: "I have become its servant by the commission God gave me to present to you the word of God in its fullness—the mystery that has been kept hidden for ages and generations, but is now disclosed to the saints. To them God has chosen to make known among the Gentiles the glorious riches of this mystery, which is Christ in you, the hope of glory. We proclaim him, admonishing and teaching everyone with all wisdom, so that we may present everyone perfect in Christ. To this end I labor, struggling with all his energy, which so powerfully works in me."

You have trusted your Savior Jesus to fulfill all God desired for your salvation. He has gone ahead to prepare a permanent place for you to walk with Him in Heaven. (John 14:2)

You need to trust your Lord Jesus with fulfilling all God desires for your sanctification. You were created in Christ Jesus for holy, fruit bearing good works. He has given you His Holy Spirit who is capable to do them through you. (Ephesians 2:10)

May that same transforming and sanctifying Holy Spirit of God be about completing the good work He has begun in you until the day our Lord Jesus returns...and your earthly walk with Him is over...and your heavenly walk with Him begins!

Chapter Five

How can I be a faithful and fruitful steward of God's gift of time?

I teach a course called, "An Introduction to Spiritual Body Building," through WALKing and TALKing Ministries, a teaching ministry of discipleship and disciple-making God gave me in March, 2010.

This chapter is probably one of the most beneficial sessions of the spiritual body building course's three components: WHY we should allow the Holy Spirit's building our spiritual bodies up in His holiness is covered in the first hour; HOW the Holy Spirit will accomplish His ongoing work is discussed in the second hour; and WHEN in our daily lives will the Holy Spirit have the opportunity to build up our spiritual bodies IN Christ Jesus is addressed in the third and final hour. As God's Holy Spirit speaks and teaches us through the Bible, daily disciples of our Savior and Lord Jesus come hungry and fed for more!

This book does not replace any course God designs and enables me to teach through WALKing and TALKing Ministries.

I am thankful for the confines of this book because of the limited time a course provides. You can go at your own pace in your own space. You can reread until it sticks in your mind. You can throw it in the slow cooker of your mind and let it simmer and savor. What this book cannot provide is the blessing of participating in real time with real people. God's Spirit is present and at work through teaching and discussion. As we prospect through God's Word with fellow disciples, we receive the blessing He intends for all those who "ask, seek, and knock!" That's why making time with fellow disciples every week is vital! (As you have interest and opportunity, send me an email for more information about offering discipleship, disciple-making, and spiritual body building courses for you and your church!)

Let me direct you, briefly, through the WHY and HOW components so that we're on the same path of the road together. Then, I'll delve further into the WHEN as we see the challenge up ahead of each of us!

I have prospected through God's Word for many references to our WALK with Him. I sought to discover and affirm our need for the daily building up of the spiritual bodies He gives us. I've shared several of them with you so far in this book. One of the central verses that speak to the NEED of having God's Holy Spirit build us up can be found in 1 Corinthians 6:19-20, "Do you not know that your body is a temple of the Holy Spirit, who is in you, whom you have received from God? You are not your own; you were bought at a price. Therefore honor God with your body."

Within our discipleship walk with Him, how often do we fail to remember what we ought to know? First, that we have a body that has become a temple of the Holy Spirit. Second, the temple isn't empty! The Holy Spirit DOES reside IN us! Third, we have received this spiritual body from God! God not only created us physically from the dust of the ground. He has shaped and formed us like clay in the hands of the Potter. God also, through baptism, gives us an inner spiritual body. What makes it spiritual? Literally, His Spirit! As we've discussed previously, our Holy God desires, demands that we become holy like Him! How can that happen unless His Holy Spirit would live and work within us?

> RM: *How have you seen the Holy Spirit creating and shaping and transforming your body into His own SPIRIT-ual body? What makes it easier for Him to accomplish His work in you? What makes it more challenging for Him to accomplish such a work in you?*

Back to prospecting the rest of the verse at hand! The remaining statement of 1 Corinthians 6:19 is a declaration! It declares the redemptive work of God the Son, who gave up His life for us. We were bought at the price of His innocent suffering and death. As we have put on Christ through our baptism, we are no longer our own! I might add, we are no longer left to be alone as well! Our Savior and Lord Jesus has enabled His Holy Spirit to be our constant companion, hasn't He? We are never on our own or left alone, are we?

> RM: *Where are there areas in your spiritual body where you lean on the Holy Spirit? How would your daily walk be if He wasn't around? Where does the Holy Spirit still need to be Lord in your spiritual body?*

What is our response? What is our responsibility? We are to honor God with our body. How can we do that? What pleases God? What gives Him glory? Again, we've spoken about this previously. We are to come to know His ways. We are to come to know Him through His Word. The Bible serves as our guide for the journey He makes with us. We allow His Holy Spirit to be actively at work in every aspect of our life every day. It's both the desire and the ability of the Holy Spirit to make us more Christ-like. He shapes and molds us to become more holy even as He is holy.

What is God's will for you? "It is God's will that you should be sanctified." (1 Thessalonians 4:3a) How would we be sanctified or holy except by the work of the Holy Spirit? 1 Peter 1:13-16 gives us a better understanding of both God's will and work for our spiritual bodies and lives. "Therefore, prepare your minds for action; be self-controlled; set your hope fully on the grace to be given you when Jesus Christ is revealed. As obedient children, do not conform to the evil desires you had when you lived in ignorance. But just as he who called you is holy, so be holy in all you do; for it is written: 'Be holy, because I am holy.'" (1 Peter 1:13-16)

> RM: *How likely is it that the Holy Spirit can accomplish such a work in your spiritual body and life? Describe the problems and praises you see in terms of self-control? Think about living under God's grace: what are some things you're still trying to do that God has already done for you? What evil desires do you still conform to rather than to God's holiness?*

Let's prospect through some more of God's Word seeking His Holy Spirit's desire and direction to build up your spiritual body. *You'll find some Road Map questions following each verse to aid you in your prospecting and pondering.*

1 Thessalonians 4:1, 7-8

1) "Finally, brothers, we instructed you how to live in order to please God, as in fact you are living. Now we ask you and urge you in the Lord Jesus to do this more and more." *Why are we urged "to do this more and more"?*

7) "For God did not call us to be impure, but to live a holy life." *Why would impurity still seek to enslave us, who are free in Jesus?*

8) "Therefore, he who rejects this instruction does not reject man but God, who gives you his Holy Spirit." *What would cause us to reject this instruction?*

2 Timothy 1:6-9

6) "For this reason I remind you to fan into flame the gift of God, which is in you through the laying on of my hands." *What is this "gift of God" and why ought it be fanned "into flame" in your spiritual body?*

7) "For God did not give us a spirit of timidity, but a spirit of power, of love and of self-discipline." *How has God's spirit of power evident in your spiritual life? How does God's spirit of love enlighten those in darkness? How has God's spirit of self-discipline been an anchor in your spiritual life?*

8) "So do not be ashamed to testify about our Lord, or ashamed of me his prisoner. But join with me in suffering for the gospel, by the power of God," *Why would the devil desire us*

to be ashamed about sharing what Jesus has and does in and through our lives? Why would God's power enable us to suffer for the Gospel? Describe such suffering in your life.

9) "who has saved us and called us to a holy life—not because of anything we have done but because of his own purpose and grace. This grace was given us in Christ Jesus before the beginning of time." *When you compare your life to that of a Lost person, what are the signs of God's grace at work in yours? Describe the holy life He enables you to lead so that the glory is Christ-centered.*

2 Peter 1:3, 5-8

3) "His divine power has given us everything we need for life and godliness through our knowledge of him who called us by his own glory and goodness." *What would you lack for your life and godliness that God can provide? Where are there areas in your life yet to be touched by God's divine power? How has Jesus' glory and goodness impacted your spiritual life?*

5-7) "For this very reason, make every effort to add to your faith goodness; and to goodness, knowledge; and to knowledge, self-control; and to self-control, perseverance; and to perseverance, godliness; and to godliness, brotherly kindness; and to brotherly kindness, love." *Where does your effort stop and the Holy Spirit's effort begin within your spiritual self? How would your faith benefit from goodness added to it? How would knowledge aid you in goodness? How would self-control be enhanced by knowledge? What does perseverance have to do with self-control? How would godliness assist you in perseverance? How would brotherly kindness flow from godliness? How does love distinguish itself from brotherly kindness?*

8) "For if you possess these qualities in increasing measure, they will keep you from being ineffective and unproductive in your knowledge of our Lord Jesus Christ." *How would God desire to see us utilize our knowledge of Jesus as our Lord? How could you see ineffective and unproductive results occur in your spiritual life if you had less and less of the qualities described in verses 5-7?*

1 John 1:6-7

6) "If we claim to have fellowship with him yet walk in darkness, we lie and do not live by the truth." *How would the devil lie to us, telling us, we have fellowship with God while walking in darkness?*

7) "But if we walk in the light, as he is in the light, we have fellowship with one another, and the blood of Jesus, his Son, purifies us from all sin." *How does walking in the light show we have fellowship with fellow disciples? What aspects of such a walk do we share? When might we would walk alone and isolated from fellow disciples? What sin can Jesus' blood not purify us from? Why would we think otherwise?*

3 John 3-4

3) "It gave me great joy to have some brothers come and tell about your faithfulness to the truth and how you continue to walk in the truth." *How does the testimony of other disciples' walk give us great joy? How would the Holy Spirit enable us to remain faithful to the truth? What can you share with*

another disciple about how you have continued "to walk in the truth"?

4) "I have no greater joy than to hear that my children are walking in the truth." *What would lead John to make such a statement? How could hearing such accounts bring him such joy? How can you relate to John's declaration? Recall such a story of a fellow disciple "walking in the truth." Write out such a story from your own Spirit-led walk and share it with another disciple.*

Physical body builders have certain necessary components at hand in order to accomplish their objective: the physical building up of their bodies. The need is not different on behalf of God's Spiritual body builders, is it? Don't we need to KNOW and enable Him to get GOing?

Let's draw upon some comparisons between physical and spiritual body builders. Let's draw up a check list and ask God to supply all we need so that He can accomplish His work in us!

For starters, adequate and dedicated work out SPACE.

1) Find the right GYM for exercise. Designate a comfortable, dedicated space in your home for spiritual exercise. Consider a place where you can go 24/7 both undisturbed and not disturbing others.

2) Make sure lighting and temperature can be easily controlled. Too much light and too much heat/cold can affect the outcome. Avoid falling "asleep in Jesus!"

3) Keep the space uncluttered and undistracted. Have enough room for all the equipment and a work out

partner. It becomes a sign of a spiritual life uncluttered and undistracted.

MY Workout Space will be: _____

Next, a source of FOOD that energizes us for growth.

1) The Word of God is our only source of spiritual food as we grow from milk (1 Peter 2:2) to meat (Hebrews 5:14). Prospecting out of a resourceful Bible is vital to our ongoing spiritual development.

2) The Bible we work out with should have

a. Easy to read print we won't strain to read!

b. A cross-referencing system usually found in the center of the page. It will establish and "tie together" other verses that relate to what we read.

c. A thorough Concordance usually found in the back of the Bible. It will supply a series of words and locations within verses that we can read.

d. If possible, Exegetical references for the layperson. You may not know God's original languages of the Bible. These references can bless you with added insights in the verse you're reading.

e. A sound theological commentary is also a blessing. God has gifted life time students of His Word, who can share the Holy Spirit's insights with you.

f. Ability to highlight and write, if you so choose, what God reveals to you. Don't be afraid you'll be leaving bleeding pages behind.

3) From our prospecting efforts, we develop a treasure chest of gold nuggets and precious jewels by writing out verses on index cards, one verse per card.

a. As we read daily, our Scripture cards are mined (written out) every day. Of course, write or print so that you can easily recall what's written.

b. We carry them around for the day and refer to them. You never know when the Holy Spirit will give you an opportunity to digest further or to share with another.

c. We comment on the back as we ponder them as Mary did. Ask the Holy Spirit to enlighten the darkness of your understanding. You can expect He will give you insights you would forget if you didn't write them down.

d. We categorize and file for future viewing. Who knows how God will speak to us or through us with a verse down the road on our walk with Him?

A source of WATER we can depend upon to keep going!

1) Just as a water bottle is necessary for refreshment and revitalization, so Prayer becomes the spiritual drink from which we draw upon as we read in 1 Peter 4:7b, "Therefore be clear minded and self-controlled so that you can pray."

2) We pray several times during our work out

a. Before we enter our gym

b. Before we begin our stretching

c. As we take up weights

d. As we take a break

e. As we resume the regimen

f. As we cool down

g. As we leave our gym

3) We want Jesus to give us the living water only He has access to by prayer. "If you knew the gift of God and who it is that asks you for a drink, you would have asked him and he would have given you living water" as He promises us in John 4:10. We also hear Jesus promise us in John 4:13-14, " 'Everyone who drinks this water will be thirsty again, but whoever drinks the water I give him will never thirst. Indeed, the water I give him will become in him a spring of water welling up to eternal life.' "

A Variety of HELPFUL WEIGHTS

1) The weights that the Holy Spirit can choose and use can be drawn upon from some 50 known Spiritual Disciplines grounded in the Word of God.

2) Beginning with Solitude and Silence, you'll find these helpful for any and all other Spiritual Disciplines.

3) From these, the Holy Spirit will guide you through the proper setting to come upon and remain in God's presence (Solitude). Invite Him to help deal with distractions that would prevent you from focusing (being still) on God, as well as being receptive to His conversation with you (being silent to hear). We'll give you a free set of weights to get you started in this book. See Chapter Six for your free set!

4) Send me an email if you're interested in learning more about the many Spiritual Disciplines the Holy Spirit can use

in your spiritual body building! I've developed courses and resources through the Academy of Spiritual Disciplines, another offering from WALKing and TALKing Ministries. They will introduce, instruct, and inspire you as you seek the Holy Spirit's will and direction in your spiritual body building. Beyond traditional in-person courses, you can inquire about "on-line" courses through the Internet. My email address is randy@walkingandtalkingministries.com

A Work Out PLAN and SCHEDULE

1) What basic plan should spiritual body builders follow? It can be tweaked based upon your response as you get under way. You can also tweak it based on your desire to proceed further in your spiritual conditioning. Consider a daily work out balanced with additional weekly work outs of worship and Bible Study with others.

2) Would you enlist a work out partner? A fellow disciple, who can be your spotter as you utilize the weights for the day's workout? The same person could be a welcomed accountability partner. You could pray for someone who will encourage you to stick to the work out plan and schedule. 1 Peter 4:8-11 offers direction for work out partners, "Above all, love each other deeply, because love covers a multitude of sins. Offer hospitality to one another without grumbling. Each one should use whatever gift he has received to serve others, faithfully administering God's grace in its various forms. If anyone speaks, he should do it as one speaking the very words of God. If anyone serves, he should do it with the strength God provides so that in all things God may be praised through Jesus Christ. To him be the glory and the power for ever and ever. Amen."

3) Pray for God's guidance and direction as your formulate your work out plan. Give it a try and see if the scheduled time actually enables some meaningful work out time and beneficial fruit. If not, make any necessary changes rather than giving up!

WHEN is the best time for the Holy Spirit to do His spiritual body building of me? Time is a gift of God we all have received. God has given us only 24 hours in a day. Some think that's not enough. I wonder if they would be any better consumers of their time if they gained a few more hours or lost a few more hours. What do you think?

Do you manage your time or does time mismanage you? Want a real eye opener? Will you make the investment of a few minutes together with a piece of paper and a pencil (Yes, please do this with a pencil so you can edit as necessary!) Ready?

Draw a circle that fills up the paper. Divide it into equal thirds. Write the number 8 in the center of each third. You should have three sections of eight, reflecting three eight hour periods in a twenty-four hour day. Now, for the hard part! You need to take some time coming up with a typical day's use of your time. Make sure it adds up to the three categories of eight. Start with the easiest one: sleep. How many hours in a typical day do you sleep? Whether you work or are retired, consider a typical week day, Monday through Friday. Write down "Sleep= " and fill in the average number of hours you sleep.

Next, take a look at the following categories to determine how much time you spend in a typical week day. Don't make it too difficult since I'm not asking for a minute-by-minute inventory.

But come up with a reasonable accounting of your time doing these things:

Rising chores, including shower and getting dressed (B)

Breakfast, lunch and dinner, including preparing, consuming and cleaning up (B)

Errands of any kind (B)

Spending time on the Internet, watching TV and movies (B)

The Job, not including commute time or lunch time (C)

The Commute to and from work on the average day (C)

Time spent with family and friends, not including meal times (B)

Volunteer time given to church, organizations or team sports played (B)

Alone time immersed in yourself not reflecting the other categories (B)

God time or devotional time or prayer time but not at church (B)

Now, total up each category of (B) and (C) and split them off into the two remaining categories of time spent. You will need to adjust the "eight's" accordingly. But, your use of time should add all three categories to equal 24 hours.

How did your 24 hours divide out and add up? Again, is this an accurate picture of a typical week day for you? Do any necessary tweaking before you read on!

Now take a look at the three main categories of SLEEP, LIFE, and WORK. Does anyone seem out of place? Too little or too much? Do you function well as you spend your time? Are you within budget?

A daily WALKing disciple of our Savior and Lord Jesus MUST have daily time focused on the Holy Spirit's access to build up our spiritual body! It can't be drawn from SLEEP or WORK because they're already dedicated to other necessary aspects, aren't they? It's in the LIFE category that we establish our "GOD" time. GOD time includes prayer and devotional reading of God's Word. It can also become times of instruction, when God the Holy Spirit is holding class. Yes, there are times when we're hearing His lecture for our walk or undergoing a "pop" test!

> RM: How much time do you give for God and His spiritual body building in your life? Is it enough to read a printed daily devotional, say a quick prayer, grab a verse or two as a quick bite from God's Word as bread for your soul on the run or on the road? Do you give God the first fruits of your time for His spiritual body building in your life? Quite a different motivation and outcome, isn't it? Instead of lousy leftovers, you give the Holy Spirit the very best of your time. When would the best time of day be for you? When is your level of alertness and responsiveness at their peak?

Why would alertness and responsiveness be so vital and necessary for spiritual body builders? There is a real devil with a real desire to prevent the Holy Spirit the space He needs to accomplish His work. Take to heart and head the message Peter reminds us of in 1 Peter 5:8-9a, "Be self-controlled and alert. Your enemy the devil prowls around like a roaring lion looking for someone to devour. Resist him, standing firm in the faith". More on the devil and his distractions to our spiritual body building in the next chapter!

You may or may not be a tither, one who gives to God a tenth of his monetary possessions as God enables him. But have you considered tithing time? Might I encourage you to consider a daily spiritual body building work out of at least two hours? You might even consider an hour in the morning as you've woken up and an hour in the evening before you go to bed. What a goal! Rise with Jesus to start the walk of your day together! Retire with Jesus to end the walk of your day together!

I would encourage you to remember the alert and responsive factor, however. I know for myself, I am best the first thing in the day. I can get up early in the morning and am rearing to go! By the end of my day, I'm like a burned down candle! There's no more wax left to shine forth the light! So, while it's a great notion to rise and retire with Jesus for an hour each, it may not work as effectively as I and He would like it to be! You have to know yourself and what changes you can make that will effect change, don't you?

Whatever it would be, you need to be on a plan for your spiritual walking. He will enable your spiritual life and the building up of your spiritual body as the Holy Spirit has His place, and space to work. You also need the encouragement and fellowship of other spiritual body builders. Gyms just don't exist to provide you access to equipment or a place to go and work out! They also serve the purpose of encouragement and accountability, as you see others working out, too!

So it is with God's gym, the Church, for God's spiritual body builders! We need to be in His gym, at the very least, on your primary worship day. For some that might be a Sunday or a Wednesday or a Saturday. That time in intimate fellowship with Father, Son, and Holy Spirit is VITAL. What's really involved in worship as we ought to come to know it and receive it?

It's the time when God comes to us to serve us, don't you know? It's not so much OUR... going, our praying, our giving, our listening, and our doing! We come to God's house so that HE can be the welcoming Host. Can't you picture our Jesus at your church? Can't you see Him wash your feet upon entry? Wouldn't He extend a kiss of peace or a heart-felt handshake to you? Of course, He would wrap His arms of forgiveness around you as you confess you've failed and need His forgiveness. He would speak to you as you listen to His spoken Word. He would teach you as you listen to His preached and taught Word. He would hear you as you come with your petitions for self and intercessions for others. Through these supplications, He promises to supply all you need. Finally, He would bless you for your journey. You leave your church to enter into a world of darkness with His blessing. You've taken the opportunity to have your light reignited. His holy heartburn within your soul has been rekindled, hasn't it?

RM: *Take an inventory of ALL that! Why wouldn't you want to receive it every chance it's offered? Why shouldn't more churches be packed with those who would receive ALL the blessings God has in store for them? Physical body building gyms aren't always filled either. What does that say about one's overall stewardship of body and soul?*

Just as a physical body building gym offers classes, so does your spiritual body building gym at church. What's the purpose of the classes? Not to replace the work out regimen, but to enhance it! How involved are you in Sunday morning Bible class? What would attract and maintain your interest and participation? How about a gender specific group for men or women? How about a relationship specific group for singles, marrieds, families or single again?

RM: *Why or why not are you weekly involved in a small group? What experiences have fueled your interest and participation or the lack thereof? If you're not currently participating in a small group, what would convince you to do so?*

Interest groups can also be found in both gyms! Consider a specific focus that would bring you together with others for fellowship and education. Don't neglect this potentially well-rounded opportunity.

Small groups are also extremely helpful when they follow a common goal. I encourage churches to form a specific small discipleship group for participants of my WALK of a Disciple, TALK of a Disciple, or Introduction to Spiritual Body Building courses. The Holy Spirit is welcome to continue the construction work He began, both inside and outside of the courses taken over time. Participants get together for at least an hour a month. They look forward to the Holy Spirit's fire being rekindled within the topic as they continue to study on their own and with each other. Prayer draws them in and keeps them in a tight circle of fellowship with each other and God!

RM: *What about reading and discussing this book in a small group or book club? How has it been helpful so that you would invite some others to read it, as well? Would it provide the opportunity to encourage their spiritual WALK and TALK?*

Consider this book for a small group study or recommend it for your next book club endeavor. It can be as simple as taking a chapter a week. Ponder in your heart what God has to say to you and discover together what He would teach you, as His daily WALKing and TALKing disciple!

Have you found the equipment and courses in a physical body building gym to be overwhelming? You may find the same to be the case as you come to see ALL God desires to give you in the building up of your spiritual body. Like with the physical gyms, the more you become familiar, the more friendly and welcoming they become. It's no different with God's spiritual gym. You just have to be out there allowing Him the place and space in your life and spiritual body for HIM to do it!

Let's take time out and pray to that end!
O God, our loving and merciful Father!
We give You thanks that You not only desire, but You enable us to have a daily disciplined disciple's walk with You!
Your Son Jesus, our Savior, made it all possible for us.
Your Holy Spirit, our Sanctifier, makes it all possible for us.
Help us each and every day to rise anew, that we might give You the thanks and praise due You.
Give us opportunity eyes and opportunity ears to see and hear You at work as Your Holy Spirit would be building up our spiritual bodies.

Give us opportunities, too, to show us how much You love the lost and the dechurched You have placed in our lives.

Give us a burden for their lostness and a Holy Spirit-ignited heartburn to tell them about You. Enable us by your Holy Spirit to share the Hope we have within us and the Hope they seek! In Jesus' Name, we ask all these things! AMEN.

Chapter Six

How do I deal with the Devil's distractions?

A Disciplined and Dedicated Disciple Deals with the Devil's Distractions! As you begin to read this chapter, the devil will not want you to apply what you learn in your daily discipleship! Expect opposition. Encounter opposition. Enable God's all mighty Holy Spirit to engage in battle for you on this front!

> RM: *Before we get started, you've got to ask yourself, "Do I really believe in a real devil? Do I know for certain he exists for the purpose of destroying any relationship God would have with me?" If you can answer, "YES," then DO continue!*

The Six "D's"

1) "Disciplined" is not just a wish or a concept to strive for. It is a lifestyle that you cannot infuse by your own passion or persuasion, your own pressure or persistence. A disciplined spirit is God's own Holy Spirit. All that you need is FOUND in Him. All that you need is to CALL upon Him. All that

you need is to LEAN upon Him. All that you need is to GET OUT of the way so that He can fully accomplish His work!

2) "Dedicated" is not just here today, and maybe tomorrow. For the spiritual body builder, it's for the entirety of his or her spiritual life. The MORE you walk with God, the more you WANT to walk with God. You will see the blessings He has always had in store for you first hand. You have tasted and seen that the Lord IS good; you want to taste and see more every day, every step He takes with you on your walk together with Him!

3) "Disciple" is who you are and whose you are! As you've read several times so far, you are no longer your own. You were bought with a price. You answered His call, "Come, follow Me!" You desire to learn and walk His ways. You no longer want to lean upon your own understanding, stumbling upon life's crooked and dark road. You've come to learn and depend upon His commitment that didn't end at the cross or the empty tomb.

4) "Deals" is where you've come to in your walk with God. You're tired of avoiding a disciplined daily walk. You're tired of an empty life, devoid of ALL the blessings of God's bounty waiting to be bestowed upon you. You're tired of asking, "Is THIS all there IS?" You desire a life that's fulfilled and complete just like your Savior and Lord Jesus promised, "I have come that they have life, and have it to the full." (John 10:10b)

5) "Devil" is not just some fictional, medieval literary figure. There is a real devil and he is really intent upon stealing

and killing and destroying you and your relationship with God! (John 10:10a) More on him throughout this chapter!

6) "Distractions" are ways that the devil very intentionally and skillfully seeks to disrupt your daily walk with God. The devil would derail the locomotive God Himself as Engineer, is driving through your life with you, as His passenger. Distractions are annoyances that may seem trivial at first. Distractions can cause us to stop walking with God over time. How easy it is to miss Sunday after Sunday of God's serving you once you begin!

God's Word is not a work of fiction. It is a fountain of fact. We can only learn about the nature, and the intent of the devil through the truth of God's Word! God reveals all we need to know to describe the devil's twisted desire and goal.

- <u>Fact</u>: The devil is a real adversary of Jesus' disciples. Just like thieves and wolves would come after what appear to be helpless, defensive less sheep, their goal is clear! Take what doesn't belong to them. Destroy what is not their own! Whose are we? We are God's. We become the targeted sheep the devil would come after, whether as a wolf or a thief, to steal, kill, and destroy! <u>Proof from God's Word</u>: John 10:10, Jesus says, " 'The thief comes only to steal and kill and destroy; I have come that they may have life, and have it to the full.' "

- <u>Fact</u>: The devil is actively out in our world, 24/7, as our enemy! He is also depicted as a roaring lion. He's hungry! He's angry! He wants us! <u>Proof from God's Word</u>: I Peter 5:8, "Be self-controlled and alert. Your enemy the devil prowls around like a roaring lion looking for someone to devour."

- <u>Fact</u>: The devil is engaged in a battle with us, not as one who is seen, but as one who is unseen. If we could see the enemy advancing towards us with his tanks and artillery, we could respond with our heat seeking missiles and stop the advance. But since it is a spiritual battle, it requires spiritual bodies equipped with spiritual weapons for spiritual battle. <u>Proof from God's Word</u>: Ephesians 6:10-18, "Finally, be strong in the Lord and in his mighty power. Put on the full armor of God so that you can take your stand against the devil's schemes. For our struggle is not against flesh and blood, but against the rulers, against the authorities, against the powers of this dark world and against the spiritual forces of evil in the heavenly realms. Therefore put on the full armor of God, so that when the day of evil comes, you may be able to stand your ground, and after you have done everything, to stand. Stand firm then, with the belt of truth buckled around your waist, with the breastplate of righteousness in place, and with your feet fitted with the readiness that comes from the gospel of peace. In addition to all this, take up the shield of faith, with which you can extinguish all the flaming arrows of the evil one. Take the helmet of salvation and the sword of the Spirit, which is the word of God. And pray in the Spirit on all occasions with all kinds of prayers and requests. With this in mind, be alert and always keep on praying for all the saints."

- <u>Fact</u>: The devil knows sinful nature, how to tempt and keep in check those he already has as his trophies, his slaves to sin. He also knows how to tempt those of us still living in these sinfully lined temporary tents known as our flesh. The flesh and the Spirit battle it out! <u>Proof from God's Word:</u> Galatians 5:16-18; 22-25, "So I say, live by the Spirit, and you will not gratify the desires of the sinful nature. For the sinful nature desires what is contrary to the Spirit, and the Spirit what is contrary to the sinful nature. They are in conflict with each other, so that you do not do what you want. But if you are led by the Spirit, you are not under the law.... But the fruit of the Spirit is love, joy, peace, patience, kindness, goodness, faithfulness, gentleness and self-control. Against such things there is no law. Those who belong to Christ Jesus have crucified the sinful nature with its passions and desires. Since we live by the Spirit, let us keep in step with the Spirit."

- <u>Fact</u>: God knows the truth. The devil has fallen. The devil is defeated. Christ has won the victory for us. <u>Proof from God's Word</u>: 1 Corinthians 15:57, "But thanks be to God! He gives us the victory through our Lord Jesus Christ."; Hebrews 2:14-15, "Since the children have flesh and blood, he too shared in their humanity so that by his death he might destroy him who holds the power of death—that is, the devil—and free those who all their lives were held in slavery by their fear of death."; Luke 10:18, Jesus replied, " ' I saw Satan fall like lightning from heaven.'"

- <u>Fact</u>: God the Father will bring an end to all things and submit them under the full and complete Lordship of our Savior Jesus Christ. We must remain patiently in battle until then! God will soon crush Satan under our feet. <u>Proof from God's Word</u>: 1 Corinthians 15:20-28, "But Christ has indeed been raised from the dead, the firstfruits of those who have fallen asleep. For since death came through a man, the resurrection of the dead comes also through a man. For as in Adam all die, so in Christ all will be made alive. But each in his own turn: Christ, the firstfruits; then, when he comes, those who belong to him. Then the end will come, when he hands over the kingdom to God the Father after he has destroyed all dominion, authority and power. For he must reign until he has put all his enemies under his feet. The last enemy to be destroyed is death. For he 'has put everything under his feet.' Now when it says that 'everything' has been put under him, it is clear that this does not include God himself, who put everything under Christ. When he has done this, then the Son himself will be made subject to him who put everything under him, so that God may be all in all."; Romans 16:20, "The God of peace will soon crush Satan under your feet."

- <u>Fact</u>: God the Father, through our Savior Jesus' death and resurrection, shares this with us through our baptism. We have become the children of God, who will overcome the world and have the victory just as He has! <u>Proof from God's Word</u>: 1 John 5:4-6, "For everyone born of God overcomes the world. This is the victory that has overcome the world, even our faith. Who is it that overcomes the world? Only he who believes that Jesus is the Son of God. This is the one who came by water and blood—Jesus Christ. He did not come by water only, but by water and blood. And it is the Spirit who testifies, because the Spirit is the truth."

- <u>Fact</u>: God gives us His power through His Holy Spirit. As His Holy Spirit resides in us, so does His power! He is able to do far more than we can ask or think in defeating the Devil and his distractions in our life! We need to commit ourselves and call upon Him in response with confidence! <u>Proof from God's Word</u>: Ephesians 3:16-21, "I pray that out of his glorious riches he may strengthen you with power through his Spirit in your inner being, so that Christ may dwell in your hearts through faith. And I pray that you, being rooted and established in love, may have power, together with all the saints, to grasp how wide and long and high and deep is the love of Christ, and to know this love that surpasses knowledge—that you may be filled to the measure of all the fullness of God. Now to him who is able to do immeasurably more than all we ask or imagine, according to his power that is at work within us, to him be glory in the church and in Christ Jesus throughout all generations, for ever and ever! Amen."

RM: *Review each of these facts to see how they've become evident in your life. If some haven't, be on the lookout. If some have, consider sharing them with a fellow daily disciple to instruct and inspire them on their daily discipleship with Jesus.*

The devil knows that everything here on earth is temporary, subject to the ultimate return of our Lord and Savior Jesus Christ. We come to understand in 2 Peter 3:3-7, 10: "First of all, you must understand that in the last days scoffers will come, scoffing and following their own evil desires. They will say, 'Where is this 'coming' he promised? Ever since our fathers died, everything goes on as it has since the beginning of creation.' But they deliberately forget that long ago by God's word the heavens existed and the earth was formed out of water and by water. By these waters also the world of that time was deluged and destroyed. By the same word, the present heavens and earth are reserved for fire, being kept for the day of judgment and destruction of ungodly men.... But the day of the Lord will come like a thief. The heavens will disappear with a roar; the elements will be destroyed by fire, and the earth and everything in it will be laid bare."

We're told in 2 Peter 3:9, "The Lord is not slow in keeping his promise, as some understand slowness. He is patient with you, not wanting anyone to perish, but everyone to come to repentance." This chimes in with God's desire that His salvation is for everyone and is complete through the work of His Son, our Savior Jesus. As we live transformed, the results will be evident we are no longer our own as we await God's final judgment. Our days would be filled with the Holy Spirit's fruitful work within our lives.

We're instructed in 2 Peter 3:11b-12a, "You ought to live holy and godly lives as you look forward to the day of God and speed its coming." What do we have now and what will we receive as the outcome of such judgment and destruction? 2 Corinthians

5:5 speaks of God having "given us the Spirit as a deposit, guaranteeing what is to come." We eagerly await this Savior who will ultimately transform our lowly, temporary fleshly body into his glorious, permanent holy body. (Philippians 3:21)

Have you ever heard life in these bodies as Paul compares them to living in tents? Yes, tents that are not meant to be permanent but temporary. 2 Corinthians 5:1-4 presents this analogy, "Now we know that if the earthly tent we live in is destroyed, we have a building from God, an eternal house in heaven, not built by human hands. Meanwhile we groan, longing to be clothed with our heavenly dwelling, because when we are clothed, we will not be found naked. For while we are in this tent, we groan and are burdened, because we do not wish to be unclothed but to be clothed with our heavenly dwelling, so that what is mortal may be swallowed up by life."

> RM: *How would you compare living in a temporary tent with living in a permanent house? How subject are you to the elements while a tent is your home? How much more easily can a tent wear down compared to a house?*

While we live in these tents, we live in the flesh. We live in these bodies that are away from the Lord in Heaven as Paul goes on to say in 2 Corinthians 5:6-9. We know as Paul confesses, that as long as we remain in these temporary, fleshly tents we will struggle with the nature of the flesh (the devil) and the nature of the Spirit (God). We will struggle with sin and the devil, the author of sin.

There's no better understanding of the struggle each daily disciple of Jesus faces than that Paul recognized in Romans 7:7-25.

While this is a lengthy section to include in its' entirety, in this chapter, it's a meaty section worth your attention. God wants you to be aware of areas that the Devil would seek to distract you from Him. Rather than provide the whole entrée in this sitting, let me give you an appetizer with the following quotes. Look to the Road Markers following the verses to get you thinking and responding. (I encourage you to take the whole section and simmer it in the slow cooker of your pondering mind on another occasion, okay?)

- Vs. 7, "Indeed I would not have known what sin was except through the law. For I would not have known what coveting really was if the law had not said, 'Do not covet.'" *How have you used God's Ten Commandments as a means to fully discover all the sins that would break such commandments? List each one on a piece of paper and then ask yourself, "Is this a commandment I struggle with or break frequently?"*

- Vs. 15, "I do not understand what I do. For what I want to do I do not do, but what I hate I do." *Get past this potential contradiction to understand our true nature as sinners living in these temporary tents. Recall some times when you could testify the truth of such a statement. Summarize in a sentence what's behind our sinful behavior.*

- Vs. 18, "I know that nothing good lives in me, that is, in my sinful nature. For I have the desire to do what is good, but I cannot carry it out." *Why do we struggle carrying out the desire to do good? Look within your own life for an example.*

- Vs. 20, "Now if I do what I do not want to do, it is no longer I who do it, but it is sin living in me that does it." *Why would Paul not want to let us off the hook when it comes to blaming sin's fault for our actions? How can we separate our responsibility for our sinful actions from the sinful entity within us?*

The devil would focus on the frailties of these temporary tents we live in to attack them. He would wear us down like a tent, wouldn't he? He would create holes in our canvass or cause our tent stakes to be lost. There would be times the devil would loosen our ropes that would tie us firmly to God. The devil dangles all those fleshly temptations in front of us and asks, "Did God really say...you...can't....?"

The devil would deceive us: "Because we're forgiven in Christ, we can go about doing those fleshly things that please us. Why else would we have God's forgiveness?" Romans 6:15-18 gives God's truthful answer in response, "What then? Shall we sin because we are not under law but under grace? By no means! Don't you know that when you offer yourselves to someone to obey him as slaves, you are slaves to the one whom you obey—whether you are slaves to sin, which leads to death, or to obedience, which leads to righteousness? But thanks be to God that, though you used to be slaves to sin, you wholeheartedly obeyed the form of teaching to which you were entrusted. You have been set free from sin and have become slaves to righteousness."

In response to the devil's desired deceptions, we need to turn to God and call upon the Holy Spirit within us to deal with them. Rather than remaining a slave to sin and the flesh, we need to become a slave to righteousness.

RM: *Consider some ways you can become a slave*
to righteousness with the helpful work of the Holy
Spirit. What would He need to do in your daily
discipleship so you would give a testimony of God
at work within you?

We know that we have moved from death to life through
the saving work of our Savior and Lord Jesus. Through our
baptism, the Holy Spirit has the daily ongoing, opportunity to
drown the old man in us, who is filled with fleshly desires to be
satisfied. As we have put on Christ, as we have received God's
Holy Spirit, we are to WALK in Him as He WORKS in us!

Romans 8 continues on with a lengthy and deep teaching I
would encourage you to again, interrupt your reading of this
book, to read further in God's book! Again, be praying for the
Holy Spirit to reveal His specific teaching and application for
you in your own life and walk with God. Make notes that you
can refer to and ponder through in your heart like Mary! As
you've done as much as time and God's Holy Spirit enables you,
come back to this chapter.

You've probably discovered that in Romans 8 you can find all
the information, instruction and inspiration God would give
you. You would only benefit more by having a prayer-filled
discussion with a fellow WALKer and spiritual body builder. If
you do have a work out buddy, get with them in person and go
over Romans 8, won't you? You will find powerful Spirit –laden
ammunition present for your ongoing battle with the devil over
your spiritual bodies and their growth!

Let me take this opportunity to highlight a portion from
Romans 8 in case you need to whet your appetite for a fuller

feasting. Romans 8:5-11 helps us see that it all boils down to who's in control of your life! *Stop at the Road Markers following each verse and ponder some heartfelt ponderings.*

Verse 5 declares, "Those who live according to the sinful nature have their minds set on what that nature desires; but those who live in accordance with the Spirit have their minds set on what the Spirit desires."*Consider your own daily, personal struggle with your sinful nature. What channel(s) do you find your mind set on to cause sinful programming to emerge? What needs to be done to change the channel or turn the TV off altogether?*

Verses 6-8, "The mind of sinful man is death, but the mind controlled by the Spirit is life and peace; the sinful mind is hostile to God. It does not submit to God's law, nor can it do so. Those controlled by the sinful nature cannot please God."

How have you experienced life and peace as a result of your mind being controlled by God's Spirit? Why do people think they can please God by their "good works"? How can we be reassured it is futile to think or do so, whether or not we're His daily disciples?

Verse 9, "You, however, are controlled not by the sinful nature but by the Spirit, if the Spirit of God lives in you. And if anyone does not have the Spirit of Christ, he does not belong to Christ." *Describe the outward signs of your inward nature being controlled by the Spirit of God. How do they give testimony to Christ in you?*

Verses 10-11, "But if Christ is in you, your body is dead because of sin, yet your spirit is alive because of righteousness. And if the Spirit of him who raised Jesus from the dead is living in you, he who raised Christ from the dead will also give life to your mortal bodies through his Spirit, who lives in you." *Describe how righteousness causes your spirit to be alive. How have you received His resurrection for your mortal body through His Spirit?*

As we have responded to our Savior's call to "Come, follow Me!" we have been invited to join Him on that spiritual walk with Him through our baptism. Romans 6:3, 5 asks, "Or don't you know that all of us who were baptized into Christ Jesus were baptized into his death?...If we have been united with him like this in his death, we will certainly also be united with him in his resurrection." Titus 3:5-7 declares, "He saved us, not because of righteous things we had done, but because of his mercy. He saved us through the washing of rebirth and renewal by the Holy Spirit, whom he poured out on us generously through Jesus Christ our Savior so that having been justified by his grace, we might become heirs having the hope of eternal life."

Through our baptism, the Holy Spirit has come to find His dwelling place within us. He dwells within us with specific passions, purposes, and plans for our spiritual body building, which we've studied previously. He can choose to use spiritual disciplines as tools to accomplish His work daily in our spiritual lives. We read of His desire and passion in Romans 8:28, "And we know that in all things God works for the good of those who love him, who have been called according to his purpose."

RM: *Consider, through the daily power and effect of your baptism, how God is at work in all things for good, in your life. How do you overcome challenges of*

> *doubt or disbelief the devil would throw in front of you*
> *in response to this promise?*

We need daily to determinedly steer clear of the devil's distractions and find ourselves even more firmly rooted in Jesus the Vine and His Holy Spirit. We can depend upon a daily walk with the Holy Spirit. Daily He helps us in every circumstance, and every distraction to remain focused upon Him. He knows our weaknesses and knows what we ought to be in prayer before God, even if we don't.

Romans 8:26-27 speaks of the Spirit's desire to help us daily, "In the same way, the Spirit helps us in our weakness. We do not know what we ought to pray for, but the Spirit himself intercedes for us with groans that words cannot express. And he who searches our hearts knows the mind of the Spirit, because the Spirit intercedes for the saints in accordance with God's will."

> RM: *How has the devil challenged you within your*
> *weakness? How has the devil sought to prevent you*
> *from praying? What obstacles has the devil led you*
> *to remain behind in terms of seeking God's will?*
> *How can these actions of the Spirit help you rather*
> *than hinder you?*

We HAVE to have a relationship with God that is truly WALKing in God's direction. Spiritual disciplines like Solitude and Silence can help bring us and keep us in God's holy presence, even while we reside in this temporary world in temporary tents!

These two disciplines, Solitude and Silence, can be seen as the two bookends of one's spiritual body building library. They can become the left and right hand weights for spiritual body building. They also can be the two disciplines the devil would love to disable. The devil would love to line up all his heavy artillery with an abundance of ammunition on the front line to try to put us out of commission!

How can God's own Holy Spirit use Solitude as a Spiritual discipline? When you think of the word, "solitude," what others words come to mind? "Alone," "only," "withdrawn," "hiding," "separate," or "one" are a few that come to my mind. A Bible concordance is a tool I would encourage you to use regularly. It can become a "pick axe" in the cavern of God's Word for you. You would use it to prospect and mine the gold nuggets or precious gems of truth God has in store for you to discover in His Word!

Chances are you won't find many uses of the specific word "solitude" in the Bible, depending upon the translation you use. However, words that are similar in meaning may turn up. You may wish to use a dictionary or synonym (similar) resource to see what you can be prospecting after.

> RM: *Grab a sheet of paper, if I've not convinced you to utilize index cards, and take a look now in your Bible's concordance for solitude, alone and only for starters. Write out the book, chapter and verse you find under each word.*

Were you surprised at all you found? Again, if you have more than one translation of the Bible that also employs a concordance, you can have another go at it and see what you find.

If you're computer and Internet comfortable, you can even go on line and use a free service called, "Bible Gateway." It will provide a variety of translations of the Bible together with search tools that are helpful. You can set as many search filters as you wish, looking for any combination of words; requesting as many verses at a time as you wish to read. You can even print them out if you wish or cut and paste them into a document for further study. The advertisers pay for your free use. You can locate this site on the Web at www.biblegateway.com

I'm using a New International Version Study Bible with the tools I mentioned in the Introduction to this book. Nothing came up looking for the word "solitude." I next looked for the word "alone" and came up with no verses utilizing "alone." What about "only"? No reference there either. I'm puzzled! Why aren't any of these words coming up? I can prospect through the Psalms and come up with three references in Psalm 62 that use the word "alone," even though '"alone" does not appear in my concordance! How about you?

> RM: *Take a look in your Bible at Psalm 62:1 and verses 5 and 6. Write out these verses, each of them, separately on an index card or sheet of paper.*

I have found Psalm 62 to be an excellent psalm describing a time of solitude with God. What do you think? As I invite the Holy Spirit to speak through God's Word, I will ask Him to turn the neon on! By that I mean, highlight for me key words like those nuggets of gold or precious stones God wants me to find in the passage I'm prospecting through. I want to pull those out, unearth them, and take them with me out of the mine of God's Word. That's why it's vital to write them out. Don't trust that you'll always be able to come back to them just by putting highlighter ink over them!

Take His Word with you like God instructed His covenant people, as we read in Deuteronomy 6:6-9, "These commandments that I give you today are to be upon your hearts. Impress them on your children. Talk about them when you sit at home and when you walk along the road, when you lie down and when you get up. Tie them as symbols on your hands and bind them on your foreheads. Write them on the doorframes of your houses and on your gates."

God calls upon His people's passion for Him and His Word that they would do several things with it. It is to be within their hearts. It is to be impressed upon their children. It is to be talked about sitting at home or travelling. It is to be talked about when retiring at night and rising in the morning. It is to be written and tied to your hands and forehead. It is even to be written out on the doorframes of your house or on your gates. In other words, make it conveniently visible everywhere you are and go! Don't let it just be His Word that you read but that you also speak and discuss. God encourages us to treat His wisdom and understanding as something valuable we would seek, "How much better to get wisdom than gold, to choose understanding rather than silver." (Proverbs 16:16)

> RM: *What are some things you can do to apply this desire of God to your daily discipleship? Make a commitment to do one thing and see how it aids in your discipleship, won't you?*

When I'm prospecting through God's Word, with my miner's hat on, I pray that God will reveal Himself to me through His Word. "Help me, Lord, find those gold nuggets or precious stones of Your Truth!" Hear this promise of God for all you prospectors out there, "Blessed is the man who finds wisdom, the man who gains understanding (in the Word of God) for she is more profitable than silver and yields better return than gold. She is more precious than rubies, nothing you desire can compare with her." (Proverbs 3:13-15) By putting on my miner's hat, I'm not wearing it to protect myself from falling rocks or debris. That thin, tin metal hat can't do that. But, it can hold a source of light to reveal what I'm prospecting for! I call upon the Holy Spirit to shine His light upon His Word in order to reveal to me what He wants me to find! "My son, if you accept my words and store up my commands within you...and if you look for it as silver and search for it as hidden treasure, then you will understand the fear of the Lord and find the knowledge of God." (Proverbs 2:1, 4-5)

> RM: *So, do you have your miner's hat? Grab your pick axe, calling upon God's seeking and revealing Spirit to show you what He wants you to find out about God and solitude back in Psalm 62. Put down this book and spend a few minutes in prayer as you enter the cavern of God's Word. Then, turn in your Bible to Psalm 62 and spend some time prospecting. Write out index cards of each verse you find is a "keeper!" Also, underline any words that "light up" and sparkle at you. If you're using a lined index card, don't write any verse on the blank side. Save that space for any additional thoughts God would choose to reveal as you ponder this verse in your heart and mind. Jot these down for present and future reflection. Come back and resume your reading after you've exited the mine shaft called, "Psalm 62".*

What did the Holy Spirit have to say to you about solitude in Psalm 62? Again, if you have a work out partner, head over to God's gym or arrange a time to share "the workout" you experienced alone. Then, encourage your work out partner to spend some time with you working out Psalm 62 to see how each of your spiritual bodies can be built up.

Solitude is a fundamental spiritual discipline to exercise in your spiritual body building for several reasons and benefits.

- First, setting the priority of "no one else but God" means just that quite literally. You will spend time with God alone and only God. You need to enter into that state of fellowship with Him. You ought to find a place and space where that can happen. Ideally, where would there be nothing surrounding you visibly or audibly to enter into your solitude space with God as an unnecessary and uninvited presence? Here, is where the devil will do his best to begin his destructive process.

RM: *What ways have you seen, or could envision, the devil doing to make sure you're not alone with God, from a physical, visual, or audible setting? How would you respond with steps to prevent such devilish activity?*

Let's take a look at how God's Word describes our Lord Jesus' approach to solitude and prayer with God. I've been able to locate ten times in the Gospels where Jesus use of solitude is talked about. As you read through them, what common words come to light?

Matthew 14:13, "When Jesus heard what had happened, he withdrew by boat privately to a solitary place."

Matthew 14:23, "After he had dismissed them, he went up on a mountainside by himself to pray. When evening came, he was there alone".

Mark 1:35, "Very early in the morning, while it was still dark, Jesus got up, left the house and went off to a solitary place, where he prayed."

Mark 6:31-32, "Then, because so many people were coming and going that they did not even have a chance to eat, he said to them, 'Come with me by yourselves to a quiet place and get some rest.' So they went away by themselves in a boat to a solitary place."

Mark 6:46, "After leaving them, he went up on a mountainside to pray."

Mark 7:24, "Jesus left that place and went to the vicinity of Tyre. He entered a house and did not want anyone to know it; yet he could not keep his presence secret."

Luke 6:12, "One of those days Jesus went out to a mountainside to pray, and spent the night praying to God."

Luke 9:10, "Then he took them with him and they withdrew by themselves to a town called Bethsaida."

Luke 9:18, "Once when Jesus was praying in private and his disciples were with him".

John 6:15, "Jesus, knowing that they intended to come and make him king by force, withdrew again to a mountain by himself."

Jesus didn't have a home He would regularly live in. He tells us He did not have a place to lay His head. (Matthew 8:20) On earth, Jesus was homeless because His home was in Heaven. But that lack of dedicated space did not deter Him from solitude with God, His Father. Several verses point out Jesus went "by Himself" or He "was alone" or "went to a deserted place" or that He was "praying alone." All of these are characteristics of what our time of solitude before God should be!

RM: *How possible is that for you? Do you live alone? Are you surrounded by spouse and children? Does it seem to be a real challenge to get some "alone time" let alone (no pun intended) with God?*

- Second, you will need to seek and establish your place of solitude. Jesus understood the challenge and how the Devil would determinedly seek to distract you from a space of solitude. Jesus recommended in Matthew 6:6 a specific location you should use, " 'But when you pray, go into your room, close the door and pray to your Father, who is unseen. Then your Father, who sees what is done in secret, will reward you."

Some translations may use the phrase, "your room," but I've also seen some use the word "closet." Whichever you prefer is not the issue. Jesus says that we need to enter that space and close the door, praying in secret or unseen by others to God, Who is unseen, so that He will reward us! You don't need to desperately clear out a closet and set up an altar and pray there exclusively. The main thing to understand and put into practice is to pray alone privately! Yes, there are times for praying together with another, or in a small group, or publically during a meeting or worship service. But, as you begin your day, you need to dedicate a time of solitude with God that's private, just between you and Him.

- Third, as you enter into that space of solitude, you will dedicate and consecrate this as God's welcome turf, God's holy ground! What would help make it holy for you? You might be led to put a cross up as a visible reminder of the love of your Savior Jesus. Some like to have a "corpus" cross displayed that has the body of Jesus hanging nailed from the cross. A cross can become a focal point for your prayer space. By looking at the cross, you can visualize the WHO, WHAT, WHERE, and WHY of what Jesus did and continues to do for you as a result of His sacrifice for you!

- Fourth, regularity of habit is essential. You are transformed into a dedicated, daily disciple of our Lord Jesus as the Holy Spirit has a regular time of free and daily access within your body, His temple. It's the way He can build your spiritual body up in Christ! Always prioritizing your practice of solitude is an outward sign of an inward relationship with God. It's how you both know how necessary alone time is in your daily walk with each other!

You've entered God's space as you've established it as a welcoming place in your heart and home. Now what? What's the other potential distraction the devil would want to put in between you and God and your time together?

I don't recall who said, "Silence is golden!" I know I've seen that phrase projected on movie screens at theatres promoting people turning off their cell phones during the show! Quite frankly, I know we live in a world that has become more noisy and busy. Our ever evolving technology appears to make it even noisier, and busier, doesn't it?

There are two kinds of silence we need to be aware of: external silence and internal silence. I've spoken about external silence already. It can be so subtle and pervasive at times and in locations. Only when we stop long enough to listen, do we find sounds like traffic, ticking clocks, dripping water, buzzing insects, settling floors and walls in old houses, the creak of a chair needing oil, and I'm sure you could add a few silence stealers of your own!

> RM: *If this is where you'll be practicing solitude and silence, take a look around for any "deal makers" or "deal breakers"! If you don't have to do much rearranging, you're set! Once you've found your place, offer it up with a prayer that God would bless and do His work there!*

When it comes to solitude as a spiritual discipline, silence comes in a close second in priority. Putting it another way, if God has blessed you with two functioning hands, your left hand employs "solitude" while your right hand employs "silence"!

You may wish to do some prospecting through God's Word regarding "silence." Illustrating how translations of the Bible can vary, if you were to go back to Psalm 62, which we prospected through in light of "solitude," you will find the New American Standard Bible and the English Standard Version (of the Bible) use the word "silence" in place of the New International Version's use of the word "rest." These two versions strengthen my understanding that God would have us link solitude and silence together as we come before Him.

One verse I've found speaks about silence in God's presence as it's designated in His place of worship. Habakkuk 2:20 says, " 'But the Lord is in his holy temple; let all the earth be silent before him.' " I am confident, no matter what the version, that it will say quite clearly, "The Lord is in His temple; let all the earth be/keep silent before Him!" God would have us understand how silence is golden to Him. There is a time to be silent and reflective. There is a time to listen for the quiet voice of God to speak. There is also a time to sing, shout, dance, pray, praise, and give thanks as well, isn't there?

> RM: *As you think about what God would teach you through solitude and silence, doesn't God's first commandment come to mind? Not having any other gods before Him? How can you come to understand and practice solitude and silence so that you would keep this commandment before God in your life and walk with Him?*

What kind of thoughts and distractions does the devil place before us during our times of silence that would prevent or break up that silence? I've even experienced fleshly thoughts trying to battle within my mind as I wanted to focus on Godly thoughts! I would either begin to be alone and silent before God or having entered into that time with God, and the devil would fire off a dart that had a sinful tinge to it! Can you see sometimes where inviting solitude and silence by closing your eyes can help deal with sinful thoughts and distractions? Knowing what they can become for you is part of the response you would ask God's Holy Spirit to make. Focusing on the things and holiness of God is a direct dart you can throw back at the devil. Do it as often as it takes in order to be rid of the devil and his distractions!

What's my prayer for you? As you have come to know and practice God's use of solitude and silence in your daily discipleship, you will want more and more time with Him. Ask any spiritual body builder if they don't increase the time and intensity of their work out because the Holy Spirit blessed them beyond their comprehension. They came away from their spiritual work out renewed, refreshed, and recharged to be used by God in great and mighty ways because God Himself and His Holy Spirit were so entrenched and visible in their daily lives, that they were enabled to bear abundant fruit through the Vine, our Savior and Lord Jesus.

Chapter Seven

How do I connect with God through communicating?

How many books have been written on the subject of prayer? I can look across my library, behind me and around me and before me, and see at least 60 different titles on prayer and just as many books containing prayers. Prayer is a subject that I spend time and money learning about and being guided through. I don't know why it's such a fascination with me.

> RM: *Do you have a similar fascination with prayer? What books do you own about prayer? What position do they hold within your spiritual library? How often do you find yourself reading books on prayer? Which books containing prayers do you depend upon daily or weekly?*

Can I trace it back to childhood? I was ten years old when my mother died of cancer. My paternal grandmother stepped in to raise my brother and I during the weekends when we visited her. Every night, before Grandma would go to bed, I would see her sit on her recliner chair with her Bible in her lap. She would read aloud the Psalms. (As you can imagine, her favorite was Psalm 23!) Around midnight, she would turn her radio on. We would hear the voice of a pastor, who had dedicated his weeknights from Midnight to 3:00 in the morning, taking phone calls and praying for people over the radio! She would listen intently, pray along with and conclude with her own, "Amen!" Most Friday nights, she might stay up at least until 2:00 am, being drawn into the prayers of a pastor she never met and for people she would never know. As a young boy, my spirit was willing to listen and pray along with Grandma and the pastor for the people who would phone it, but my flesh was weak. I just couldn't endure for the whole stretch and would usually walk up stairs and go to bed.

Saturday and Sunday mornings were usually the same. Grandma would pray and spend time with God FIRST! She would always have time alone in the quiet before sunrise, and before us boys would rise! She'd continue once we came downstairs, taking another half hour or so before finishing. Saturdays were leisurely, but Sundays were more structured and schedule sensitive. While Grandma never went to Bible Class or took us boys to Sunday School, she would always get us and her to worship at least a half hour early. She liked the quiet time in the pew, reading the bulletin along with the prayers in the hymnal.

> RM: *How about you growing up? Were you blessed to grow up in a Christian home where your parents prayed and set the example for you? Did you have a fixed time when everyone assembled for family prayer time?*

My parents weren't the types to pray with us growing up. We didn't have the classic night time "Now I lay me down to sleep" prayers. Nor did we intercede with blessings for mom, dad, brother, grandpa and grandma. We didn't have any prayers at all. I don't hold that against my mom or dad. But as I stayed with college friends at their home over break, I noticed some that had devotional time around Dinner. The dad would reach for his Bible after dessert and pull out a small devotional book that he or another family member would read from. Nothing fancy or lengthy. Not even moments of intercessory prayer. Just a bit of quiet time together around the dinner table.

What about now during your WALK with your Lord and Savior Jesus? As you went through chapter five and reviewed your stewardship of time, were you satisfied with how much time you spend with God? As you read about solitude and silence in the last chapter, what kinds of thoughts floated to the surface? How much of a challenge is it already to find time for God, let alone time alone and in silence? Perhaps you're not thoroughly convinced that you need any more time with God or that He needs any more time with you. I can't do anything to change your mind. No amount of words or chapters in this book or any other on prayer could convince you otherwise.

You will come to know and love the fruit of prayer as your relationship with God brings you into closer, more intimate steps through prayer. When God tells you in His Word, "Oh, taste and see that the Lord is good!" (Psalm 34:8) do you believe it? Do you believe it because you HAVE tasted and SEEN Him as good? You could take a look at all of Psalm 34 as fuel for your prayer life. David wrote this psalm as he did many, from his own heartfelt experience. I believe David had a steady dose of holy heartburn! You can tell the intensity of the Holy Spirit's flame within him based upon the intensity of the words God speaks through him! Have you ever had such a time of prayer as that?

For as many books as have been written about prayer, I have come to see as many different definitions, applications, and practices of prayer emerge. From the time of early childhood, whether human calendar years or spiritual growth years, we have come to understand prayer as being as uncomplicated as, "We speak, God listens." That is fundamentally so, but not entirely extent within the boundary of prayer.

Have you ever asked, "Why pray?" I've heard non-Christians ask that question. They'll often go on to say, "It won't help! So and so is dying. Prayer isn't going to change anything!" I've heard lukewarm Christians sigh that sentiment, "Why pray? I've never seen God heal anyone. If medicine can't do it, nothing can!" When I asked my Sunday morning Bible Class why they thought prayer mattered, the replies didn't surprise me. Here, were daily WALKing disciples assembled around the Word. They KNEW prayer mattered! One dear sister even said, "When the need is desperate, I always phone so and so! I KNOW she's a woman of prayer! I can depend upon her prayers to comfort me and the person she's praying for!"

When I phrased within the title of this chapter, "we speak," it was quite intentional. Prayer is not just for soloists. Prayer is for small groups and large communities. There is strength and comfort knowing others are in tune with you and each other before God. Sometimes what matters more is not the answer, but the request! None of us knows how God will answer our petition or intercession. We know He will answer! He promises us that! We know the answer will be according to His good and gracious will for each of us! But, through prayer, for and with each other, we recognize that we're not in this circumstance alone! God has given us the community, the body of Christ, for just such a blessing as that!

We have a responsibility to pray for each other that goes beyond obligation or necessity. It becomes a responsibility because the love of Christ compels us! Look at the beginning or the ending of any of Paul's pastoral letters in the New Testament. Often specific requests from and to the community of faith are shared and requested. Take, for example, the first chapter of Romans verses 8 through 12. Here, Paul goes beyond words of greeting and blessing to say, "First of all..." and proceeds to offer up a prayer of thanksgiving for the body of Christ in Rome hearing (or reading) his God inspired words! He reveals in verses 9-10, "God, whom I serve with my whole heart in preaching the gospel of his Son, is my witness how constantly I remember you in my prayers at all times." (Romans 1:9-10)

How encouraged they would both be by each other's faith! Before Paul concludes his letter with personal greetings and instructions, he calls upon them again to be in prayer with him before God, writing in Romans 15:30-32, "I urge you, brothers, by our Lord Jesus Christ and by the love of the Spirit, to join me in my struggle by praying to God for me. Pray that I may be rescued from the unbelievers in Judea and that my service in Jerusalem may be acceptable to the saints there".

> RM: *Have you ever thought to pray for a person's spiritual strength and welfare? What unique challenges, if any, would such a prayer about one's spiritual life be in contrast to illness, for example?*

Having a spiritual work out partner is one significant reason to start regularly praying along these lines. At a loss, as to what to pray for? Let's take a look at Paul's words to those Ephesian brothers and sisters. How can they serve as a guide for us as he bows his knees before God on behalf of them in Ephesians 3:14-21? *I'll provide you with some Road Marker questions in italics following each Scripture passage. Make sure you stop and let the Spirit ponder His thoughts within you!*

Verses 14-15, "For this reason I kneel before the Father, from whom his whole family in heaven and on earth derives its name." *According to this verse, as we kneel before God our Father, what name do we derive as people who pray to Him?*

Verses 16-17a, "I pray that out of his glorious riches he may strengthen you with power through his Spirit in your inner being so that Christ may dwell in your hearts through faith." *What does the Holy Spirit provide within you? What about your spiritual WALK would you ask God to strengthen?*

Verses 17b-18, "And I pray that you, being rooted and established in love, may have power, together with all the saints, to grasp how wide and long and high and deep is the love of Christ". *Being rooted in Christ's love, what fruit would you like to see borne by Him in you? Consider what you would ask in the form of a petition.*

Verse 19, "and to know this love that surpasses knowledge— that you may be filled to the measure of all the fullness of God." *Why would you pray to be filled with all the fullness of God? How would God's love surpass the knowledge you would possess?*

Verse 20, "Now to him who is able to do immeasurably more than all we ask or imagine, according to his power that is at work within us". *What would we count upon God to do working within us? What impossibilities would we present to God through prayer? In what ways would we pray or experience prayer as a faith builder?*

Verse 21, "to him be glory in the church and in Christ Jesus throughout all generations, for ever and ever! Amen." *What outcome or testimony would God's work within us or through us provide? What might become some of the perpetual praises we would offer up as God is at work?*

Can you see how helpful it can be to study these openings and closings of the Epistle writers? Beyond the specific people identified along with their intercession, there are great prayer helps we can learn and employ in our own prayer time.

> RM: *Go back through each verse above from Ephesians and write out for yourself a petition that you would pray as an intercession. Consider how you find comfort and strength knowing someone was praying along those lines for you.*

What a great spiritual gift to give to another, when you invite the Holy Spirit to pray along such lines on their behalf through you!

Paul wasn't the only daily walking disciple who talked about and encouraged prayer in his letters. James concludes his letter with instructions regarding intercessory prayer before each other and God. We read in James 5:13-16, "Is any one of you in trouble? He should pray. Is anyone happy? Let him sing songs of praise. Is any one of you sick? He should call the elders of the church to pray over him and anoint him with oil in the name of the Lord. And the prayer offered in faith will make the sick person well; the Lord will raise him up. If he has sinned, he will be forgiven. Therefore confess your sins to each other and pray for each other that you may be healed. The prayer of a righteous man is powerful and effective."

> RM: *What has been your experience in intercessory prayer with members of your church? What would encourage or discourage you from inviting an elder to come, anoint and pray with you when you are sick? What is the connection James makes between confessing sins and being healed? Why is it necessary?*

The Letter to the Hebrews is one of my favorite wellsprings to draw our Lord Jesus' living water from. I'm encouraged to offer a cold cup in His name to a thirsty fellow disciple! Especially when it comes to an understanding of the role our Savior and Lord Jesus has taken upon Himself, under the direction and authority of God the Father. He ascended for just such a purpose as to sit at God our Father's right hand in order to be our Great High Priest and Intercessor 24/7!

It's here where we find Jesus first spoken of as our Great High Priest as we read in Hebrews 4:14-16, "Therefore since we have a great high priest who has gone through the heavens, Jesus the Son of God, let us hold firmly to the faith we profess. For we do not have a high priest who is unable to sympathize with our weaknesses, but we have one who has been tempted in every way, just as we are—yet without sin. Let us then approach the throne of grace with confidence, so that we may receive mercy and find grace to help us in our time of need."

We can receive these words both as an encouragement and an admonition. An encouragement because Jesus knows what we're going through as His daily WALKing and TALKing disciples. He KNOWS our weaknesses and temptations because He's been there. Yet, Jesus never fell victim to sin's alluring temptation! We can also receive these words as an admonition. They're given to us in response to encouragement as if to say, "Now, be confident knowing this about Jesus and draw near to Him. In your time of need, you will receive mercy and find grace to help in your need!"

What's your opinion of a friend who faithfully phones you, unloading everything that's on their mind, spending a fair deal of time centered on self? At the end of the conversation, they've hung up. You've never had the invitation or opportunity to share with them anything about yourself and what you may be going through on life's journey. Does it seem like you're in a mutually exclusive relationship? Does it seem it's exclusive, all right? Exclusively focused on them to the point of excluding you? They might as well have a doll to speak to for as much as you are encouraged with any interaction or dialogue. After all, dialogue has "two" implied in a conversation, doesn't it? No, you didn't have a dialogue. Could you call it a "unilogue?"

> RM: *So, when it comes to putting the person of God in human terms, how could we expect any less of a thought or response from God? How would we find it unselfishly and not conditionally, self-seeking as we might be? Does God take offense if we just call upon*

Him, finish our prayer with an "Amen", and leave?
Would God be still there in our presence saying, "But
wait a minute! I've got something I want to share
with you!" How have you ever thought along those
lines?

We can surmise from God's description of Himself that He's not like us in terms of what we think or act. Is that comforting or distressing? He tells us through Isaiah 55:8-9 that the thoughts and ways of man and God are not the same. As a matter of fact, God goes on to say that while they're different, His ways and thoughts are high above ours! Yes, I've come to realize as I looked at the lives of those who walked with God in chapter one in this book that not everyone saw their capabilities in the same light as God. Wouldn't you agree? How about your own self evaluation? Do you believe God would think more highly of you than you do of yourself? If so, what does that have to say about the kinds of things God would want to share with us through our time of prayer with Him?

Is there any Biblical basis or support for this subheading if we asked the question, "Through prayer, does God speak and are we listening?" We have read already in chapter one of the many dialogues God has had with His children. Sometimes, God has to get our attention or talk loudly for His voice and message to get through, doesn't He? Can you think of a time in the Bible when that happened?

While it was anything but corrective, persuasive, or condemning, God sends His angels as messengers. Seldom does God choose to speak directly to us by His own voice. Luke's gospel is the only one showcasing several opportunities where God had a message His children needed to hear. God sent an angel of the Lord to appear to Zechariah as a result of his prayers being heard by God on behalf of his wife Elizabeth. Not only would she, who was barren and advanced in years, have a son. This boy would not be just any boy! The angel gave him specific instructions as to his name, how he would live and what he would accomplish! Of course, this was the foretelling of the birth of John the Baptist who would come to prepare the way for Jesus. (Luke 1:5-25)

As this account ends, the next one unfolds (Luke 1:26-38), again with a specific messenger angel, named Gabriel, who would be sent from God to Mary, a virgin found in favor with God. He would explain she was chosen as the mother of the Son of the Most High, Jesus. As he explained and responded to her disbelief, Gabriel even pointed out a fellow angels' message to her cousin Elizabeth. Mary was convinced as was Zechariah. God had spoken directly to them through His appointed angels. They listened. They heard. They responded just as God asked them.

The next time we hear the voice of God, it's in conjunction with the baptism of Jesus by his cousin John. Only identified as a voice coming down from heaven, the message was one that all would hear. Jesus would be identified with God as His Son in whom God was well pleased. (Luke 3:21-22) The only other time a similar occurrence occurs is in Mark 9:2-8, where a voice comes out of a cloud identifying who Jesus is, "my beloved Son" but also with an admonition, "listen to him." God certainly had a message for Peter, James and John to hear, didn't He?

But, does God directly respond with a voice during our time of prayer? I believe He can if He chooses. God is Almighty, all powerful and tells us His ways and thoughts are higher than ours! Then again, neither would I believe God would have to limit Himself to an audible voice. As ones who are following God, we must let Him BE God, taking the lead in all aspects of our WALK, including prayer!

Having a lot to learn from Him, what's a valuable and vital aspect of learning? Listening! As He chooses to speak, He responds in the best way He knows He is capable of doing to get His message through to us! Are we listening?

Without doubt or argument, God has chosen to reveal as much about Himself through the Holy Spirit inspired and inerrant Word of God as we have it preserved in The Bible. Because it IS the Word of God, I believe and operate with the understanding that God Himself inspired His Word. Since He is The Truth, it can only contain the truth and be inerrant (without error)!

In order to back up such a claim, I provide you with several proof texts that point to the Bible as inspired by God.

2 Timothy 3:16-17 states, "All Scripture is God-breathed and is useful for teaching, rebuking, correcting and training in righteousness so that the man of God may be thoroughly equipped for every good work." Think of God's Word as the tool box He provides with all the tools He gives us for the tasks He would accomplish through us. We also read of God's inspiration in 2 Peter 1:20-21, "Above all, you must understand that no prophecy of Scripture came about by the prophet's own interpretation. For prophecy never had its origin in the will of

man, but men spoke from God as they were carried along by the Holy Spirit."

As to the Bible being a truth-full testimony of God, thereby it being without error, we can turn to several references. Luke 24:27 says, "And beginning with Moses and all the Prophets, he explained to them what was said in all the Scriptures concerning himself." Jesus again speaks about the benefit of studying God's Word in John 5:39, "You diligently study the Scriptures because you think that by them you possess eternal life. These are the Scriptures that testify about me".

One of my favorite testimonies of God's Word within His Word comes from John 20:31, "But these are written that you may believe that Jesus is the Christ, the Son of God, and that by believing you may have life in his name." Peter testifies to the command of Jesus for the apostles to tell all they had seen and heard, even as the prophets were cited, with his words found in Acts 10:43, "All the prophets testify about him that everyone who believes in him receives forgiveness of sins through his name."

Finally, Paul gives testimony to the powerful work of Scripture in the life of Timothy. He encourages him in 2 Timothy 3:14-15, "But as for you, continue in what you have learned and have become convinced of, because you know those from whom you learned it, and how from infancy you have known the holy Scriptures, which are able to make you wise for salvation through faith in Christ Jesus."

> RM: *How have you responded to those who were skeptical about God actually authoring the Bible through human beings?*

To seal the connection between prayer and God speaking to us through His Word, I'd like to take us on a mini-Bible study. Yes, it's time to get out your prospecting gear again! Grab that miner's hat, making sure the light's working brightly. Grab your pick axe, as we'll have to prospect through some passages to discover the gold nuggets or precious stones God has placed for us to take with us and ponder. Let's go down into the cavern of God's Word with our stop in the mine shaft found in Psalm 143! Get your Bible out, something to write with and write upon, and let's prayerfully begin!

As I was prospecting through Psalm 143, I came up with four veins of thought that I dug into. I'd ask you to begin first by prayerfully looking at the following verses, one section at a time: Psalm 143:1; then verses 5 and 6; followed by verse 8, and end with verse 10. Take time to read, reread, read aloud, write out and read a last time the same verse(s). Underline any words that leap out or click the light on within your mind. Any thoughts that come forth over any underlined words make sure you capture in writing underneath the verses. Once you've gone through all four sections, then pick up this chapter as I share with you what God has spoken to me through His Word, okay?

Psalm 143:1, "O Lord, hear my prayer, listen to my cry for mercy; in your faithfulness and righteousness come to my relief."

GOD's Message:

Our RELATIONSHIP with God brings us to an understanding and dependence upon Him IN prayer. We KNOW He hears us! The answer we seek from God comes because of His

FAITHFULNESS towards us. We would not want, nor would we ask for any other answer from God unless it be grounded in His own RIGHTEOUSNESS...unlike ours or any sinful human being.

MY Reflection:

WHAT do you ask from God as He hears you...that would reflect His righteousness towards you?

HOW do you ask in confidence that God will extend His faithfulness again to you through this prayer?

Psalm 143:5-6, "I remember the days of long ago; I meditate on all your works and consider what you hands have done. I spread out my hands to you; my soul thirsts for you like a parched land."

GOD's Message:

OUR MEMORY blesses us richly as we recall the mercy of our God in His daily dealings with us. We consider His mighty work of creation and restoration and preservation...not just on earth, but also in the lives of His people, both LOST and FOUND.

MY Reflection:

WHAT kind of gesture can our response in prayer be? What would we surrender to His all-sustaining power?

HOW do you seek Him, who would satisfy your parched self with the rich water only He can provide?

Psalm 143:8, "Let the morning bring me word of your unfailing love, for I have put my trust in you. Show me the way I should go, for to you I lift up my soul."

GOD's Message:

CAUSE me! We can only call upon God's own Spirit to bring about the change we need and seek! Our relationship cast in trust would cause me to hear of His loving kindness. CAUSE me to know His way, the only way I should walk!

MY Reflection:

HOW is His unconditional, ever faithful love for me present every day I begin IN HIM? How do I KNOW and SEE and SPEAK of it to others, Lost and Found? HOW is His way for my walk EVIDENT? What challenges must I overcome by His causal work in my life...that I might remain daily WALKing in His way alone? What impedes us? Slows us down? Diverts our path away from His?

Psalm 143:10, "Teach me to do your will, for you are my God; may your good Spirit lead me on level ground."

GOD's Message:

GOD has MUCH to teach us. Do you want to learn from Him? Will you prioritize the time HE alone gives you? Would you sit alertly before Him, ready to listen and take notes? Would you welcome His testing how much you desire to learn from Him?

MY Reflection:

If I pray for PATIENCE, am I ready to endure whatever God would give me?

If I pray for COMFORT, am I ready to suffer through whatever God would give me?

If I pray for PEACE, am I ready to succumb to any turmoil God would send me?

HOW would you share your relationship with God to the Lost, who would want to know Him as you have come to know Him in your walk? HOW would you share your relationship with God to the Found, who would want to depend upon Him as you have come to know Him in your walk?

I am confident that as you invited the Holy Spirit to come along side your personal study of the selected passages in Psalm 143, God fed you, and you were nourished. I am also confident the Holy Spirit came along side both of us as we studied and reflected upon the selected passages in Psalm 143. God fed both of us and will continue to feed and nourish us as we work through these "message" and "reflection" sections.

Yes, I encourage you to ask the Holy Spirit to help you prospect through the points He raised through me to you as well! Again, think of the blessings in store between you and your spiritual work out partner if you together had such a study! Let it be more than just a nudge or suggestion. Schedule some time this week for such an endeavor. Begin to pray NOW for God's still, present voice to speak to you through His Word as you are enabled to listen!

Through the Word of God, we feed, He nourishes and sustains us for WALKing with God as we battle the devil!

Do you hunger for God? How would you describe your appetite? Minimal satisfying or starving? I am convinced that the more time we spend with God IN His Word and in a mutual hearing/ speaking dialogue with Him, the more we hunger! The more time we would beg, yes, BEG to have with Him. He's more than able and capable to give you ALL the time you would WANT and USE! Would you agree?

So, what's preventing you from such satisfying opportunities? Who's preventing you? Yes, the devil will always be out there! My fellow spiritual body builder, the devil is always trying to put aside or weaken God's efforts as you've come to know them. Weaken, you say? How is that if I believe the Scripture passage that says, "...the one who is in you is greater than the one who is in the world." (1 John 4:4)

I DON'T doubt God is greater. I also don't doubt that the devil takes his own work seriously. The devil firmly believes he's going to take as many people with him as he is able. Read our Lord Jesus' own words in Luke 24 and come to appreciate the fact that the devil is hard at work where God is at work. Where God is at work, through the lives of daily walking disciples, these are those farthest away from the devil. Wouldn't it be a true trophy if the devil could bring down a daily walking disciple? How the devil rejoices and celebrates when a pastor or a well known Christian is caught in his sinful ways, in the media! It's as if contrition, repentance and forgiveness are not possible!

I'm not condoning the sinful actions of any person, whether they are God's shepherd or servant! The blood of Jesus covers any sin, none seen any least or greater in the eyes of God. The forgiveness won by Jesus' own work for us on the cross WILL be given to anyone who is sorry for their sins, confesses them, and desires by the power of God's Holy Spirit to amend their way! And not only does God forgive, but God also forgets. Just so your clear on this forgetfulness of God, let the power of these two passages cover your understanding, as well! God Himself tells us in Isaiah 43:25, " 'I, even I, am he who blots out your transgressions, for my own sake, and remembers your sins no more.'" We also read in Jeremiah 31:34b, " 'For I will forgive their wickedness and will remember their sins no more.'"

Why should we hold on to the memory of any forgiven sin if God doesn't? The devil wouldn't want the power of God's forgiveness, through the blood of Christ, to be even considered in light of any sin, including those sins we would consider extreme or harmful, would he?

Dear daily disciple and spiritual body builder IN Christ Jesus our Savior and Lord! We only know we have this day, today, to walk with our Lord Jesus, as His Holy Spirit within equips, enables, empowers and expects us to BE His disciples. As we've read God's expectations for us as His branches, connected to His vine, would you not agree there is no more time left? We must ABIDE in Jesus every step of the way and every day He gives us!

We HAVE to come to KNOW His Word more faithfully. We have to invite Him and ask Him to spend more concentrated hours as He gives them to us. We have to be out WALKing His walk and let His Holy Spirit be TALKing His talk through us! John points this out to us, as we read about what it means to abide in Jesus in 1 John 2:5b-6, "This is how we know we are in him: Whoever claims to live in him must walk as Jesus did." We may be sure we are in Him! How? If we say we abide in Him, we are to WALK the same way Jesus WALKED! We have to know all about Jesus as His life and teachings were revealed through the eyewitnesses God called and spoke through. We each experience the power of God's Word as we come to know it, call upon it, and take it up as the weapon God intends for it to be in this spiritual warfare!

Later, in 1 John 4:12b-13, John again reminds us what it means to be abiding in Christ, "but if we love one another, God lives in us and his love is made complete in us. We know that we live in him and he in us, because he has given us of his Spirit." As we love one another, God abides in us. His love perfects us! We KNOW that we ABIDE in Him and He in us because we have His Spirit. The devil would have us know very little and fear knowing much more about the Holy Spirit. The devil knows what the power of the Holy Spirit can do in the daily WALKing and TALKing life of God's spiritual body building disciple! Do you?

It's quite likely we have forgotten two things: Time is short and Hell is hot! Two things the devil surely would have us forget, would you agree?

So, let's start taking this WALK with God seriously. Let's start taking the time in prayer and in reading God's Word far more seriously than we ever have. Let's start calling upon God's Holy Spirit to have complete Lordship over us as our Lord Jesus would expect! Let's start committing a regular amount of the first fruit time God gives us in response to His call, "Come, follow Me!"

I trust and pray that's why God made it possible for me to write this book.

I trust and pray that's why God enabled you to read this book.

I trust and pray that's why God will work His work through you through this book.

There's no inherent power in this book. It's ALL in His Book, the Bible, the very Word of God. It's "the power of God for the salvation of everyone who believes." (Romans 1:16)

Won't you come, hungry before Him, asking for every slice of bread He provides in His Word? Remember Jesus' word to the devil in response to bread?

We would not live by physical bread alone but by every word that comes from God (Matthew 4:4)! Time to DIG IN, daily disciple of our Savior and Lord Jesus!

Chapter Eight

How does God enable His spiritual body building within me and His church?

God desires an intimate daily relationship with you. How much do you believe that? Enough to honor Him with worship once a week? Enough to go beyond that minimum to include Sunday morning Bible class? How about participating in the extras, like additional classes or worship services? Volunteering in whatever capacity for whatever responsibility you are asked?

If you had to measure how much you participate in an intimate daily relationship with God, would it be based on the structured, organized and visible church? Or would it be more walking with God as a part of the invisible body of Christ? How are they different?

Think about it this way. If you joined an organization that required attendance and participation as part of membership, how much of a member would you be? Superficial or sustaining? Just doing enough to meet the minimum? Or if you left, would there be a crisis? The organizations that men design and run look and function much like that, don't they?

God is a different designer, isn't He? You would expect what He designs and supports to be different as He is different (Remember our reading of Isaiah 55:89-9?)

The invisible body of Christ, as God designs, equips, and sustains it, is not like the visible church man creates and maintains. Purely from the perspective that visible churches come and go, are built and sold, grow like gangbusters or wither away ought to show some of the differences. Yes, even the visible church of God is subject to decay, as are all things made with human hands on this earth.

The continuing trend within many North American churches is to design them like companies that are budget driven and results evaluated. Shepherds have become CEO's; Elders have formalized into a Board of Directors; volunteers have become paid employees; God's vision for ministry has become a cost-effective, budget driven plan for measured, profitable success. While God's invisible church has remained a living organism, the visible church has been designed to run like a mechanized robot.

When you look at the contrasting difference between the invisible body of Christ (aka "the invisible church") and the visible church (aka the "visible body of Christ"), you wonder if God truly desires that they become so misunderstood and interchangeable?

Did God desire to have His Son our Savior die on the cross so that we would create visible organizations that could come and go based upon the whims and fancies of its' members?

Does God desire that we steer clear of the membership driven mechanism and budget driven ministry today's visible church has become? Ought we to rediscover how the Acts 2:42 church became to be, grow, and go forth to disciple and make disciples?

> RM: *Do you think the average Lost person is lost because they're not in a daily discipleship with their Savior and Lord Jesus? Or are they lost because they lack some "dues paying membership" in the visible church? Do you think the average Dechurched person, who chose to leave the visible church they belonged to for some specific reason, is looking for another membership opportunity more favorable to their way of thinking or feeling? Consider how your own local church responds to both. Cite some examples where they were successful or less than successful in attracting and ministering to them.*

Are we asked by God to become members and make members at a local church? Or are we asked by our Savior and Lord Jesus to come follow Him and walk according to the way He walked? Would these be the kinds of disciples He would want to be out making other disciples?

In the midst of all my questions, let me proceed forward with a few answers that will help you see my position clearer and with a bit of renewed confidence.

There exists the invisible and visible church or body of Christ. The invisible is created and sustained, united under one Head, our Savior and Lord Jesus. The visible is established and run much like a business, having become fragmented under many differing views of mission, purpose and visible organization and structure.

Many people are members of both. Membership in the invisible church or body of Christ is God's free gift to you through your baptism. Membership in the visible church is your decision to join a local church. The invisible church is driven by God Himself as He outlines how His Church will function within the Word of God. The visible church is driven by elected members operating under member-devised constitutions that meet to limit ministry opportunities based upon money available that can be well spent according to its' objectives.

I can hop, skip and jump through more than one visible church in my lifetime. I can even adopt the consumer practice of brand comparisons while I'm shopping for my next church. Not so with God's invisible church. What He fashions and sustains are for all eternity! There's no question one would be satisfied with what God offers; no need to find something else, is there?

Finally, within the visible church man designs and operates, there are all kinds of levels of membership available. Not so with God's invisible church! God wants you only at the hot, daily walking discipleship level. The visible church will gladly sustain your membership at the entry, Sunday service only level. You will never have to move out of lukewarmness to anything resembling God's hot, daily walking discipleship level.

This is the TRUTH as our Savior and Lord Jesus would identify within His Church and Word. There will be some overlaps from God's invisible church and man's visible church, where the visible church has truly caught the vision for God's mission.

But, how many of them out there are discipling and making disciples the way God intends the whole world to become His invisible church?

It's time we rediscover what God's desire is for His invisible body, the Church, and respond in obedience to His righteous command.

God desires that His light be transformed out of darkness. God desires that each of us become transformed from being LOST to being FOUND. God desires that each of us no longer walk in DARKNESS but in His LIGHT.

Jesus was on a mission. Luke 19:10 reminds us, "For the Son of Man came to seek and to save what was lost." 1 Peter 2:9 reminds us, "But you are a chosen people, a royal priesthood, a holy nation, a people belonging to God, that you may declare the praises of him who called you out of darkness into his wonderful light."

> RM: *What would Jesus have us do in response to being no longer lost and no longer in darkness? Consider some concrete things you would see Him accomplishing through you for such a purpose. Would Jesus not desire that we be baptized, receive the Holy Spirit, learn His teaching, and go and let Him make disciples through us? Yes, God's Word confirms that and because I've shared enough references from God's Word in the previous pages, I'll refrain from reproducing them here!*

That's what the WALK of a Disciple is all about! We're made His disciples through baptism so that we would walk in His ways and teaching! Remember where we've come from? Remember how many are still there?

Paul reminds us in 2 Corinthians 1:9, who we should depend upon! "Indeed, in our hearts we felt the sentence of death. But this happened that we might not rely on ourselves but on God, who raises the dead." We read further the desire of God's work in 2 Corinthians 1:21-22, "Now it is God who makes both us and you stand firm in Christ. He anointed us, set his seal of ownership on us, and put his Spirit in our hearts as a deposit, guaranteeing what is to come."

Why? Wouldn't Satan, the devil, want to take advantage of us? We would confirm by our reading of 2 Corinthians 2:11, "in order that Satan might not outwit us. For we are not unaware of his schemes." What are some of Satan's schemes? Jesus confirmed during His time of temptation by Satan how much Satan wants God's place in our lives. Jesus condemns Satan in Matthew 4:10, " 'Away from me, Satan! For it is written: 'Worship the Lord your God, and serve him only.' " Jesus also said to Peter how Satan asked to sift him as wheat (Luke 22:31). We also know Paul's description of Satan's activity in our present age, "The god of this age has blinded the minds of unbelievers, so that they cannot see the light of the gospel of the glory of Christ, who is the image of God." (2 Corinthians 4:4)

> RM: *You have heard the description of Satan as "your enemy the devil prowls around like a roaring lion looking for someone to devour." (1 Peter 5:8b) How would it become easier or difficult for Satan to come sniffing around you? How would your lifestyle and walk as a daily disciple provide opportunities for the devil's obstacles?*

God desires and continues to transform us. He always leads us in triumph over the devil IN Christ! 2 Corinthians 2:14 describes the outcome of God's work in our lives: "But thanks be to God, who always leads us in triumphal procession in Christ and through us spreads everywhere the fragrance of the knowledge of him." We are to be that fragrance of Christ as we read in the next verse of 2 Corinthians 2:15, "For we are to God the aroma of Christ among those who are being saved and those who are perishing."

Remember, we are not in any position to think it's from us or what we do that generates that salvation fragrance of Christ. We come to understand in 2 Corinthians 3:5, "Not that we are competent in ourselves to claim anything for ourselves, but our competence comes from God." As God is at work within our daily discipleship, we would see God actively behind every opportunity for such work! What's God's desire for us? We find it in 2 Corinthians 3:18, "And we, who with unveiled faces all reflect the Lord's glory, are being transformed into his likeness with ever-increasing glory, which comes from the Lord, who is the Spirit."

As I've mentioned before, God is very specific. God has a very specific plan for each of us as we read in Ephesians 1:11-12), "In him we were also chosen, having been predestined according to the plan of him who works out everything in conformity with the purpose of his will, in order that we, who were the first to hope in Christ, might be for the praise of his glory." God has carried out that specific plan for our salvation through the work of our Savior Jesus. God continues to carry out His very specific plan for our sanctification through the work of His Holy Spirit.

It's even in the words of the benediction Paul shares with the spiritual body builders in 1 Thessalonians 5:23-24, "May God himself, the God of peace, sanctify you through and through. May your whole spirit, soul and body be kept blameless at the coming of our Lord Jesus Christ. The one who calls you is faithful and he will do it."

> RM: *How have you seen in your daily discipleship the commitment God has for you to "sanctify you through and through"? Give some examples of His construction work in your life. Consider some big opportunities God has called you to allow His work through you. How did He show you His faithfulness and ability to "do it"?*

We are so blessed to have so much of our Lord Jesus teaching at our fingertips. When you want to learn ALL of Jesus teaching verbatim, make sure you've got a "words of Christ red letter" edition. It makes it so much easier to get around those quotation marks to hear again, first hand, ALL Jesus wants His present day daily disciples to learn from Him.

Yes, He is our Lord. Yes, He is our Savior. Yes, He is also our Teacher. Many times throughout the gospels, Jesus is referred to as "Teacher" and we disciples as "Students." That's the direction our relationship with Him has taken. We're enrolled in our Teacher Jesus' Academy. There are no semesters or quarters, with limited weeks of instruction, assignments, and no final exams.

We have one WALK with one Holy Spirit to instruct us in all we need to know to become holy as God is holy! Our instruction is not just limited to the kind of information we would find in the

Epistles of the New Testament. No, we can draw from several different subjects including Old and New Testament History; God's Poetry; God's Words of Comfort through Prophecy and more! Aren't these some fascinating subjects to get immersed in? Where will you start? I'd encourage you to read some of each and have yourself a well-rounded outlook on your walk together!

Of course, it's not enough to learn and know. We have to put it into practice, as Paul would remind our Teacher's students in Philippians 4:9, "Whatever you have learned or received or heard from me, or seen in me—put into practice. And the God of peace will be with you." I like how Paul includes what we see in each other as being imitated, not just words of teaching. Part of that learning, Paul goes on to say, is to learn to be content whatever the situation. No matter what the contrasting circumstances, what's the one constant that remains? Philippians 4:13 tells us, "I can do everything through him who gives me strength."

> RM: *How have you learned such a lesson yet? What have been some circumstances, weak though you thought you were that were opportunities for God to demonstrate His strength through you?*

In preparing this book, I have been reminded again of ALL the wealth and wisdom God shares with us through His Word. KNOWing becomes WALKing when we allow the Holy Spirit to rekindle His Holy Heartburn in our lives on His walkway. Timothy was a blessed daily disciple. He had the opportunity from childhood to know God's Word; how that it's God-breathed and useful for teaching, rebuking, correcting and training in righteousness. God gives us His Word so that we might be thoroughly equipped to use it. That's the motive Paul makes for every spiritual body builder, seeking to be built up in Christ and His Teaching! We read in 2 Timothy 3:14-17, "But as for you, continue in what you have learned and have become convinced of, because you know those from whom you learned it, and how from infancy you have known the holy Scriptures, which are able to make you wise for salvation through faith in Christ Jesus. All Scripture is God-breathed and is useful for teaching, rebuking, correcting and training in righteousness, so that the man of God may be thoroughly equipped for every good work."

Don't be content with God's ten pound weights for your training in daily discipline! Make sure you call upon the Holy Spirit to condition you to keep growing and going beyond the minimal through to the maximum!

I spoke about direction before. How many of us have come to depend upon Global Positioning Systems (GPS) in our cars to get us from the unknown to the known? They're great at directing us!

God's Word can be seen as a GPS device. However, God doesn't just teach us from His Word. He also teaches us according to the circumstances we will encounter together on the WALK. He's committed to us. Are we committed to Him? Or do we start having second thoughts when the road gets rougher than we expected?

With God, isn't it a continual walk that leads to growth? So, you've got to expect that as God toughens you up from a faith muscle stretching time, you will be better prepared for the next more challenging stretch...and so on...and so on! Don't give in and yell, "I give up!" If you do, that means you won't have future opportunities to soar higher and farther as God's eagle. You would be telling God and yourself you would rather dwell in the nest than soar above as His eagle!

God's committed to you soaring like an eagle! How about you? Do you find yourself leery about being in a nest too high up? Do you get airsick if you're at too high an altitude? Who's really to decide that anyway? Isn't God the One doing the leading? Isn't God the One doing the equipping? Can't you trust Him to take you up higher than you've been? As He calls you to do a faith jump, can you trust the One who packed your parachute?

It's clear from 1 Thessalonians 2:4 that God "tests our hearts." God wants to test you because He wants you to become stronger and more faith-filled in your walk with Him. He's prepared us well. We need to keep advancing towards our ultimate goal... becoming more Christ-like!

God also wants us to take Jesus' yoke and learn from Him, as He tells us in Matthew 11:29, " 'Take my yoke upon you and learn from me, for I am gentle and humble in heart, and you will find rest for your souls.' " The yoke is meant to keep you in line, walking a straight path, with your partner. Yoked to Jesus, we can't help but walk in the direction He walks.

Of course, we let HIS strength and will dominate. Peter had a hard time with that. It seemed to be Peter's desire to do things his own way, according to his own experience and direction. How many of us would see ourselves in the same driver's seat?

But, what a difference when we let Jesus take the wheel, or the direction of the nets in the fishing boat in the case of Peter?

Don't we want an abundant WALK with Jesus? That's why He came, remember, to give us abundant life. Who else, where else, and how else can we find it except in Him? What more do we need to convince us to let Him be yoked to us?

What's God's intentional outcome for His daily WALKing disciples? "For we are God's workmanship, created in Christ Jesus to do good works, which God prepared in advance for us to do." (Ephesians 2:10) We don't have to worry what these good works are. We don't have to wonder how they will be accomplished. We don't have to second guess their reality. It's just like the plan God put together for our salvation and Jesus our Savior implemented. It's all HE, not me! "For it is by grace you have been saved, through faith—and this not from yourselves, it is the gift of God—not by works, so that no one can boast." (Ephesians 2:8-9)

As we studied previously, Jesus relationship to us as the Vine means He has been appointed by God, the Vineyard dresser, to take us on as His fruit bearing branches. As long as we remain and abide IN HIM, He will be able to grow such fruit of holiness in our lives. People will see the outcome of such holiness only through those fruits the Holy Spirit can grow through us including love, joy, peace, patience, kindness, goodness, faithfulness, gentleness and self-control. These are outlined for us in Galatians 5:22-23. Jesus, the Vine, makes it possible in His plan for us. "Since we live by the Spirit, let us keep in step with the Spirit."(Galatians 5:25)

RM: *How would God's Spirit enable us to keep in step with Him? What would "not keeping in step with Him" look like?*

The Writer to the Hebrews gives us a good snapshot of all God would see as His planned outcome through each of us. Follow along in Hebrews 12 as we see the Holy Spirit's desire and dedication to fulfilling God's plan for each of us: to be reconnected and walking with Him in holiness!

Why is holiness so important, such a priority, in God's eyes? Beyond a priority, a necessity? Why are we told in Hebrews 12:14, "Make every effort to live in peace with all men and to be holy; without holiness no one will see the Lord"? Clearly God IS holy. We cannot be in the presence of a holy God unless we are holy. That's the mark of the relationship God had with Adam and Eve before their fall into sin. God would walk among them because they were holy as He was holy. Once sin entered the world, He would no longer be able to have such a rich communion with them in the cool of the day

God loves you so much, He didn't want to let that remain the chasm between you and Him. He wanted to restore those walks with you, didn't He? And He HAS through the blood of Jesus His own Son! Such grace and mercy extended to each of us! Won't you forever in eternity give Him His due thanks and praise? We're doing so even now!

As God tells us, the Devil is actively trying to get us tied up, confused, frustrated and ready to quit the race even after a few miles. God tells us, "let us throw off everything that hinders and the sin that so easily entangles, and let us run with perseverance the race marked out for us" (Hebrews 12:1). What are those things that hinder us? What are those sins that so easily entangle us?

Why would we have our eyes fixed on Jesus? Ask Peter! With his eyes on Jesus, Peter walked on water! He walked within arms length of Jesus. Could the same be said of us at any point in our daily discipleship? We read on in Hebrews 12:3, "Consider him who endured such opposition from sinful men, so that you will not grow weary and lose heart" especially as the race gets more and more challenging.

Yes, it can be a struggle and a challenge posed by the Devil. When would we welcome God's discipline? Why would we welcome God's discipline? First, because we ought to be thankful we're His sons and would want us to be treated as His sons! Hebrews 12:7 points out to us, "Endure hardship as discipline; God is treating you as sons. For what son is not disciplined by his father?" Don't you like being considered and treated by God as His sons and daughters?

Second, because God knows what is good for us, including the discipline that will lead to sharing His holiness! Hebrews 12:10 reminds us from our history lessons in the Bible, "Our fathers disciplined us for a little while as they thought best; but God disciplines us for our good, that we may share in his holiness." How can God be assured of such an outcome in us?

Third, God will produce in us and through us what we cannot ever produce! And all because of His discipline? YES! "Later on, however, it produces a harvest of righteousness and peace for those who have been trained by it." (Hebrews 12:11b)

RM: So how do you suppose God will discipline you in order that such a harvest of righteousness and peace will be produced in you? Will you go along with such discipline or will you need further convincing? Not only understand the "why" or "why not," but be able to state the implications!

God has given us prayer and His Word as the two chief weights His Holy Spirit would use in building up our spiritual bodies. Let's see how Jesus finishes His final lesson with His disciples before His death on the cross with a time of prayer in John 17.

As you will see in John 17, Jesus splits up His prayer in light of three persons He is led to pray for!

- Himself

Jesus reveals to us that God the Father granted Jesus the authority necessary from God over all people. They would all be subject to receiving God's gift of eternal life. Only God could wrap and personally name tag that many gifts, couldn't He? Jesus sets the example for us before God when it comes to fruit bearing. Just as He asked us in John 15:8, " 'This is to my Father's glory, that you bear much fruit, showing yourselves to be my disciples," so Jesus acknowledges in John 17:4, " 'I have brought you glory on earth by completing the work you gave me to do.' "

- His Disciples

Jesus, as Teacher, has fulfilled all God's teaching assignments. He has taught them all the words given to Him by God. They have received all the lessons. He will be leaving them behind. He knows the world will hate them, and He has told them so! He also knows the Devil will hate them and seek after them because Jesus has given them God's Word. Holiness and sanctification are those things necessary in their lives. These can only come about by God's very Word which is truth!

- All Those Who Will Believe Through Their Message

Even then, Jesus was thinking to pray for you and me! Jesus desired that all the invisible church be built up in the Father and Son. The unity that Jesus sought and prayed for could not come about in the visible, physical world where the Devil would seek to divide even Jesus' disciples into fractions. But, in the invisible body of Christ, God's own invisible Church would be one in glory with the Trinity. Jesus work, even through us, doesn't end. He continues until the Father calls Jesus to return to bring final judgment upon the earth. We have such a call from Jesus, too! We're to be working until He brings it all to an end.

How has God been answering Jesus prayer through His daily walk with His disciples? We can see from the days following Jesus ascension and the descent of the Holy Spirit on Pentecost, God continued to empower His disciples with everything they needed.

Aren't you empowered to read after Jesus' gave them the promise of the Holy Spirit, "and you will be my witnesses... to the ends of the earth" (Acts 1:8)? Can't you imagine as each one looked in the eyes of their crucified and risen Savior, and Lord Jesus, THEY were empowered to do everything exactly as He had taught them? It must have been so because Acts 1:10 says they were looking intently at Jesus while he was going up to heaven!

When they returned, what did they do? Go their separate ways? Take a much deserved, well earned vacation from such a stressful time? First, they remained together. Theirs was an unspoken strength they could draw from each other. Have you ever experienced the sweet sincere fellowship only brothers and sisters IN Jesus can have and share? Acts 4:32 is a testimony to the transforming power of God's unconditional love IN Christ. We are told, "All the believers were one in heart and mind. No one claimed that any of his possessions was his own, but they shared everything they had." (Acts 4:32) How else could this have happened if it were not for the transforming power of God to move from self-centered to selfless? Would the same be said of us in our day!

Second, they were constantly in prayer. Paul tells us in Romans 1:9b, "how constantly I remember you in my prayers at all times." "I pray also that the eyes of your heart may be enlightened in order that you may know the hope to which he has called you, the riches of his glorious inheritance in the saints." (Ephesians 1:18) "And pray in the Spirit on all occasions with all kinds of prayers and requests. With this in mind, be alert and always keep on praying for all the saints." (Ephesians 6:18) What would they be praying about? Whom would they be praying for? Why would prayer be their constant activity? Can you see the value and power of corporate prayer in your witnessing as they did? Can you see how important the time of prayer is in your spiritual body building workout with your workout partner?

There is so much value and importance we can learn from the Acts 2:42 church. What was it about this visible church in its' day that has unraveled into the visible church of our day? All the components were there; all the basic stuff necessary can be found in what they were devoted to in that one verse! How could we have strayed so far away that we have so many buildings dotted across the landscape, doing their own thing to survive, that you wonder why the light is even still on?

If we would only get back to the Acts 2:42 church! How was it so different from the visible church today? Some visible churches are so concerned about capturing and maintaining worshippers' time and interest. They believe they have to become as entertaining as a 60 minute TV show, minus the commercials! No one wants to hear any good old fashioned preaching from the Bible! Devotion to the apostle's teaching is not enough anymore ! What did Paul say to young Timothy about such times as these in 2 Timothy 4:3-4? "For the time will come when men will not put up with sound doctrine. Instead, to suit their own desires, they will gather around them a great number of teachers to say what their itching ears want to hear. They will turn their ears away from the truth and turn aside to myths." Many have referenced today's prosperity preachers and teachers as being the ticklers. Would you agree?

True New Testament fellowship seems to have snuck out the back door, as well. We have more dinners as fundraisers than potlucks! Don't you think in today's hurry up world, folks would appreciate a "home cooked meal" in the church Fellowship Hall?

"The breaking of bread" refers to the Lord's Supper or Holy Communion. They knew then what it was. Review Paul's definitive teaching in 1 Corinthians 11:23-32 to understand what was present and happening as they ate and drank, proclaiming the Lord's death until He comes! The visible church is divided and confused over the true meaning and celebration. Many churches seldom offer this sacred meal. Many disciples seldom draw His power and assurance from such a gift!

What about prayer in a worship setting? Are our prayers limited to the litany of pre-prescribed sentences spoken in response? If we dare spend five minutes or more standing or kneeling in prayer, would we hear complaints after the church service? Do we even consider offering prayer time outside of the church service? What kind of attendance numbers would we get if we offered a prayer service at any time on any day? Would we take a false sense of pride in responding that it's always the "faithful few" who come out for these events?

I don't believe technology and a sped up world ought to become the reasons why we can't become communities of daily devoted disciples who are spiritual body builders! It's great to use technology for worship to be offered "live streaming" to all parts of the world. Think of the impact throughout the world, where Islam is the only voice? How innocent can such a broadcast appear to be on the surface level to penetrate a wall of stone or a curtain of iron?

Yet, the availability of real time worship services ought not replace the assembling of each other on a Sunday morning for worship. "Let us not give up meeting together, as some are in the habit of doing, but let us encourage one another." (Hebrews 10:25) No matter how tempting it would be to gather around our laptop in our pajamas for worship. Nor do I believe people's attention spans and expectations have become so limited and fragmented by over stimulation, that we can't derive a fruitful experience that lasts longer than a television program!

I believe a prayer-filled look at the visible church in light of Acts 2:42 is the assignment for God's daily disciples to take to heart today! I believe that's the message of WALKing and TALKing Ministries through this book and the courses God leads me to teach.

The devil is working relentlessly at fragmenting the visible church. Even now he's doing all he can do to turn down the heat of the Holy Spirit's fire. The devil desires to disengage more daily disciples from the fruit bearing our Lord Jesus prayed for in John 17! Think of how much the devil would benefit if we continued down the path we've been continuing down in the "growth" of the visible church! Yes, I know these are hard statements to hear. They are even harder to say!

By becoming His daily WALKing and TALKing disciple, what will you let the Holy Spirit accomplish in you? What fruit will be borne on your branch? What will your daily discipleship show the rest of the visible church?

Won't you join me in prayer for the revival and reformation necessary in our day? Won't you pray with me that both the visible and invisible church would be one as Jesus' prayed for us in John 17?

Heavenly Father, we thank You for your untold and abundant mercy and grace which You alone have extended to and through Your church, visible and invisible. We ask in these days, O Holy Spirit, that You would rekindle and reignite the hearts of Your children, the church. We ask that we might become again the Acts 2:42 church and exceed the fruit borne through them by You. Help us to be those witnesses You have called us to be!

Help us to have Your Spirit at work through our life and word witness. May our testimony of You, O God, at work in and through us give glory and praise to You alone! Bring the revival of Your church and reformation of Your church so that we can become those vessels of clay moldable and useful according to Your perfect will. In Jesus' Name, we ask this! Amen.

Chapter Nine

What is God's commitment to my WALKing with Him?

What is my commitment to my WALKing with God?

It always amazes me when I stop and think about how much God loves me! Jesus loves us by extending both arms as far as they will go hanging on the cross for us. Yes, God not only showed us then, He continues to show us every day and in every way, doesn't He?

I believe that's a lot behind the prayer Jesus taught us! It's got everything in there that a daily WALKing disciple of our Lord Jesus needs to be reminded of as prayer points! It's all about our relationship with God! Unlike any other religion of the world, Christianity is all about a relationship with God. As I like to say it, "Christianity is not a religion, it's a relationship!"

So, let's take a look at this relationship which God has gone to great lengths to establish and maintain. It begins before we begin, doesn't it? Within Psalm 139, we read David's testimony pointing to his relationship with God. It's a testimony that points to a life-long commitment of God walking with us. God commits to us because His love always accepts us where ever we're at. We would say with David in verse 4, "Before a word is on my tongue you know it completely, O Lord." (Psalm 139:4) God has a comforting and surrounding presence around us like a warm blanket on a chilly night! And no matter how dark that night becomes, He will be the light we need to be at peace.

Verse 13 is a powerful text used often in pro-life circles, "For you created my inmost being; you knit me together in my mother's womb." (Psalm 139:13) As we come to know all the intricacies of a human life, we are amazed! How does God do it? Verse 14 moves us to respond, "I praise you because I am fearfully and wonderfully made; your works are wonderful, I know that full well." (Psalm 139:14)

What would the fruit be of God's creative work in each one of us? His plan and outcome for each of us are not a mystery nor a series of random acts. No, verse 16 tells us with certainty, "All the days ordained for me were written in your book before one of them came to be." (Psalm 139:16)

> RM: *Take some time out to recall what some of those days have been. What do you say to God in response for all His planning on your behalf? What do you remember as one of the most memorable actions He's taken on your behalf?*

Moving from the Old Testament to the New Testament, we're reminded of Paul's words to the Ephesian Christians and us in Ephesians 2:10, "For we are God's workmanship, created in Christ Jesus to do good works, which God prepared in advance for us to do." Recall His fingerprints and handprints on your life. Don't these two passages from God's Word interlace together well? Here are a few more cross references to both of these passages that further explains the claim God has placed on each of us!

God has a deep down desire to have a relationship with each of us, even those who are lost. He says in Isaiah 43:6-7, "I will say to the north, 'Give them up!' and to the south, 'Do not hold them back.' Bring my sons from afar and my daughters from the ends of the earth—everyone who is called by my name, whom I created for my glory, whom I formed and made." To what lengths will He go to rescue, reclaim, and redeem ALL whom He has created?

Read God's creative comparison of our creation in Isaiah 60:21, "They are the shoot I have planted, the work of my hands, for the display of my splendor." God takes both love and pride in all He makes. That's why He went to great lengths to bring us back to Him...and still does for those out there still lost and far away from Him!

We can find several references to the hands of God at work in creating ourselves: Psalm 119:73, "Your hands made me and formed me". Have you ever stopped to consider what has God made and formed you to become? How has God reformed you throughout your daily discipleship walk? Job asks, "[Did you not] clothe me with skin and flesh and knit me together with bones and sinews?" (Job 10:11) God's relationship goes beyond creating us as we read in verse 12, "You gave me life and showed me kindness, and in your providence watched over my spirit." (Job 10:12) Isaiah records God's testimony, "This is what the Lord says—he who made you, who formed you in the womb, and who will help you" (Isaiah 44:2). He not just formed us in the womb, but wants to help us!

God knew our deepest need as sinners needing His forgiveness. Again, God testifies as our Redeemer, " 'I have swept away your offenses like a cloud, your sins like the morning mist. Return to me, for I have redeemed you.' " (Isaiah 44:22) God not only upholds us since conception, but carries us beyond birth, "Even to your old age and gray hairs I am he, I am he who will sustain you. I have made you and I will carry you; I will sustain you and I will rescue you." (Isaiah 46:4)

> RM: *Which of these verses could you cling tightly to as a promise fulfilled in your life? Write it out in the form of a prayer of praise and thanks to Our Father, Creator, Redeemer, and Sustainer!*

We could gather from the prophet Jeremiah the kind of relationship God desired to have with him. As we hear God say in Jeremiah 1:5, " 'Before I formed you in the womb I knew you, before you were born I set you apart; I appointed you as a prophet to the nations.' ". What a power-filled responsibility God expected and fulfilled in Jeremiah! Even we could receive God's words through Jeremiah and be so blessed.

David describes our relationship with God as being filled with thanks and praise! What is God's personality, seen through His activities? Psalm 145:8-9 tells us, "The Lord is gracious and compassionate, slow to anger and rich in love. The Lord is good to all; he has compassion on all he had made." I cannot comprehend such grace and compassion. Can you? I like how God puts it in Ecclesiastes 11:5, "As you do not know the path of the wind, or how the body is formed in a mother's womb, so you cannot understand the work of God, the Maker of all things."

I've spoken of the testimony of God at work in our lives. His work and words become our testimony as He is involved intimately in our daily discipleship. In Psalm 138:6-8, David shares God's testimony of actively being at work in David's life. "Though the Lord is on high, he looks upon the lowly, but the proud he knows from afar. Though I walk in the midst of trouble, you preserve my life; you stretch out your hand against the anger of my foes, with your right hand you save me."

What's God's response? How does God preserve our life? His hand stretches out and saves us from our enemies because God's intention is to fulfill His purpose for each of us!

> RM: *What would you confirm has been God's fulfilled purpose in you? What may be on His list, yet to be completed?*

Two more psalms of David testify to this relationship God desires and has with His created beings. Within Psalm 62, David speaks of our soul resting in God alone, Who is our rock and salvation. We ought to trust in God at all times and pour our hearts out to Him, who is both strong and loving! Then, next door within Psalm 63, David speaks of our earnestly seeking, thirsting, and longing for such a God as we have! We ought to cling to Him because His right hand upholds us! We would lift up our hands, and praise Him in response for all God does for us!

I don't doubt you could find any more testimony of God's love and desire for you as demonstrated in His Word among His children. But, sufficeth enough to say, "Yes, God loves you! Yes, God cares for you! Yes, God redeemed you!" for a purpose-full daily relationship with Him as His child and disciple!

Yes, God's commitment to you is clear and backed up, isn't it? So, what about our response to Him? What is our commitment to this God, our God?

> RM: *Go back over Psalms 62 and 63 for a moment. David talks about his own behavior towards God in specific terms. Would you find yourself chiming in with David? Take a personal inventory as I lead you through those two Psalms with a bit more detail, okay?*

Looking into Psalm 62

(vs. 1) "My soul finds rest in God alone; my salvation comes from him." *Is our relationship with God based more on our salvation through Him for eternity and less upon our daily need for Him? Would we look elsewhere, including our own strength, to find our rest?*

(vs. 2) "He alone is my rock and my salvation; he is my fortress, I will never be shaken." *What can we handle and what would we choose to let God handle in our lives? Ought we to keep the "easy stuff" and hand off to God the "tough stuff"?*

(vs. 5) "Find rest, O my soul, in God alone; my hope comes from him." *Who and what is your hope based in? In what ways does such hope help you? Why would you be at rest during difficulties?*

(vs. 6) "He alone is my rock and my salvation; he is my fortress, I will not be shaken." *What shakes your foundation? What past occurrences in your daily discipleship have caused you to see the wisdom of depending upon God only and totally?*

(vs. 8) "Trust in him at all times, O people; pour out your hearts to him, for God is our refuge." *What have you poured your heart out to God about? How did you feel before, during, and after such an opportunity?*

(vss. 11-12) "One thing God has spoken, two things have I heard: that you, O God, are strong, and that you, O Lord, are loving. Surely you will reward each person according to what he has done." *How would you describe the strength and love of God as He's shown it in your life?*

Looking into Psalm 63

(vs. 1) "O God, you are my God, earnestly I seek you; my soul thirsts for you, my body longs for you, in a dry and weary land where there is no water." *When and why did you ever earnestly seek God? How was He found by you? Describe a time when your soul thirsted for such a God. Describe a time when your same body longed for Him. How did you know you could go to God for such a response as His?*

(vs. 2) "I have seen you in the sanctuary and beheld your power and your glory." *How have you seen God's power and glory through your worship experiences? How would this encourage you to remain faithful in your corporate worship every chance you get?*

(vss. 3-4) "Because your love is better than life, my lips will glorify you. I will praise you as long as I live, and in your name I will lift up my hands." *How easy is it for you to respond to*

God's faithful gifts and work in your life? How often is your private and public prayer life filled with words and gestures that would glorify God and praise Him with lifted hands?

(vs. 6) "On my bed I remember you; I think of you through the watches of the night." *Why would your sleep time be a great time to reflect upon God's relationship with you? If you were to wake up, how would your response be reflecting upon God's presence and protection and provision for you?*

I encourage you to spend lots of time in the Psalms. Can you see why? You can find many prayer passages worth prospecting like precious jewels or nuggets of gold! You can respond to God through such words and prayers within a life that bears clear witness to the work of God, walking as His disciple! How have you come to know God in such a way? How have you truly tasted and seen how good God is? What fruit would God produce through you, remaining connected and abiding in Jesus only?

How is every day different in your discipleship walk? If every day as Jesus' disciple seems to be the same, then could something be wrong? What I have found invigorating about a daily walk, focused on Jesus as His disciple, is that every day IS different! In what ways, you may ask? Allow me some room for personal testimony, won't you? And please, recognize at the onset that there really is nothing different about me as far as disciples go.

I believe God treats us all the same way. He gives us the same love. He has expectations for us as we find Him outline them for us in His Word. But, I might add, my daily discipleship has not always been daily nor always discipleship-focused. Each day, I have allowed more and more room in my life for the Holy Spirit. He desires to become actively at work in and through my life as Jesus' disciple. Without that as a starting point, the Holy Spirit really doesn't have our permission to be at work and so He won't!

No, don't get me wrong...it's not what we do, but it's what we allow God to do...because of the free will God has chosen to give us and abide by!

So, for starters, we need to have the mind of Christ at work in us as we read in 1 Corinthians 2:16. To have the mind of Christ is to be IN Christ. We find ourselves in such a relationship with God through our baptism. Our daily recognition and invitation of the Holy Spirit is to drown the old man in us. The new man emerges. That new man emerging is nothing more than the mind of Christ replacing our sinful desires. You'll find this to be the case as it's confirmed by God's Word as follows.

Ephesians 4:22, 24, "You were taught, with regard to your former way of life, to put off your old self, which is being corrupted by its deceitful desires"; "and to put on the new self, created to be like God in true righteousness and holiness."

2 Corinthians 5:17, "Therefore, if anyone is in Christ, he is a new creation; the old has gone, the new has come!"

Romans 6:6, "For we know that our old self was crucified with him so that the body of sin might be done away with, that we should no longer be slaves to sin".

Titus 3:5-8, "he saved us, not because of righteous things we had done, but because of his mercy. He saved us through the washing of rebirth and renewal by the Holy Spirit".

Galatians 3:26-27, "You are all sons of God through faith in Christ Jesus, for all of you who were baptized into Christ have clothed yourselves with Christ."

As we read Romans 12:1-2, "Therefore, I urge you, brothers, in view of God's mercy, to offer your bodies as living sacrifices, holy and pleasing to God—this is your spiritual act of worship. Do not conform any longer to the pattern of this world, but be transformed by the renewing of your mind. Then you will be able to test and approve what God's will is—his good, pleasing and perfect will," we have to ask ourselves, "How much am I minding my response to all God has done for me in my baptism daily?

> RM: *How do you daily offer your body as holy and pleasing to God as a living sacrifice? How do you daily no longer conform to the world's ways and lifestyles? How do you allow the Holy Spirit to transform and renew your mind to become like Christ's? How do you daily test and live according to God's good, pleasing, and perfect will for you?*

Philippians 4:6-8 prescribes the motivation each of us needs to allow the Holy Spirit the place and space within each of us to accomplish His daily work. Take a look, verse by verse, at this prescription.

(vs. 6) "Do not be anxious about anything, but in everything, by prayer and petition, with thanksgiving, present your requests to God." Don't be nervous about anything. Take that anxious energy and call upon God through prayer for everything! Don't withhold anything from God. Be specific and persistent in your prayers. Give thanks with a heartfelt trust and confidence that you can bring everything to God!

(vs. 7) "And the peace of God, which transcends all understanding, will guard your hearts and your minds in Christ Jesus." Be prepared to receive such a peace from God like no other because that's what God give you when you give Him all your burdens. He stands ready to guard your hearts and minds IN Christ Jesus. (See, there's the mind of Christ at work in you again!)

(vs. 8) "Finally, brothers, whatever is true, whatever is noble, whatever is right, whatever is pure, whatever is lovely, whatever is admirable—if anything is excellent or praiseworthy—think about such things." Imagine how your life's attitude will be as you think on things that are true, noble, right, pure, lovely, admirable, excellent and praiseworthy!

We would come to understand and depend upon God's promise to us, begun at our baptism, and carried out daily within our discipleship as we find in Philippians 1:6, "being confident of this, that he who began a good work in you will carry it on to completion until the day of Christ Jesus." Our part? Allowing God to do so! We would not get in the way or ahead of God at work! If only God would plant a big sign in front of us: GOD AT WORK! How would that make a difference in our response?

How would we see God at work? How would we see the devil at work? God's Word describes who the devil is and what he desires to accomplish! Yes, there IS a devil! We can find an accurate description of who the devil is within the Word of God. Let's turn to a couple of passages that speak about him. I John 3:8 points out, "He who does what is sinful is of the devil, because the devil has been sinning from the beginning. The reason the Son of God appeared was to destroy the devil's work." Jesus points out who the devil is in John 8:44, " 'You belong to your father, the devil, and you want to carry out your father's desire. He was a murderer from the beginning, not holding to the truth, for there is no truth in him. When he lies, he speaks his native language, for he is a liar and the father of lies.' "

Paul explains in Ephesians 6:12, "For our struggle is not against flesh and blood, but against the rulers, against the authorities, against the powers of this dark world and against the spiritual forces of evil in the heavenly realms." Yes, we would recognize we are in a struggle against powers we cannot see, but are, nevertheless, very real!

Of course, the most recognized warning comes to us from Peter, who tells us in 1 Peter 5:8-9, "Be self-controlled and alert. Your enemy the devil prowls around like a roaring lion looking for someone to devour. Resist him, standing firm in the faith, because you know that your brothers throughout the world are undergoing the same kind of sufferings."

Would the devil want to devour you? You better believe it! The devil would just as soon take the precious Word of God sown in you as Jesus describes in Mark 4:15, " 'Some people are like seed along the path, where the word is sown. As soon as they hear it, Satan comes and takes away the word that was sown in them." Hebrews 2:14 says of Jesus, "...by his death he might destroy him who holds the power of death—that is the devil". John tells us in 1 John 3:8, "He who does what is sinful is of the devil, because the devil has been sinning from the beginning. The reason the Son of God appeared was to destroy the devil's work." James response to the devil? Take to heart his admonition in James 4:7, "Submit yourselves, then, to God. Resist the devil, and he will flee from you." I once heard a helpful hint, "When the devil comes knocking at your heart's door, send Jesus to answer it!" I like to sing very loudly for all, including the devil and his demons to hear, "Jesus! Jesus! Only Jesus!"

Do you see the obstacles that the devil would throw in the midst of your daily walk as Jesus disciple? Yes, all kinds of obstacles! Often they are fleshly based, not just sexual lust, but lust for anything that you can see! They are obstacles that are the worldly based stuff of this world. And what kind of world do we live in but a sinful world? And so, if our minds and hearts are set on the world and the things of this world, then they are in direct opposition to God and the things of His heavenly world, aren't they? John points this out in 1 John 2:15-17:

"Do not love the world or anything in the world. If anyone loves the world, the love of the Father is not in him. For everything in the world—the cravings of sinful man, the lust of his eyes and the boasting of what he has and does—comes not from the Father but from the world. The world and its desires pass away, but the man who does the will of God lives forever." (1 John 2:15-17)

John leaves no potential obstacle out of the devil's inventory and arsenal, does he? Verse 16 indicates "everything in the world"! You can't get by without finding something in this world that the devil will throw at you. Remember, he wants to throw you off God's path to holiness. It can be the things we see, we crave, what we would even boast about possessing! None of these would come from God our Father...but rather the father of all lies and sin, the devil!

None of us is exempt; We will all become the devil's targets. Paul says our sinful nature lives in us. That's why we must call upon God's Holy Spirit to live in us and daily drown this sinful nature! We might have the desire to do God's good, but we fail to carry it out as Paul points out in Romans 7:18, "I know that nothing good lives in me, that is, in my sinful nature. For I have the desire to do what is good, but I cannot carry it out."

Until God crushes Satan under our feet (Romans 16:20), we must be on the alert! We must let the peace of Christ transcend us as we allow the mind of Christ to navigate our steps on the daily walk as His disciples. We, like Paul, can be confident, as he says in 2 Timothy 1:12, "...I know whom I have believed, and am convinced that he is able to guard what I have entrusted to him for that day." What would we entrust to the Lord each day we rise, having the Holy Spirit drown the old man with all the devil's obstacles rolled up in him?

We would come to recognize and depend upon our circumstance IN Christ Jesus. God would take the devil's obstacle and either obliterate it or transform it into an opportunity for our good IN Christ Jesus! Isn't that what's behind the promising words of Romans 8:28? "And we know that in all things God works for the good of those who love him, who have been called according to his purpose." This is another promise of God we ought to commit to memory and recite whenever and wherever the devil would throw an obstacle our way!

Are you convinced that our God works for your good in and through all things, even the devil's obstacles? Paul writes for our confidence and assurance these words in Romans 8:35, "Who shall separate us from the love of Christ? Shall trouble or hardship or persecution or famine or nakedness or danger or sword?" Haven't we come to know nothing can separate us from the love of Christ? Therefore, no obstacle from the devil can be so great that it can remain in the sight of God and His beloved children!

We, you and me, have become, as it says in Romans 8:37, "more than conquerors through him who loved us." We have seen and can testify with God at work in our lives, "For I am convinced that neither death nor life, neither angels nor demons, neither the present nor the future, nor any powers, neither height nor depth, nor anything else in all creation, will be able to separate us from the love of God that is in Christ Jesus our Lord." (Romans 8:38-39)

> RM: *Think back to an obstacle of the devil to prevent you from depending upon the promises of God. In what ways did the devil get in between you and the love of Christ? How was the obstacle of the devil obvious or subtle? How did you come to overcome and become a conqueror through Jesus?*

We can say with Paul as he heard from Jesus, " 'My grace is sufficient for you, for my power is made perfect in weakness.' Therefore I will boast all the more gladly about my weaknesses, so that Christ's power may rest on me." (2 Corinthians 12:9) As Jesus daily walking disciples, all the grace of Jesus is more than enough for us...it satisfies us! Jesus' grace becomes the strength we need and can depend upon throughout any days of weakness.

> RM: *Where are there some aspects in your life that you clearly see as weakness? How can Jesus grace turn these into His strengths as we surrender them to Him?*

It's as if we need to make sure we're wearing the right clothing, the strong garments of Him Who overcame death and the devil. Romans 13:14 advises us, "Rather, clothe yourselves with the Lord Jesus Christ, and do not think about how to gratify the desires of the sinful nature." I know for myself, the more I think about and focus on sinful desires, the more I will give in! I know that for myself! The more I dwell upon how good and satisfying the sin would be, I think less of the sinful consequences, and more about the sizzling satisfaction. How about you?

So, we must call upon Him who stands ready to aid us! As Paul tells us in 2 Thessalonians 3:3, "But the Lord is faithful, and he will strengthen and protect you from the evil one." Yes, we have a Lord who faithfully strengthens and protects us from the devil. As he also tells us in 2 Timothy 4:18, "The Lord will rescue me from every evil attack and will bring me safely to his heavenly kingdom." That's why prayer is so important together with being in God's Word often, often, often! And especially when the devil tries to throw that latest and greatest obstacle our way!

> RM: *What should you be IN prayer about as you see the devil attacking you or someone you know? Give God thanks for his ample supply of strength and protection!*

I can imagine most of us have a hard time understanding the necessity of armor in our lives. After all, chances are most of us are not active duty military. We also don't live in a time when we have to be on guard to defend ourselves or our possessions against those who would be armed for battle. Did you ever wonder, then, if this is where we have to change our way of thinking? We have to recognize we ARE in a spiritual battle and have to be outfitted accordingly? Remember again those words I quoted previously from Ephesians 6:12, "For our struggle is not against flesh and blood, but against the rulers, against the authorities, against the powers of this dark world and against the spiritual forces of evil in the heavenly realms." We can't see with our eyes any visible warfare, but it exists. We may see the aftermath of such warfare, however.

So, we have to get serious about wearing the armor of God over the spiritual body God gives you! Paul outlines those components or pieces God knows are necessary for each one of His soldier-saint sons and daughters in Ephesians 6:10-18.

(vs. 10) "Finally, be strong in the Lord and in his mighty power." Our first God given response is to be strong in the Lord and in God's mighty power! We draw upon God's strength through prayer and His Word, don't we? Don't you see why WALKing daily disciples need to be daily WALKing IN His Word, if not for just such a purpose as that, to draw upon God's mighty strength and power?

(vs. 11) "Put on the full armor of God so that you can take your stand against the devil's schemes." Yes, the devil will have all kinds of schemes and obstacles to put before us. That's why we need the full armor of God, not just a piece here or there, or even worse, only what "we" think we need wear!

(vs. 12) "For our struggle is not against flesh and blood, but against the rulers, against the authorities, against the powers of this dark world and against the spiritual forces of evil in the heavenly realms." It is a REAL battle we will undergo at times. Often, we may be at our weakest point! (Remembering then, for sure, to recall and recoil upon our Lord Jesus' strength, as promised in 2 Corinthians 12:9b, "Therefore I will boast all the more gladly about my weaknesses, so that Christ's power may rest on me.")

(vs. 13) "Therefore put on the full armor of God, so that when the day of evil comes, you may be able to stand your ground, and after you have done everything, to stand." The evil day WILL come, but we will be able to stand our ground, and we will stand because of the overpowering will of God.

Note all the remaining pieces we need to have put in place and ready for their use in verses 14-17, including Jesus' truth buckling our waist, His righteousness covering our chest, feet ready to move, being shielded by our faith IN Jesus that can extinguish all the devil's flaming arrows, and carrying about the Word of God as the sword the Holy Spirit will use on our behalf!

(vs. 18) "And pray in the Spirit on all occasions with all kinds of prayers and requests. With this in mind, be alert and always keep on praying for all the saints." PRAY! PRAY! PRAY! No request should be left unspoken on any occasion. And we ought to be praying for our fellow disciples in the trenches of battle, doing all we can do, to allow Christ's power to work through us to aid them (as we would ask them to do on our behalf, as well)!

Our response, empowered by God's own Holy Spirit, is our only means of victory over the devil's obstacles. This response needs to become the Spirit's regimen at work in us every day without fail! As necessary as food and water are for our physical body's survival, so are prayer and the Word of God necessary for our spiritual body's survival. And both require the Holy Spirit's active access to our daily discipleship life and walk! Both require all the attention we would give to be on alert for the obstacles the devil would gladly throw in our daily walk.

Be alert from the moment we get up from a night of sleep, throughout a day filled with obstacles and opportunities, through to the evening hours leading us back to bed for the night! Look at your twenty four hour day. How are we allowing Him the space and place to work most effectively and fruitfully? Not just in response to the spiritual warfare constantly waging against us and the Body of Christ, but also for our spiritual growth and development.

> RM: *So, as we asked in Psalm 63, how much do you hunger and thirst for the things of God? How earnestly do you seek God and the ways of God? How have you beheld God's power and glory, so that they also would be put to work in and through your life as His disciple?*

I can't help but go back over Psalm 62. I need to take some necessary time to inventory my daily walk. I understand the devil's desire to throw obstacles in front of me. How can I testify truthfully and confidently as David did in Psalms 62, 63?

What strategy and schedule will it take? Getting up an extra hour or so...staying up an extra hour or so? Prospecting through the Word of God for the precious gem or nugget He wants me to have for the day, written out on an index card, and then carried and referred to throughout the day? Fixed times of prayer balanced with spontaneous prayer opportunities as they pop up? Incorporating a mindset of prayer devoid of any petition or supplication for the first 30 minutes of prayer-filled fellowship I invite God the Trinity to engage with me? Becoming more praise-filled and thank-filled in my response to God? Inviting God's Spirit to show me what He wants me to learn for this day, for this hour, for this response to the devil's obstacle before me? REMEMBER, it's not me, it's HE! It's not how much or how often I do...it's ALL about what the Holy Spirit wants to do!

I've tossed out plenty of God's Word as the Holy Spirit has shown us within the confines of the 3-I's, "Introduction, Instruction, and Inspiration," just how MUCH God will enable His daily relationship with you to exist. How much will you bend and break your will to respond to such a Fatherly desire as He has for you? Here are some pieces to prayerfully allow the Holy Spirit to put in place in your daily disciplined discipleship with Jesus!

- Now BE in prayer with your heavenly Father as you confess your need for Him and your desire to live in a close and intimate fellowship with God the Father, Son and Holy Spirit.

- Determine your daily discipleship regimen, including the first fruits of your time, consciousness, and heartfelt desire for fellowship with God through prayer. Determine the opportunities for the Spirit's spiritual feeding and strengthening of you through ample time in His Word.

- BE on GUARD for the devil's increased response to the changes the Holy Spirit will make in your daily discipleship regimen. Call upon God's power and strength to overcome every obstacle. Ask Him to transform every opportunity into one that is God-pleasing and fruit bearing in your life as only HE can do them!

- Don't neglect the fellowship of believers. You're in a race with others, you know? It's not a competition to be a better disciple in comparison to others. It's a perseverance God enables you to endure so that you can endure the race and complete it. So, pray with and for others, won't you? You have been blessed for what purpose? To be a blessing! BE a blessing to others, won't you?

Wouldn't it be great one day, when God decides to fold your tent, that you might have the opportunity to exclaim, "It is finished!" and fall asleep in Jesus? Wouldn't you then be ready to claim your heavenly reward won for you by Jesus? Every day you can pray and invite God to give you a fresh and forgiven start. Through the power He works within your baptism, He will drown the old man and the devil's empty lies. As that new man emerges, as you are clothed with Christ, and think as one with the mind of Christ, so you will take every step with Jesus ever nearer and closer to the finish line.

My prayer for you is this:

Father God, thank You for ALL you have done and continue to do for each of us, as Your beloved sons and daughters. Dear Lord Jesus, thank You for ALL you have done and continue to do for each of us. We ask You to hear and bring our prayers before our Father. Holy Spirit, thank You for ALL you have done and continue to do for each of us. You alone have brought us into a faith based, and blood bought personal relationship with God. May You continue to have all the place and space to work. Work Your holy and sanctifying work in and through us each and every day. May God the Father, Son, and Holy Spirit grant this for Jesus' sake! Amen!

Chapter Ten

My Brother Steve, LOST and FOUND, as a Daily WALKing and TALKing Disciple

God IS GOD. Recognizing and experiencing the depth and width of God within these dimensions remains the challenge for the daily WALKing disciples of our God. The Word of God, from "in the beginning" through to "even so, come Lord Jesus!" describes such a God, for as much as He allows. For as much as we know, there still remain opportunities to question God's depth and width. Often such questioning can be summarized with such a heavy and burdensome question as, "Why?"

Just as I had finished the first draft of Chapter Eight of this very book, looking forward to another week of writing and revelation from God, I got a phone call from Helena, Montana.

My brother Steve had been estranged from my family for nearly 25 years! Our dad died not knowing the whereabouts of his first born son, my brother. Unfortunately, their relationship had ended in anger and separation across many miles and many years.

Out of the blue, I received the following email:

>Subject: Steve Wendt
>
>From: Jim M.
>
>To: Randy Wendt
>
>Date: August 21, 2011 9:12 PM
>
>This may be something that is a false lead, but one of our friends at First Presbyterian Church here in Helena, MT is a man named Steve Wendt. He indicated he grew up in Detroit, MI and had a brother, Randy, in the pastorate in Detroit. Steve works in a center for the handicapped, Goodwill Industries. Steve seems to be healthy. We got to know him through serving coffee hour with him in our church.
>
>I forgot exactly how old Steve said he was, and he is pretty slow to make a lot of information available to others, but he indicated it would be all right if I contacted you. When he was here, he seemed to think you were his brother, when we looked you up on the computer and said it was OK to contact you. He is approximately 50 years of age. We have known him for about 8 years. I get the impression he does not keep up with you very well.
>
>Just thought you would wish to know he is OK.
>
>Jim M.

Can you imagine your response, if you received such an email, about your brother, given up for lost or worse dead after all these years? I was floored! I couldn't believe it! I wanted to be reconnected with Steve! Here's my reply:

> Subject: Re: Steve Wendt
> From: Randy Wendt
> To: Jim M.
> Date: August 22, 2011 8:44 AM
> Dear Jim,
>
> Thank you for contacting me. I am very interested in finding my brother Steve. My cell phone number is listed below. You are welcome to forward it to him and ask him to call me.
>
> The last I had heard from him was a letter from a post office box in Pocatello, Idaho in the mid 1990's. I live in suburban Atlanta but will not be at this address for much longer.
>
> Thank you for doing the work to track me down!
>
> Randy Wendt

I have an aunt who lives near me, who knew Steve from birth. After I told her the story up to this point, she replied, "You know Steve isn't going to call you. You need to contact him!" She was excited for the prospect of reconnecting with him after all these years, as well!

After several weeks passing with no communication, I took my aunt's advice. I tried to track down Steve's phone number on the Internet. Believing I had found it, I began phoning late at night and early in the morning, letting the phone "ring off the hook!" There was no answering machine or voice mail attached to leave Steve a message. I just let the phone ring and ring in mounting frustration. "Why wasn't he picking up the phone? Why wasn't he trying to reach me? What's preventing us from reconnecting?"

On October 16th, I decided to send Steve a card and an invitation to contact me. I figured by the weekend, I would hear from him. Nothing happened, until Monday night October 24th, when Jim M. phoned me. He asked if there might be some way to confirm I was Steve's brother. I emailed him a photo of the three of us, my Dad included, after my college graduation in 1981.

Within minutes, Steve's friend phoned back. "Without a doubt, I'm sure Steve is your brother. He was killed this morning crossing a street while walking to work."

The wind was knocked out of me! "What?" was all I could eek out! After a bit of a pause, Jim explained it had happened this morning around 7:00 am in a dark and rainy intersection. I couldn't believe it! I couldn't believe it! I could tell in his voice that the news was still difficult for him to speak of. I could hear grief in his voice. Jim went on to say that his pastor would like to speak with me as they would begin to make funeral arrangements.

I sent the following email to family and friends the day after the news of Steve's death:

> Dear Family,
>
> It is with great shock and sadness to share with you the death of my brother, Steve, who had been living for over 20 years in Helena, MT, unknown to me until a few weeks ago. I had received an email from a member of the Presbyterian church Steve had been an active member of for over 11 years, inquiring if I was Steve's brother. Not sure, I encouraged the man to give Steve my cell phone number and contact me. I phoned several times, at all hours of the day and night, and never got connected to an answering machine or voice mail. This past Tuesday, I sent Steve a card asking him to contact me.
>
> Jim M., his friend from church, had visited Steve on Sunday at his apartment. Steve told him he had not contacted me. The attached news story link will fill you in with as much as I know at this date. I'm awaiting 9:00 a.m. Montana time to contact the coroner and police

in Helena. I spoke with Steve's pastor last night and am confident my brother Steve had a daily walk with His Savior Jesus. I draw upon that hope we can all have as we call upon Jesus to be such a Savior for each of us.

Things are still being determined. I hope to go to Helena next Monday and participate in a Memorial Service, being held at Steve's church on Tuesday, which happens to be All Saints Day! My Uncle Mike, Steve's Godfather, will join me there. I will share more with you as I come to know it! Meanwhile, please pray and give thanks to God that Steve came to know Jesus as his Savior and Lord. Also, that it appears he died without undue suffering or pain at the scene of the accident. Also, pray for the family of the 17 year old whose vehicle struck Steve. Thanking you in advance for your prayers and support,
Randy

For the rest of the week, as I received phone calls and emails from family and friends, "What?" turned into "Why?" While "What?" has been answered, "Why?" remains unanswered... and probably will this side of Heaven. The question became more fully developed than just three simple letters. "Why didn't Steve ever contact me?" "Why didn't Steve ever pick up the phone when I called him?" "Why didn't Steve have an answering machine? Why couldn't I at least have left a message?" "Why did I wait so long to send the card?" "Why didn't I try harder to get a hold of him?" (I'm probably leaving out a few more "Why's?" ... some of which have been answered!)

As the saying goes, "So close, and yet, so far!" As more of the "what?" was revealed, some of the "why's?" were answered as well. Steve didn't have long distance service nor an answering machine for his phone. Steve made it a habit of turning off his phone when he went to bed early each night. Steve was seldom in his apartment. Steve may have been waiting until that upcoming Wednesday to try and contact me by phone. But, Wednesday never came.

Why Wednesday? Steve had been living under treatment and fully employed with Schizoaffective Disorder for nearly twenty years in Helena, Montana. I knew nothing about where he was, what he had, or even whether he was alive. You can only imagine how reassuring and comforting it was to know Steve had a good life, independent and successful! Steve's case worker for twenty years, having recently retired, thought Steve would wait until he met with his new case worker and ask if he could call me. But, that meeting never happened. Wednesday never came for Steve as he died on that Monday morning.

Uncle Mike and I began a journey of discovery in Helena that was indescribable! Every person we met, every conversation we had, told a story both very strange and unknown to us. For over twenty five years, this brother of mine was both LOST and FOUND. Unfortunately, a lot of the specifics for several "Why's" have gone on with Steve. They will be answered following the Resurrection, when I'll be finally reunited with him for eternity because of our Savior Jesus! Until then, I can only pray to be content with the answers I have received!

Yes, Steve had been spiritually LOST while living with us in Detroit. Steve had been spiritually FOUND while living in Helena all these years. Steve had been physically lost, whereabouts unknown until late August 2011. Steve had been physically found, lying dead in an intersection early October 24, 2011. Yes, the "bitter and the sweet" I would further encounter during those hours in Helena.

I won't go through any more details of Steve's death or any ironies that surfaced. Sufficed to say, my brother Steve had been both LOST and FOUND, both physically and spiritually. I am SO THANKFUL to God for letting me know in time. Those two days in the church year calendar will never be the same: Reformation Day (October 31), when we held the Family Hour and Prayer Service and All Saints Day (November 1), when we held the Memorial Service, Internment and Luncheon.

I decided I had to write a chapter based on what I saw and heard. I took my video camera with me for several reasons, and I am so glad that I did! For the sake of my own "fact finding," it would be helpful to recall what folks said about Steve. They would also serve as a testimony to Steve's life and faith. I wanted family and friends to see and hear "first hand" what these folks had to say about Steve. Bringing back their stories and a video copy of the memorial service, I could remember and write a turning point in this book that will hopefully turn your head and heart as mine have been. I pray they will turn every reader towards the God my brother Steve found, worshipped, adored, and served.

Understand the starting point to all of this: my brother Steve was diagnosed with Schizoaffective Disorder. It is a mental illness still under much discovery and investigation. Commonalities exist as do exceptions. Each person is seen uniquely and treated accordingly. Steve had been under doctor's care and daily medication. He would have periods of depression. He heard voices saying he was a bad person and encouraging him to do bad things. Most would be unable to hold down a job or support themselves.

Part of the transforming work of God can be seen in Steve's work history before and after his diagnosis. His days in Helena were filled with praise recognized by his peers, whether fellow workers or supervisors at Goodwill Industries. You'll be able to hear that shortly as you "hear" them speak. The other transforming work of God, evident in his life, was that he WAS a daily disciple of Jesus. Part of that proof he wrote in his Bible, "Jesus lives in my heart 24/7". The rest you'll also be able to hear shortly as fellow disciples speak.

I invited attendees at the Family Hour to describe Steve "on camera" during a videotaping. I had a healthy dose of skepticism present in my questioning. I didn't want to encourage a lot of "nice things" said about my brother that weren't warranted by examples they could cite. Even more importantly, I would respond that there were good people out there doing good things because they cared for others. Why wouldn't this have been Steve? Was this Steve's motivation? Or was there something or Someone more who made a difference in his life?

A starting point was shared by a fellow Church member, Steve O, who arranged Steve's pre-paid funeral arrangements. Steve had arranged a year and a half before his death everything necessary. Please understand that my brother made an hourly wage at a bit above minimum at a Goodwill Industries Donation Center. He also received SSI benefits. He gave a fair amount of his earnings to good causes that touched his heart. He supported a child overseas.

Despite all of that and quite to the surprise of Steve O, my brother was able to write a check for $8000 to pay for the funeral plans without hesitation. Incredible! Here's how Steve O, described it in italics, with my follow-up questions in standard type:

Steve lived a simple life. He worked at Goodwill. He walked wherever he went. He wanted to have a Christian service. He was a very Godly man. He didn't have a clue when he was going to die, but when he did, he wanted to be sure it was completely taken care of and that nobody else had to have the burden of making these decisions.

What was the way that you knew Steve was a Godly man? What was the sign of that? What was the fruit that you saw?

Probably the peace in his life. It didn't seem there was much that would bother him. He was waiting at the church before 7:00 am on a Sunday because he usually made coffee for the congregation every Sunday. The things he would say in small groups. He was very well founded scripturally. And he lived a Christian life. You could see that.

In what way? *The way he would treat people. The way he viewed the world. The prayer for world peace. He didn't like the violence and the fighting. He wanted people to love each other. I think he was very loving.*

There can be and are many good people out there, good natured people. You know, people who have a lot of genuine compassion, do a lot of philanthropic things. How would Steve's life have been any different? How would it be more of a testimony that God was in the center of his life if you believe that to be the case? *When you talk to people that are good people and aren't Christians, you don't hear them talk about God. But, Steve would. He was concerned with treating people the way Christ would have treated people. That's what his concern was. You could just see that in him.*

Many people recounted how Steve would never start a conversation. He was a very quiet person and usually said very little. His favorite reply to most inquiries was, "Not too bad." He said it so quickly that it sounded like one word instead of three! But, even if he knew you, trusted you, and had a long standing relationship with you, Steve wouldn't start a conversation. But, if invited to engage, he would contribute and respond in his own way.

Steve didn't shy away from congregational life and small group ministry. He participated in many small groups over the course of his discipleship at First Presbyterian Church in Helena. Often he would be part of two different groups per week, one meeting on Tuesday and another on Thursday. He didn't sit silently by nor did he lead discussions. He did contribute, however, in his own way.

Often, Steve would say things with such a depth of understanding the Scriptures that folks thought Steve must have had a seminary education, even though he hadn't! It was apparent to them Steve read his Bible. As I looked through his

Bible, many pages had highlighted sections with comments handwritten in the margins.

One of his dear friends, Rita P, spoke at the Family Hour about Steve's participation level in small groups:

Was Steve still that shy, quiet guy in small groups? *Yes, but the longer we would go on, the more comfortable he would get. But when he prayed, you knew it was from the heart.* He prayed aloud? *Oh, yes. Oh, yes, a lot of times at the end of our session. Some people who came weren't comfortable praying out loud. But, we would have a popcorn prayer, where someone would start it, and people would say a name of somebody they wanted to have prayers for and not really say what it was for. Steve would pray out loud and for the people whose hand he was holding. Oh, yes, and for other people.*

Tom R, another small group member with Steve, described Steve's participation at their meetings: *Steve didn't say a lot, but it was always worth listening to. He had really thought things through, and he always came prepared. He always studied the subject we were going to talk about in the group. He'd spend a lot of time thinking about it. Like I say, he didn't always say a whole lot, but, boy, what he said was worth listening to. In the small group, when we would get talking about people getting saved or someone was struggling with their relationship with the Lord, you could just see that concern in his face. When Steve prayed, he would pray for somebody's child mentioned in the small group. And then you would see him reaching out to that child and trying to talk to them. Just be friendly with them, just say "Hi" to them, just to let them know the community was there supporting him. When you first met Steve, you kind of wondered because he was so quiet. Then, the more you got to know him, it was just a depth there that I think he was a lot deeper than we realized. I've thought about that a lot this week since he's been gone. Our church community is really going to miss him very much.*

I brought up again with Tom this notion that there are a lot of good people out there, people who do good things, who seem to have care and compassion for people. Might you say Steve was like that? Or was there anything more about him that might make you think there was something different about him? In terms of where he was at in his relationship with God, let's say? Here's Tom's reply: *There's no question in my mind that he was saved, that he knew the Lord as his personal Savior. I just don't have any doubt about that whatsoever. What would make you think that way? The things he said in small group. When he talked about the need to reach out to people and the fact that he prayed daily, and he had a walk with Christ on a daily basis.*

[Another close friend Jim M. joined in on the conversation]: *And you saw it in that he walked what he talked. He walked what he talked.* [Tom continued] *And he didn't talk a lot. It was mainly walked. Quite often he would pray about world peace. That was really on his mind. I don't have an answer why, but it was really very important to him. I think he cared about people. If there was a lot of turmoil on the news, it bothered him. And I think he cared about people's salvation. I really do.*

Jim M was the person who first contacted me about Steve through an email. He had last seen Steve alive a day before he died, having stopped by his apartment with home grown tomatoes. Jim confirmed with Steve that he had not tried to contact me yet. Jim and his wife Charlotte often befriended Steve, having him over for meals, even having Steve spend Christmas Day with their family! Jim described Steve's self-driven greeting card ministry: *Steve was so quiet. He didn't let you in very much. I saw him with a stack of cards frequently to give to people at church, remembering their birthday or their anniversary. Just frequently. I think he got it off our church calendar and newsletter every month.* Tom chimed in: *If I think he had any connection with people, all of a sudden, there would be a card, and I'd think, 'Wow, he remembered!' and it just kind of took me back that he cared that much about me.*

Jim described another ministry of Steve's, making coffee on Sunday mornings for an average 220 worshippers: *Who's going to do coffee hours now? Steve was responsible for close to 50% of the coffee hours over the last seven or eight years, I would say. For one person to take that on is pretty big.* Tom added: *And he was quietly there doing it.* Jim went on to say, *He sure didn't put himself forward. We'd just "chit-chatted" with him, and tried to respect his boundaries. And then he would slowly open up. He was not a very outgoing person, not on the surface. But I think, deep in he was an ambassador. I bet if you talked, I'll bet there were 25% of the people in the church that got cards from him one time or another.*

Wondering if there was any motive for Steve's participating at his church, I asked them both, "Was he lonely? Was he looking to get out of this loneliness by going to these things?" Jim replied: *I don't know, don't know.* Tom answered: *You know, that's maybe a good observation, but he came across caring. Not that it was something for him, but it was something he cared about other people. So, he wanted to be involved. You see, when I talked with him, it seemed like he was always involved with things at work, and when I thought of him walking many times from where he lived clear down to the* Goodwill [about two miles from his apartment] *and working there for eight to ten hours, there might have been some filling in of time, but it always seemed like he was doing things.* Jim added: *I think he had a need to nurture and it probably worked with his need to be private. He was a very private individual. But, he also had a need to nurture. I think he needed to feel like he was there for people. Be there with cards. Be there contributing with the small group.*

Two fellow employees from Goodwill shared comments about working with Steve and the kind of person Steve was. Myrna described Steve: *He's been a good friend. He couldn't have had a better heart. His heart was just so full, and he touched everybody. He was a friend to everyone that came into the store. He couldn't have been any better. He made coffee for us. He looked out for Mickey Mouse things for me all the time. He was such a sweetheart. He didn't want to put anybody out. He had just a heart of gold.* Do you think God was in his life? *Oh, definitely!*

How could you say that with confidence? *Because of the way he was. Understanding, caring, not wanting to hurt anybody's feelings. Steve never talked bad about anybody.* But, there could be a lot of people like that. *No! He was just special. Chris and I were just saying we think he's our angel now, taking care of us at Goodwill.* Chris replied: *I've known him about two years. He would give you the shirt off his back. He'd stop at McDonalds and bring two bags filled with sausage muffins for us or he'd bring cookies in. It's not the same around there without him. He was a very smart man. You could tell the way he talked. He was very intelligent. A funny guy.*

Back in 2003, Steve was nominated by his store for Employee of the Year. Out of over 330 nominees in the state of Montana, Steve received the award. He travelled all expenses paid to Great Falls, Montana for the Annual Banquet. It was "a night to honor consumers who have achieved significant levels of independence in their lives, dedicated volunteers, community supporters and staff receiving special recognition." Steve received the Employee of the Year award from the Board of Directors President, Michelle Belknap.

Remember, Steve was a person with Schizoaffective Disorder, many of whom are challenged to maintain employment. She said the following as he received the award: *"Steve Wendt, a janitor and plant processor at Helena Goodwill, is our Goodwill Employee of the Year. Steve started at Goodwill in June of 2000 as a janitor with very little assistance from his job coach. Within three months, he had added donations processing to his job description. He learned his duties in record speed and demonstrates a terrific attitude. He has consistently challenged himself to be the best employee he can be. Steve is dependable, punctual, and his attendance is flawless. He sets an excellent example in following policies and procedures, and he is respectful of all customers, donors, coworkers and staff. Store Manager Toni Svaleson says that Steve is an unbelievable individual, with a character that is unmatched. He has maintained maximum independence and shines as one of our most valuable employees. Congratulations, Steve."*

Myrna described why Steve was chosen as Employee of the Year: *He was loyal, dependable, always there, and friends to everyone!*

His picture, name, and a quote appeared on the Helena store collection truck, bigger than life!

At the memorial service the following day, well over 250 people were in attendance! It was overwhelming to see such a response. Pastor Jim F spoke of *"his friend Steve,"* who gave him a variety of gifts over the years, usually with a golf theme, together with many cards for many occasions including Clergy Appreciation Day. Steve had been a member of his small group and drove Steve many times to their gathering.

Yvonne W, a fellow employee at Goodwill, also shared at the service about the response to Steve's death on behalf of the customers at Goodwill: *There's been an outpouring of warmth from our customers at Goodwill. It's amazing the things people have been saying, and the common thread is that Steve touched a lot of lives in a positive manner. I'm not an expert on these things, but I believe it's because he always put God first. He put himself last. He loved everybody. It's just an outpouring of love. I could talk about him for a long time. I count him as a dear friend. He shared his faith with me many times.*

Mary O, one of Steve's first case managers for seven years, said: *Work and his faith were the most important things to Steve. But even though he was very proud of that* [Employee of the Year award], *Steve was never proud full. He was very, very humble in everything that he did.*

I took the opportunity to share a poem I wrote about our relationship as it began, developed, and ended. My concern was to reach out to anyone who was LOST or Dechurched who knew Steve and would be in attendance. I have always valued Memorial Services as prime opportunities to share a faith such as the one my brother Steve exemplified.

Following the luncheon, I set up a video camera and invited anyone to come and share their thoughts about Steve. A few people took me up on the opportunity. A man well in his seventies said: *We should pray more prayers that we should be like Steve because Steve was so God like. That was his total life's ambition. He did the things that the rest of us normally don't do as fervently. We weren't big pals or anything, but I took Steve for a few rides from time to time to Small Group and some dinners and so on. He was a man of few words because he only needed a few words. You would ask him something, and it was short and concise. But he always worked a discussion of Christ or God or Christianity into his statements.*

Another elderly woman who was involved in the church's response ministry said: *Steve was a person that exemplifies Christ, and you'd of been proud of him and we are all proud of him, too!* I believe this woman was Joyce B, who had given Steve two thank you cards I brought home with me, dated a week or so before his death. Sixteen women personally signed one of the cards sent to him!

Mary O, his first case worker, spoke again about Steve: *Because of Steve's problems, he had a very hard time expressing his emotions. So he gave of himself by buying* [gifts and cards] *for people and being with people. Any kind of card you can imagine, Steve gave. He gave with his heart. It was the way he told us all how much he cared about us. And we all cared about him. He was a very loving Christian man, who gave me more, I'm sure, that I could ever, ever give him.*

The funeral home had an online guestbook for Steve, open for anyone to leave comments. See if you can picture the kind of person Steve had been transformed by God. Tonna S writes: *Steve, we are going to miss your smiling face and jokes at First Presbyterian. We are going to miss you making coffee for everyone in the morning. Steve, we are going to miss you so much!* Michelle B, the Goodwill Board of Directors President, wrote: *Steve will be missed by the ESGW. He was a great* addition to our Helena Goodwill store. We so appreciate his years of dedication and service. He made the store a fun place for staff and customers. My thoughts are with his family and the staff that worked closely with Steve. I always appreciated his thank you cards he sent after he received his birthday card. He was very thoughtful.

Connie P wrote: I worked with Steve for a year or more at the Goodwill store. Everyone liked him because he was so nice, and his demeanor never changed from day to day. He was one quiet guy unless I got him started with a small conversation. He worked hard and tended to his own business. He was always so polite to me when I would go into the store to shop. If I was looking for something special, he seemed to know just where to find it! There were a few times that I gave Steve a ride home from work. He never had much to say unless I again started the conversation. He seemed peaceful all of the time. I will miss him saying "Hi" when I go into the store. (He would always help me find stuffed toys for my pets in the store. He will be terribly missed by all of the GW staff and all of their regular customers.

Darla H wrote: I will always remember working with Steve at GW. He always had ideas to make the day brighter and he loved to come up with ways to help others. Brenda M, then the current store manager at Goodwill, wrote: Steve and I worked together at Goodwill. He was the kindest person that I had ever met. He was always thinking of other people before himself, even my dog Tiffany. Steve would ask every day, "How's Tiffy?" and was always bringing treats for her also. Steve will be very missed and very loved by many. Toni S wrote: A true humanitarian, who was such a humble and *gentle man, only kind words did he ever speak. Always a smile and a hello for his friends. He said little, but he always knew what to say and how to say it. My friend Steve, I will miss you very much.*

I think the most touching entry was from Sherryl H: *We will truly miss Steve. He was my sister Patty's best friend. He was so good to her as she is blind. He always checked her mail for her and took her downstairs to eat. Steve was an angel on earth, and I know he is an angel in heaven. We love you, Steve. I cry, but I know we will see you again. In Jesus' arms you rest. Thank you for all the kindness and gifts you gave to Patty.*

After the lunch of homemade soups, sandwiches, and pies, Kathy Z, his case worker for over twenty years, took Uncle Mike and myself to Steve's apartment. We had met many residents of the low income residence where Steve had lived. Looking around, I remarked how much it reminded me of a college dormitory. The layout of the public areas, dining room, and individual apartments gave me the impression that Steve lived a dorm-style life.

Kathy wanted to be sure I would have the opportunity to bring back home any of Steve's personal effects. I had hoped as Steve wished that the Goodwill Store would receive the bulk of his items along with any items his church might want. There was too much to go through since it was apparent we both had the "pack rat" spirit about our living quarters. But, what I did take back on the plane, I will always cherish: Steve's Bible! Yes, he highlighted passages throughout, wrote notes, even included stickers. What is the most precious testimony of Steve's Bible?

As I said earlier, inside he wrote with an ink pen, "Jesus lives in my heart 24/7" What a power-filled statement!

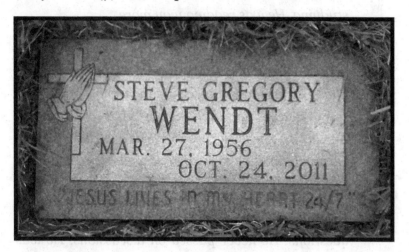

I made sure that in addition to his name, dates of his birth and death, that statement was included on his memorial marker at the cemetery.

I was fortunate to be able to attend his Tuesday night small group that evening. These were the fellow disciples Steve studied with at Rita and Gale P's house Tuesday nights. As members went around the room with their recollections, I captured their comments on video. [My intent is to put together a short video that will be a testimony to Steve's WALK and TALK as Jesus' daily disciple. While I have no video of him doing either, those left behind have adequately represented him!]

The folks didn't self identify on the video, shot over six months ago, so I'll share their comments without the benefit of a name.

- *Steve studied his Bible a lot. I sat by him quite a bit and he had it highlighted and marked. He knew where stuff was at.*

- *I think he read his Bible every day and studied it every day. And it wasn't just what the small group was studying. He was reading way more.*

- *When we'd be going around, I remember, with a question from our study, people would be talking, and Steve would be quiet. And then somebody would say, 'What do you think, Steve?' And he'd respond. And he just knew. He was right. He was always right. He knew his Bible. He knew it well. He was a good Christian man.*

- *He always knew in Small Group, he had answers to questions. He never passed on discussions. He was really an active member of our group.*

- *He was a scholar. He was a Biblical scholar. He really was. No matter what we were studying, he knew. He was familiar with it. You asked us how did we know he was a Christian? I think one of the gifts he had was contentment. You know how we're always wanting more. We keep searching. Steve was just content. He was content with his life. He was content with his work. He didn't need or want a lot. But, he enjoyed sharing what he did have with others. He was just content.*

Well, wasn't that cool? How Steve's life unfolded here, just coming in alone, no money, and how God had placed all these people in his life for him to have a good life here. And placed him in our lives!

What a BLESSING God was to my brother Steve! Jesus met Steve where Steve was at. Jesus transformed Steve's life from being LOST to being FOUND. Jesus took care of his Schizoaffective Disorder so that it didn't interfere with Jesus' work through Steve!

Steve wasn't a good person, who was lucky to have run out of money on the bus from Pocatello, Idaho to have ended up in Helena, Montana! LOOK at what Jesus our Savior did for Steve! Did you HEAR the testimony of those surrounding him who would say it was God in his life, not good works, that he will be remembered for?

I never got to connect with Steve. The card I had sent to Steve postmarked October 20, 2011 was never opened. It must have sat in Steve's mailbox. It was returned to me unopened and processed on November 20, 2011 with the following message on its' yellow label: "Return to Sender. Moved Left No Address. Unable to Forward." I guess that's what happens when God folds your tent. You've moved, leaving no address, and are unable to forward!

I've created a binder of keepsakes as a result of that trip to Helena. I've included newspaper articles and several of the many cards sent and received. I was able to gather up and display photos given to me that I didn't have of Steve during his last Helena days. One of his fellow employees ran out of the store as we were leaving. She had the Hot Dog costume he wore a few days earlier for a store Halloween Party. She felt I had to have the costume, which I did bring home.

It also was the last picture of him alive.

What more can I say than has been said by so many already? A lot remains unanswered. I look forward to that time when I'll be finally reunited with Steve. I'm counting on him saving me a seat next to him at the heavenly welcoming banquet God will give us. I can't say with certainty that I will see my Mom or Dad there. I don't know if they came to accept God's free gift of salvation wrapped up with His grace and a name tag that says, "For Irene!" and "For Hugo!"

THANK-fully, Steve got his present from God with plenty of time to enjoy it. Now, he's in God's presence awaiting the final judgment and that permanent dwelling place with all the saints.

Steve's life, affected by sin and mental illness, was washed clean by the blood of Christ. Steve's life was transformed by the only One who would have the power to do so...and the desire to do so! What a testimony! ALL thanks to God that He allowed me the connection after so many years of disconnect... so that I could know Steve was no longer LOST, physically and spiritually! What a blessing to be able to be there for Steve's memorial service. Thank you, Uncle Mike, for making it possible to attend and being a witness to it all, too!

I can't think of any more suitable segue to Part Two of this book than the testimony of the disciples in Helena, Montana, who saw and heard the WALK and TALK of my brother Steve, can you?

PART TWO:

TALKing as Jesus' Disciple

- "Come and listen, all you who fear God; let me tell you what he has done for me."

    Psalm 66:16

- "But in your hearts set apart Christ as Lord. Always be prepared to give an answer to everyone who asks you to give the reason for the hope that you have. But do this with gentleness and respect."

    1 Peter 3:15

- Jesus promises: "But when they arrest you, do not worry about what to say or how to say it. At that time you will be given what to say, for it will not be you speaking, but the Spirit of your Father speaking through you."

    Matthew 10:19-20

- "When they saw the courage of Peter and John and realized that they were unschooled, ordinary men, they were astonished and they took note that these men had been with Jesus."

    Acts 4:13

- Peter and John replied, "For we cannot help speaking about what we have seen and heard."

  Acts 4:20

- "Pray also for me, that whenever I open my mouth, words may be given me so that I will fearlessly make known the mystery of the gospel."

  Ephesians 6:19

Chapter Eleven

"You know, I wasn't always this way!"

I wasn't born into an "every Sunday we go to church" family. My parents were raised as church goers but didn't seem to carry on the practice as their children grew up. As my mom became hospitalized the last two years of her life due to cancer, my dad took us to his mother's house for weekends. Grandma Wendt, a faithful daily disciple of Jesus, made sure my brother and I were in church every Sunday morning.

Being in church was a fun outing for me. I enjoyed the singing and worship services. I didn't really get to know other kids until I carried on the practice beyond my mom's death through my times in High School. While in High School, I came to receive a fuller understanding of all that had happened at my baptism as an infant. Receiving a year of instruction with others regarding the basics of the Christian faith within the Lutheran Church-Missouri Synod, I stood before God's altar to profess my faith in Jesus and my desire to become a confirmed member of His church there in Detroit, Michigan.

I got involved in youth group activities, Sunday School, and even participated in a singing group with about 25 others from a neighboring church. It was a great time as I was given the opportunity to read the Sunday Scripture lessons during worship services. I enjoyed utilizing a God given gift to speak publically.

Between my Junior and Senior year, I felt a strong urgency to become a pastor. I had no clue where, when, or how. But speaking with my pastor, he encouraged me to check out the local Lutheran college, Concordia-Ann Arbor. I spent a few weeks in a special summer program for high school students. I took two classes and lived on campus. It was fantastic! I got the opportunity to see what a Christian college was like. I met and lived with students who were preparing for some type of church work.

When it got to be time to decide where to apply for college, it was a "no-brainer" for me. Not applying anywhere else, I got my acceptance letter for Concordia and was so glad for the opportunity God was making available. As I finished High School, I continued in my faith life, but rarely spoke to anyone about God or what He had done for me.

> RM: *How about you? Think back to your childhood. Were you part of a church going family? Did your life of discipleship grow and go outside the boundaries of worship as a teenager or young adult? Recall and think about any regrets you may have had.*

At Concordia, it appeared to be heaven on earth. People knew people. People hugged people. People loved people. People cared for people. It was like some large protective dome hung over our bit of paradise! Graduation was a hard time for some folks. They didn't want to leave or move on! I know some folks ended up on the "five year plan" just to suspend the inevitable!

But, graduate we did and move on we did! Outside that heavenly, protective dome, we found life hard, gritty, and challenging...at least those of us that didn't venture on to seminary. That was me! For so many years I wondered if I had done the right thing. I just seemed to have lacked that "deep down sense of joy about serving the Lord as a pastor" that my pastor impressed upon me. He said if you lacked it, you would be better off not going. So, I didn't on both counts!

As far as witnessing or sharing my faith goes, I heard about it from time to time, but I didn't seem to "go out of my way" to talk about my faith to strangers. Sure, it was easy to talk about Jesus and share Bible verses with the "found" inside the doors of a church. But, I seldom ventured out to the street corners or watering holes to ask people questions like, "Do you know Jesus as your personal Lord and Savior?" Or the real popular one, "If you were to die tonight, where would you be? Heaven or Hell?"

> RM: *How about you? Describe honestly what kind of TALKing disciple of Jesus you were then? How has it changed? What can you point to that caused such a reaction and behavior in and through you?*

I did all the things "a pew warmer" would do within "safe" bounds. Even though, I always thought of myself as an outgoing person, I was seldom out going and talking about my faith in

Jesus with someone who was Lost! If anything, I felt more the nagging need to be speaking about Jesus in response to that oft quoted verse, "I am not ashamed of the gospel of Christ"! I don't honestly know if I was ashamed. I think this outgoing guy just lacked the burden to do so.

Do you know what I mean about "lacking a burden"? My favorite story in the Bible was about the road to Emmaus. I never sensed the spiritual heartburn those two disciples of Jesus had on that Easter evening! I might have cared about whether a family member or friend were going to go to Hell. But, I sure didn't care enough by talking about their only way out, Jesus!

Yes, it seems easy now to be so honest! But back then, I wouldn't have had the guts to 'fess up that I didn't share my faith in Jesus, especially with those who really needed to hear it! I led many devotions and Bible Studies, but I never gave a presentation or followed an outline testifying to Jesus. I never memorized so many verses from the Bible so that a Lost person might become Found!

When I went to seminary, after twenty five years of waiting, I realized, pastoral ministry was not for me! I confirmed God's intention and mine not to become a Pastor. God's desire for me, however, could still be found within that list He came up with. You know the one that says, "And some he gave pastors, teachers, evangelists...."? Evangelists? Maybe that was what I was supposed to be? I just didn't seem satisfied enough with "Teacher". I felt I had to be more than just a teacher. Hopefully, in the process, I would tackle and overcome whatever phobia there was to verbalizing my faith with Lost people!

RM: *How about you? Recall times when you wondered what was God's plan and purpose for you as a disciple. How have you struggled or deliberated over mission or church work? How did you finally confirm God's will for you vocationally?*

Of course, I kept reading and re-reading passages from God's Word like, "Always be prepared to give an answer to everyone who asks you to give the reason for the hope that you have." (1 Peter 3:15b) Or, "Don't you know that you yourselves are God's temple and that God's Spirit lives in you?" (1 Corinthians 3:16)

And then, I would hear those hymns and join in them loudly: "Stand up! Stand up for Jesus!" or "Here am I! Send me, send me!" But, I wasn't standing up, and I wasn't being sent! How about you? Did they ever pull hard enough on your heart strings?

I'm not sure if I should credit a part-time job as being the opportunity where "the rubber met the road?" I took on a 15 hour per week position as an outreach coordinator for a local Lutheran church. As the first year folded into four more, I participated in plenty of "educational" opportunities regarding evangelism. While the church board I worked with carried that label, I kept the softer and friendlier sounding "outreach" label for the activity I had invited people to take part in.

I came to a better understanding, however, as I would research and write about what I did and encouraged each one to do. Whether it was "evangelism" or "outreach," I understood the response I was receiving. Often, people were silent, non-committal, or just didn't respond to any article or half-sheeted insert I would put together. In the end, I came to one sobering conclusion: It was hard to encourage church members to join me in making disciples. It may be because they weren't disciples of Jesus?

They were moved or motivated enough to drive to church, having done the right thing for that week. Like so many checked off activities in their lives, what were they giving and what were they receiving?

> RM: *How about you? Do you share a similar conclusion when it comes to fellow church members? How do the ones actively involved in outreach stand out? What kind of fruit is being born in and through them? Are you in their company? Why or why not?*

During those five years of part time work, I eased up my apprehension. I eased into talking about what God was doing in my life. I became a living "Guidepost" story...you know the magazine that says on every cover, "True Stories of Hope and Inspiration"?

I started seeing in my life the importance of daily discipleship. I wanted to model it for the people I was seeking to equip for ministry. I wanted to let them, and me know, I wasn't ashamed or afraid to speak about Jesus to strangers, Lost or Found! I got out on the streets of Atlanta during times when we fed the homeless. I would walk up to folks in the line for food and ask, "Can I pray about something for you?" I gave devotionals as well, publically testifying of what God had been doing in my life. Far from being a soapbox standing, megaphone speaking street preacher, it seemed I lacked the "whatever" that would have prevented me from doing so years before! I felt good about doing it, too!

I've come to a deeper, more Scripturally sound understanding of the conversion process. As I've come to understand it within my Lutheran Christian outlook, it's ALL God at work, none of me!

The power of baptism, whether infant or adult, is just as real and saving in the life of any sinful human being. It's ALL the Holy Spirit at work to create a willingness or receptiveness to receive God's free gift. It's only free because we don't have to buy it. God desires to give us the gift of His forgiveness and eternal life. It's a gift with our name on the name tag. Jesus came down to earth in human flesh, untainted by sin so that He would overcome sin, death, and the grave for each of us. What Jesus accomplished, we can't! We can only receive this precious gift. We can only allow Jesus to live and work in and through each of us as branches connected to His vine!

Such opportunities lie with the work being done by the Holy Spirit through the baptism He performs on each believer. Yes, they become a believer through baptism, not the other way around (ie. They become a believer and then "get baptized".)

Why do so many differences of understanding, like so many shades of grey, exist when it comes to baptism? In the clear light of God's Word, I cannot understand, except to say that the devil truly doesn't want us to be in clear agreement or in our understanding. Salvation through baptism is truly ALL of God's work. Salvation is nothing that we can or need contribute to. When Jesus proclaimed from the cross, "It is finished!" IT

WAS! The kind of gift God gives us has nothing necessary from us wrapped within the paper, bows, and name tag, marked personally "For You!"

How can our sinful hands come to create or contribute anything to the sinless sacrifice expected by a holy God? Jesus' work was fulfilled and accepted totally and completely for you and me.

There is no room for doubt! Our baptism is a total and complete rebirth or regeneration. We have moved from death into life through the water and the Word! We cannot do anything to earn or merit God's forgiveness or gift of eternal life, nor does He expect anything from us...except a grace-filled acceptance and acknowledgment that "Jesus is Lord!"

That's what we have in the baptism Jesus offers us...and commands us to offer others. As we would go into all the world, the Holy Spirit is at work to make disciples by baptizing them first. He continues His work by teaching them all Jesus has taught us. Otherwise, Jesus would have changed the order around in His command, wouldn't He?

I won't repeat the battery of proof texts in the Bible that support this understanding. You'll find them in the next chapter. Like with everything about God, we have to accept it as God presents it. We would have God's own Holy Spirit at work in our hearts and minds to cause us to receive it and believe it just as God says. That's why over the course of every chapter of Part One of this book, I've been very intentional to explain based upon God's Word how God has designed and delivered HIS plan of salvation for all that would receive Him and HIS gift. It's so vital now to confess that with me because Part Two of this book will emphasize the TALK of a Disciple.

It's as much as WHAT and HOW the Holy Spirit will speak through us, that a person believes and receives God's gifts. It's not having to memorize outlines or Bible passages so that a person will come to faith in Jesus. Let me be simple and clear: "It's NOT me...It's ALL HE!" The "HE" is the Holy Spirit, who only works through the means of grace. What's that? The Word of God and the Sacraments of Baptism and Holy Communion. What do these two sacraments do? Baptism brings us into a faith-based relationship with God. Holy Communion keeps us into a faith growing relationship with God. Together, they enable us to GO forth with the power of the Holy Spirit, who desires to choose the person, place, and possibility for His life changing work to be done!

All that we are is an empty glove. God would fill us with the necessary power to become useful and purposeful for His work. The Holy Spirit becomes the hand needed to fill the glove. Do you see? It's only with the power of the Holy Spirit that God can accomplish what He sets out to do. Doesn't recognizing that "It's NOT me...It's ALL HE!" take a tremendous burden off of our shoulders? Doesn't the devil want to place and maintain such a burden to witness upon our shoulders? It is a favorite and oft used obstacle of his. It has stood in the way of the Holy Spirit speaking through a disciple's mouth.

When we realize that, like within our salvation, there is nothing we do to bring someone to faith in Jesus Christ, then what's the result? WE CAN'T screw it up! WE CAN'T mess it up! WE CAN'T fail or get it wrong! And if we encounter a question we don't know the answer to, we honestly say in response, "I don't know! Can I find an answer and share it with you?"

Yes, it is that simple and that satisfying to your conscience. You do not need to feel guilty or burdened or bullied into talking about Jesus. No matter what the devil's thinking would be or how true are his lies! Unfortunately, you cannot expect that anything you say or how you say it will make any difference in a person's receiving God's gift!

Yes, you may become law-oriented and downright hateful towards folks as you may have seen and heard the guy behind the bullhorn on the street corner! They aren't allowing the Holy Spirit to speak through them. They're trying to yell over the Holy Spirit's voice. Remember His directive to speak "with gentleness and respect"? The devil would have these folks just as falsely convinced. Casting guilt instead of the Gospel cannot be seen as the bait on the hook necessary to reel in the fish they believe God wants them to catch.

So, have you've come to the same understanding about salvation as I have from God's Word alone, and no other source? Then you're encouraged to read on from this Biblically based, Christ-centered perspective. I pray you will understand more fully how the Holy Spirit stands ready to TALK through you, His daily WALKing disciple!

Chapter Twelve

"You mean it's NOT me?"

Now that you're still with me, let me share with you in more detail the proof texts from God's Word alone that would point you to a clear understanding of what it means to become a daily TALKing disciple of Jesus. It's important to study and be familiar with these verses. The Holy Spirit may choose to speak them through you. Let them become a part of you just like God instructed Israel, "These commandments that I give you today are to be upon your hearts. Impress them on your children. Talk about them when you sit at home and when you walk along the road, when you lie down and when you get up. Tie them as symbols on your hands and bind them on your foreheads. Write them on the doorframes of your houses and on your gates." (Deuteronomy 6:6-9) I believe the modern day application would include computer wallpaper, cell phone or internet home pages, index cards you can review and memorize, even the popular wristbands!

> RM: *Have you been convinced and have you bought into the practice of writing out and reviewing God's Word? When do you find yourself more likely to*

*follow such a practice? What outcome do you expect
to receive from such a practice?*

Again, becoming familiar with proof texts from the Bible will
aid the Holy Spirit's work. They will become seeds planted by
Him through our speaking them. Let's tackle the means and
method GOD Himself chose and states "over and over again"
IN His Word, the Bible, no matter what version you use, to
cause this "free gift of God" to become ours...through baptism!

Titus 3:5-6 tells us, "He saved us, not because of righteous
things we had done, but because of his mercy. He saved us
through the washing of rebirth and renewal by the Holy Spirit,
whom he poured out on us generously through Jesus Christ our
Savior." It's NOT me...it's ALL HE!

John 1:12-13 tells us, "Yet to all who received him, to those
who believed in his name, he gave the right to become children
of God—children born not of natural descent, nor of human
decision or a husband's will, but born of God." We CAN'T
decide to follow Jesus! No matter how much we, family, or
friends would want us to be a child of God, it won't happen
because of OUR will! It's NOT we...it's ALL HE!

You've heard me point previously to Jesus' own words
describing our relationship with Him, Who says quite clearly
in John 15: 16, "You did not choose me, but I chose you..."

Our life before God is without hope if we would have to depend
upon ourselves for our salvation. As Paul says in Ephesians
2:1, "As for you, you were dead in your transgressions and
sins..." Everyone born a human being is in need of God's
righteousness and can receive it, as Romans 3:22 reminds us,

"This righteousness from God comes through faith in Jesus Christ to all who believe. There is no difference, for all have sinned and fall short of the glory of God..." This is not just a New Testament doctrine or understanding. The Old Testament has many proof texts for man's sinful condition and his fruitless attempts to do good in God's eyes. David would confess on behalf of all of us, "Surely I was sinful at birth, sinful from the time my mother conceived me." (Psalm 51:5) He also says in Psalm 53:3, "Everyone has turned away, they have together become corrupt; there is no one who does good, not even one."

We could never do enough to please God. "The sinful mind is hostile to God. It does not submit to God's law, nor can it do so. Those controlled by the sinful nature cannot please God." (Romans 8:7-8) God would look at the good we would do and conclude through Isaiah 64:6, "All of us have become like one who is unclean, and all our righteous acts are like filthy rags". Did you know the meaning of "filthy rags" in the original Hebrew language this Psalm was written in? The filthy rags spoken of here is referred to as the cloths a woman uses during her menstrual period when she is considered unclean.

God not only sets the standard, He expects us to keep it! "Be holy, because I am holy." (I Peter 1:16; Leviticus 11:44) How can we? We would have the Law to be our guide to leading a life of holiness. But which of us has kept God's Law as He intends us to? "All who rely on observing the law are under a curse, for it is written, 'Cursed is everyone who does not continue to do everything written in the Book of the Law.' Clearly no one is justified before God by the law, because, 'The righteous will live by faith.' " (Galatians 3:10-11)

It's not even the purpose or power of God's law to save us. Paul says twice in Romans God's convincing words, "Therefore no one will be declared righteous in his sight by observing the law; rather, through the law we become conscious of sin." (Romans 3:20) The law lacks the power to save us. We read in Romans 8:3, "For what the law was powerless to do in that it was weakened by the sinful nature, God did by sending his own Son in the likeness of sinful man, to be a sin offering."

> RM: *In response to the salvation won for us by Jesus, why do you think people struggle with their role? Were you of an opposing understanding at one time? How did you come to know and testify to the truth?*

NO, it won't be faith in ourselves or our good works. Only IN Jesus can we find the righteousness fit for God's acceptance. It is Jesus' good works, not ours, that merits God's assurance of our salvation. Jesus took upon Himself our curse by fulfilling the Law, "Christ redeemed us from the curse of the law by becoming a curse for us." (Galatians 3:13) Be assured God "condemned sin in sinful man, in order that the righteous requirements of the law might be fully met in us..." (Romans 8:3-4) We could do nothing; Jesus did everything for us!

YES, "For it is by grace you have been saved, through faith-- and this is not from yourselves, it is the gift of God--not by works, so that no one can boast." (Ephesians 2:8-9) The writer to the Hebrews chimes in with Paul's words, "Without faith, it is impossible to please God." (Hebrews 11: 6) With such a gift from God in our possession, we are no longer enemies of God. "For if, when we were God's enemies, we were reconciled to him through the death of his Son, how much more, having been reconciled, shall we be saved through his life!" (Romans 5:10) We are restored as His children through the righteous work of Jesus! We have become His sons and daughters in Jesus. God has done it ALL, hasn't He?

How does this happen? "You are all sons of God through faith in Christ Jesus, for all of you who were baptized into Christ have clothed yourselves with Christ." (Galatians 3:26-27) Our salvation comes to us through our baptism into what Jesus has done for us, "Or don't you know that all of us who were baptized into Christ Jesus were baptized into his death? We were therefore buried with him through baptism into death in order that, just as Christ was raised from the dead through the glory of the Father, we too may live a new life." (Romans 6:3-4)

As Jesus tells us to go into all the world and share this good news to all creation, He also says, "Whoever believes and is baptized will be saved...'" (Mark 16:16a) Baptism has that power! "...baptism that now saves you..." (I Peter 3:21) It is the work of the Holy Spirit by water and the Word of God in baptism, "But you were washed, you were sanctified, you were justified in the name of the Lord Jesus Christ and by the Spirit of our God." (I Corinthians 6:11) "Faith comes from hearing the message, and the message is heard through the word of Christ." (Romans 10:17) "The word of God...is at work in you who believe." (I Thessalonians 2:13) "I am not ashamed of the gospel, because it is the power of God for the salvation of everyone who believes..." (Romans 1:16)

This work of God brings us into fellowship with each other as the church and as His holy people, "...just as Christ loved the church and gave himself up for her to make her holy, cleansing her by the washing with water through the word..." (Ephesians 5:25-26) It's through our baptism that we're finally made holy, as God is holy, only through the work of Jesus on our behalf!

It is SO MUCH the work of God for ALL, that one can see God's Word justifying all to include even the baptism of infants! Yes, infants and children, who don't have to wait until an age when they can figure out and decide to receive God's gift. (Remember John 1:13 tells us, we do not become children born of God based upon "human decision"!)

What proof texts would affirm and support infant baptism? Peter states that the promises of baptism are "for you and your children and for all who are far off—for all whom the Lord our God will call." (Acts 2:39) Whom does the Lord our God call? Jesus said, "Let the little children come to me, and do not hinder them, for the kingdom of God belongs to such as these. I tell you the truth, anyone who will not receive the kingdom of God like a little child will never enter it." (Mark 10:14-15) Jesus says also in Matthew 18:6, "If anyone causes one of these little ones who believe in me to sin..." So, infants and children are not exempt from being part of the world that Jesus came to save...and we are to bring the saving grace of God to them through baptism as Jesus instructs us to do!

Jesus again demonstrates His love and desire, even for babies, to come to Him, as we read in Luke 18:15-17, "People were also bringing babies to Jesus to have him touch them. When the disciples saw this, they rebuked them. But Jesus called the children to him and said, 'Let the little children come to me, and do not hinder them, for the kingdom of God belongs to such as these. I tell you the truth, anyone who will not receive the kingdom of God like a little child, will never enter it." How can a little child receive the kingdom of God unless it is God Himself who does everything possible for the little child, or anyone for that matter, to receive it? God calls ALL, not just adults! "It's NOT me...it's ALL HE!"

> RM: *Why do some Christians have a hard time accepting infant baptism? What have you come to understand as their arguments for or against infant baptism? How can you, in the light of the proof texts presented here from God's Word, make an adequate defense for the truth?*

The power of God resides in God within His Word and baptism. God chooses to use us to speak that Word of God as I've referenced earlier in this chapter. It's seen by Paul as a treasure belonging to God, yet residing in us as His Holy Spirit is! "But we have this treasure in jars of clay to show that this all-surpassing power is from God and not of us." (2 Corinthians 4:7)

I can take all the confidence God wants to give me. He lets me know clearly, "It's NOT me, it's all HE!" when He tells me the Holy Spirit is responsible for ALL HIS work! Here are two promises of God I would cling to when the devil would attempt to confuse me. See if you can recognize within these a false belief the devil would put as an obstacle between me and the Lost person hearing the truth of God's Word:

"This is what we speak, not in words taught us by human wisdom but in words taught us by the Spirit, expressing spiritual truths in spiritual words." (1 Corinthians 2:13) It's the Holy Spirit's word and teaching, not ours, when it comes to things spiritual. It's the Holy Spirit as Jesus testifies, "But when he, the Spirit of truth, comes, he will guide you into all truth." (John 16:13)

It's NOT Paul, the messenger or speaker speaking on his own. It's not his abundance of knowledge and demonstrated ability speaking God's Word. His confession of who truly is at work is to encourage us, "When I came to you, brothers, I did not come with eloquence or superior wisdom as I proclaimed to you the testimony about God.... I came to you in weakness and fear, and with much trembling. My message and my preaching were not with wise and persuasive words, but with a demonstration of the Spirit's power, so that your faith might not rest on men's wisdom, but on God's power." (1 Corinthians 2:1, 3-5)

Jesus talks about the TALK the Holy Spirit will speak through us. When we would make a defense, much like Peter and John did before those opposed to God and His free gift and powerful work, read the outcome: "Then Peter, filled with the Holy Spirit said to them.... When they saw the courage of Peter and John and realized that they were unschooled, ordinary men, they were astonished and they took note that these men had been with Jesus.... 'For we cannot help speaking about what we have seen and heard....' 'Now, Lord, consider their threats and enable your servants to speak your word with great boldness.' " Acts 4:8,13,20,29)

As Jesus is with us as the Holy Spirit is within us, we can't help but speak what we have seen and heard with great boldness, can we? That was the case with Peter and John. It was evident to those who saw and heard them! It is the same Jesus and the same Holy Spirit that has been given to us ordinary men and women. For the same purpose? YES! Jesus speaks of the opportunities only the Holy Spirit can create and operate through, "But when they arrest you, do not worry about what to say or how to say it. At that time you will be given what to say, for it will not be you speaking, but the Spirit of your Father speaking through you." (Matthew 10:19-20) You can also read these confirming words of Jesus in Luke 12:11, 12.

> RM: *Did that obstacle of fear, of not knowing what to say, of messing it up, just slide off your shoulders? Did that obstacle of the devil detonate into a billion tiny pieces in response to the truth of God's Word at work in your hearing? Write out and share with a fellow daily disciple what you have come to understand as the Holy Spirit's role in sharing your faith.*

I trust SO! We would know God's Word even from our infancy because these holy Scriptures are "able to make you wise for salvation through faith in Christ Jesus." (2 Timothy 3:15)

God's plan for communicating His gift to us IS a planned series of events, utilizing the work of the Holy Spirit through the Word of God and baptism. His plan is often spoken or conducted through His disciples, like you and me! We have to recognize and state emphatically what that plan is and our response to it!

Martin Luther, in his summary of the third article of the Apostle's Creed, speaking of the Holy Spirit, says it simply and clearly, based upon the same Word of God I've already laid out for you:

"I believe that I cannot by my own reason or strength believe in Jesus Christ, my Lord, or come to Him; but the Holy Spirit has called me by the Gospel, enlightened me with His gifts, sanctified and kept me in the true faith. In the same way He calls, gathers, enlightens, and sanctifies the whole Christian church on earth, and keeps it with Jesus Christ in the one true faith." (Luther's Small Catechism, Concordia Publishing House, St. Louis, MO, 1986, p. 144)

Did you catch all that? Luther joins with God's Word to say, "It's NOT me...it's ALL HE!" doesn't he? Here is God the Holy Spirit at work "in a nutshell" or in a few simple steps that occur over time and receptivity (or willingness on behalf of the receiver to receive them)!

The power is IN the Word of God much like a seed has the potential to no longer remain a seed but become fruit. (Remember Romans 1:16 telling us the Gospel is the power of God for salvation to all who believe?) Isaiah describes God's word as being like such a seed with a purpose or outcome in Isaiah 55:10-11, " 'As the rain and the snow come down from heaven, and do not return to it without watering the earth and making it bud and flourish, so that it yields seed for the sower and bread for the eater, so is my word that goes out from my mouth: It will not return to me empty, but will accomplish what I desire and achieve the purpose for which I sent it." Just as seed has a life-giving, fruit-bearing purpose, so the writer to the Hebrews says "the word of God is living and active."' (Hebrews 4:12)

The Word of God would be spoken by the Holy Spirit as He creates the opportunity when the hearer is receptive. We are actively used by Him for such a purpose. We are out and about sowing the Word of God. The Holy Spirit gives it to us and through us to all kinds of people, like all kinds of soil. Jesus describes the different kinds of responses to God's Word, sown and cast like such seeds, in Matthew 13:19-23. " 'When anyone hears the message about the kingdom and does not understand it, the evil one comes and snatches away what was sown in his heart. This is the seed sown along the path. The one who received the seed that fell on rocky places is the man who hears the word and at once receives it with joy. But since he has no root, he lasts only a short time. When trouble or persecution comes because of the word, he quickly falls away. The one who received the seed that fell among the thorns is the man who hears the word, but the worries of this life and the deceitfulness of wealth choke it, making it unfruitful. But the one who received the seed that fell on good soil is the man who hears the word and understands it.' "

> RM: *As you begin to think about the Lost person God has placed in your life who needs to hear about Jesus in their life, what kind of soil is present in their life that God's Word would land upon as a seed?*

As it takes root and grows, God's Word is at work through the seed within the person, the soil, upon which it is received, watered, and a harvest of fruit is cultivated after growth. Through this Holy Spirit generated faith such fruit is borne in our lives so that we are no longer dead, but made alive with Christ. "For you have been born again, not of perishable seed, but of imperishable, through the living and enduring word of God." (1Peter 1:23)

God does accomplish through His Word and work of baptism what He desires, "For God did not send his Son into the world to condemn the world, but to save the world through him." (John 3:17) God truly does desire ALL to be saved and patiently waits. God is like that father of the prodigal son waiting for His lost sons and daughters to come home, back to Him, and celebrates! Jesus describes the father's response in Luke 15:20, 32, " 'But while he was still a long way off, his father saw him and was filled with compassion for him; he ran to his son, threw his arms around him and kissed him....' 'But we had to celebrate and be glad, because this brother of yours was dead and is alive again; he was lost and is found.'"

The unconditional love God has for each Lost and Found person is patient but with a purpose He will fulfill. "The Lord is not slow in keeping his promise, as some understand slowness. He is patient with you, not wanting anyone to perish, but everyone to come to repentance." (2 Peter 3:9)

> RM: *How can you see God's patience prevailing in a Lost person's life to the point where they may believe they have "all the time in the world" to come to terms with God and eternal life? What might you say to help them see while God is patient, it doesn't last forever? Nor do they know when God will fold their tent and their time will be up?*

God is waiting patiently for all the Lost to receive His gift of forgiveness and eternal life. God calls and invites, through the words of Isaiah, " 'Seek the Lord while he may be found; call on him while he is near. Let the wicked forsake his way and the evil man his thoughts. Let him turn to the Lord, and he will

have mercy on him, and to our God, for he will freely pardon.' "
(Isaiah 55:6-8). God is waiting! But, God will not wait forever!

Here are some proof texts from the Bible that spell out clearly
and confidently God's plan for judging both the Lost and the
Found:

"...now [God] commands all people everywhere to repent. For
he has set a day when he will judge the world with justice by the
man he has appointed." (Acts 17:30b-31a) This verse refers to
judgment of non-Christians, based on whether or not they have
received God's free gift of eternal life and forgiveness of sins.

"For we will all stand before God's judgment seat.... So then,
each of us will give an account of himself to God." (Romans
14:10b, 12) This verse refers to the judgment of Christians, who
will describe the good works done through them by God.

"For we must all appear before the judgment seat of Christ,
that each one may receive what is due him for the things done
while in the body, whether good or bad." (2 Corinthians 5:10)
God expects us to be His daily disciples, through whom He
will bear fruit as we allow Him. We will not be compared with
others quantity or quality of good works or fruit. No, it will be
specific to what we have or haven't done "while in the body."

What would we expect to receive for what we have done? What
would any of us say in response to God's just judgment? "But
they will have to give account to him who is ready to judge the
living and the dead." (1 Peter 4:5)

Do Christians need to fear Jesus judgment of them? We would
be afraid if we chose not to allow Jesus to bear His fruit and

good works through us. We would be afraid if we chose to become Sunday only walkers with Jesus, a sure sign of our lukewarmness towards God's desire and design for each of us. Remember, we would want to do those things pleasing to God by our life and our good works. "Now we ask you and urge you in the Lord Jesus to do this more and more." (1 Thessalonians 4:1)

We know that the will of God for each of us is to be holy and to love one another. These things God Himself will be about doing in our spiritual bodies because we would allow Him to! It's the subject of Paul's heartfelt prayer for the Thessalonians (and for us!), when he writes, "May the Lord make your love increase and overflow for each other and for everyone else, just as ours does for you. May he strengthen your hearts so that you will be blameless and holy in the presence of our God and Father when our Lord Jesus comes with all his holy ones." (1 Thessalonians 3:12-13)

We want to be ready for Jesus return. Not just because He comes to bring an end to this world through judgment and destruction. But, also so that we can each receive the reward He so lovingly desires to bestow upon us beyond our salvation from damnation and Hell! It's all about remaining faithful and fruitful in our abiding relationship with Jesus as branches to His vine, isn't it? BE confident with these words from John:

"We know that we live in him and he in us, because he has given us of his Spirit. And we have seen and testify that the Father has sent his Son to be the Savior of the world. If anyone acknowledges that Jesus is the Son of God, God lives in him and he in God. And so we know and rely on the love God has for us. God is love. Whoever lives in love lives in God, and God in him. In this way, love is made complete among us so that we will have confidence on the day of judgment, because in this world we are like him." (1 John 4:13-17)

> RM: *Taking an inventory of your spiritual life and daily discipleship, write out signs of your confidence for your day of judgment before Jesus. Would there be some areas where you are less than confident? If so, what would your prayer be as you would seek God's commendation, rather than His condemnation?*

Our WALK in Jesus is walking IN His love! Our TALK of Jesus is talking about His love! Yes, the Holy Spirit can make it so simple that anyone, even a child, can believe and have faith in Jesus! We ought not try to complicate it any further. We ought not allow the devil to place any burdensome obstacles between ourselves and the Holy Spirit's working through us.

How are God's desire and the devil's desire in conflict? Jesus describes twice these two opposing forces in anyone's life, "I am the gate; whoever enters through me will be saved. He will come in and go out, and find pasture. The thief comes only to steal and kill and destroy; I have come that they may have life, and have it to the full." (John 10:9-10)

Is Jesus your good shepherd? He promises, " 'I am the good shepherd; I know my sheep and my sheep know me--just as the Father knows Me and I know the Father--and I lay down my life for the sheep. I have other sheep that are not of this sheep pen. I must bring them also. They too will listen to my voice, and there shall be one flock and one shepherd." (John 10:14-16)

As we enter Jesus' flock, the church, we recognize, "There is one body and one Spirit—just as you were called to one hope when you were called—one Lord, one faith, one baptism; one God and Father of all, who is over all and through all and in all." (Ephesians 4:4-6)

> RM: *How have you experienced that oneness that God has called you to? How would you describe the one hope you have to someone who has yet to receive that hope in their lives? How would these become words of testimony to God at work in your life and discipleship with Him? What prayer of thanks would you offer up in response?*

Who still remains outside of Jesus' flock, the church? Who has yet to receive God's free gift of forgiveness and eternal life? Who remains outside of that relationship with God that we find ourselves in? Who lives without that hope we have as we have come to know "one Lord, one faith, one baptism"?

Who has God placed in your life who needs to know about Jesus in their life?

Do you hear the love of God in Jesus' voice as He tells us, "I have other sheep that are not of this sheep pen. I must bring them also. They too will listen to my voice, and there shall be one flock and one shepherd" (John 10:16)?

Who is this person you know that Jesus describes in this parable? " 'Suppose one of you has a hundred sheep and loses one of them. Does he not leave the ninety-nine in the open country and go after the lost sheep until he finds it? And when he finds it, he joyfully puts it on his shoulders and goes home.

Then he calls his friends and neighbors together and says, 'Rejoice with me; I have found my lost sheep.' I tell you that in the same way there will be more rejoicing in heaven over one sinner who repents than over ninety-nine righteous persons who do not need to repent." (Luke 15:4-7)

Who is that person? Who is that one lost sheep? Wasn't it you? Wasn't it me? At one time, yes! But, thankfully no longer! What words would you confess before Jesus as your grateful thanks for His finding you? Don't you desire the same for "your" lost sheep? God does! That's why He's equipped you with the Holy Spirit, Who CAN accomplish His work if you allow Him to!

Did you ever stop to think how each person of the Trinity is a distinct person? Each with a unique purpose joined together for the ultimate demonstrated love and care of each created being? That's why God IS God! Only God IS and HAS the love and life designed for each of us that goes beyond the just results of our sins in this human flesh. Wouldn't we expect a loving God to be fair and treat each person equally? What is that equality we would all share as sinners, who are no longer Lost but Found? "For the wages of sin is death, but the gift of God is eternal life in Christ Jesus our Lord." (Romans 6:23)

One day God will fairly and justly exact the wages of sin through the physical death of each of us. These temporary tents, these bodies that are susceptible to the decaying results of sin and disease, will be folded by God. Paul helps us understand the outcome that every sinner's "earthly tent we live in is destroyed...for while we are in this tent, we groan and are burdened" because of sin! (2 Corinthians 5:1a, 4a)

But, God's demonstrated love and desire is that death would not be the end for us! He wants us to have "a building from God, an eternal house in heaven, not built by human hands." (2 Corinthians 5:1b)

As God, through His Spirit, has revealed ALL He desires to give you, as He has spoken to you through His Word, the Scriptures, do you have the Holy Heartburn? You remember, the holy heartburn He would impart to you as Jesus did to the two WALKing disciples of His on that Easter evening while on the road to Emmaus? (Luke 24:36) Do you have a God-given, Holy Spirit-ignited burden, burning in your heart for this one lost sheep?

Isn't that what it's going to take? In order for you, yourself, to be receptive and responsive to the Holy Spirit's desire? Hasn't He placed them on your heart, and mind so that they would no longer be Lost? Wouldn't you want them to have His Holy Heartburn, too?

Let's talk more about just what the Holy Spirit wants to do through you and others in the next chapter. But, before we do, let's identify who they are! I trust you know who this one lost sheep is. Are you ready to commit God's Spirit to be at work in and through you as HE desires?

Let's pray for such an outcome together!

Dear Holy Spirit, You have worked Your work in my life. Thank the Lord, I, who once was blind, now see! Thank the Lord, He paid in full all the debt I owed God through my sinful life and actions. Thank the Lord, I have seen and heard all that He has shown me through His Word alone...what each sinner's condition is, as helpless as it is, apart from the acceptable work of our Savior and Lord Jesus. You have placed this Lost person in my life for a purpose. You desire to use me and others to speak Your powerful words of the life changing Gospel into their ears and heart...so that they would receive Your free gift by faith through Your wonder working water in Baptism for their salvation. I ask to be used by You in whatever way You would desire. I ask to restore and renew and revive Your Holy Heartburn within me for them! I ask you to create any and all opportunities so that they would hear Your Word and respond as You keep knocking on the door of their heart and life! Guide and direct me in these remaining days before You choose to fold their tent and mine! In Jesus' Name, I ask this, Amen!

ON to Chapter Thirteen and HE, the Holy Spirit!

Chapter Thirteen

"Me, Thee, and S–HE?"

Who has God placed in your life who needs to know about Jesus in their life? That's the prayer-filled question you would invoke Matthew 7:7 before the Lord, " 'Ask and it will be given to you; seek and you will find; knock and the door will be opened to to you.' " Do you suppose Jesus expects us to ask, seek, and knock only once? That once is enough? Do you think Jesus would want to know "how much" you desire what you are asking, seeking, and knocking for? Wouldn't that imply then that you ought to "keep on" asking, "keep on" seeking, and "keep on" knocking until you knew you had or didn't have your answer?

I would challenge you to look at the application of Jesus' words in light of a specific situation, the salvation of a soul Jesus died for: your family member, friend, or an associate you're involved with. You may not know who this person is yet. You may have had a particular person on your mind and heart for awhile. Now is the time to ask God to reveal or confirm who this person is through prayer! In light of the previous paragraph, I would suggest it is not enough to pray once or once in a while. You would make a minimal daily commitment to pray for them, at the very least. Would you agree?

As you consider who this person is, you'll want to consider several questions to help you understand your starting point with them. How much do you care if they perish spiritually? We all ought to have a certain level of compassion for every soul, right? Desiring to see a saving and sustaining faith in this person, we've got to start with ourselves and see where we stand. Are there some lingering unforgiven relations between us and them? What impact could that hold? What obstacle might the devil try to place between us and God's words? Maybe they won't be as receptive to hear God's Good News for them through us? Maybe that's been on your mind more than need be and so they've not been hearing it from us!

> RM: *Take a few minutes to discover your answers to those questions in the last paragraph. As you think about how you would answer, begin in prayer. Ask the Holy Spirit's guidance to reveal what He knows about your relationship with them. Don't be so quick to come up with a profile. Make some time to let this remain in your slow-cooker, won't you? As you've learned to practice silence and waiting upon the Lord, exercise it here for discernment and direction from the Holy Spirit.*

Consider the starting point could very well be seeking their forgiveness, no matter who's to blame! What a starting point that would be! Talk about an ice breaker? You might be on the edge of a glacier becoming bitty icebergs by the power of the Holy Spirit! It starts with Jesus' loving presence in your life. It starts by your confessing your desire for the other's forgiveness. It starts by praying specifically that God would change your head and heart if you're having a hard time forgiving, let alone forgetting!

Beyond your care if they perish, be reminded how much Jesus cares! Picture Jesus' extended arms hanging on both sides of the cross! Jesus died to bring you forgiveness. You live daily in the assurance His death on the cross was enough to cover your sins in God's sight. Jesus would extend those same arms and nail pierced hands to your family member, friend, or associate! How much more will they learn about the forgiving grace of God? How would your example of extending forgiveness to them be used by God? (Especially if it's a challenge for you?) Begin with a prayer-filled attitude as you get started! Invite other fellow daily disciples at your church or within your fellowship to do the same won't you?

Commit yourself to them for the long haul! Thank the Lord for them daily. Remind yourself that you have a relationship with them. How would this relationship be complete and fulfilling unless the Lord completes and fulfills it? Be committed and determined, you'll not give up on them just as Jesus won't give up on you! You know you can't do anything to bring them into a faith based relationship with God. You know the Holy Spirit can!

- You would agree with God and His other disciples that (fill in their name here) is in need of His blood bought forgiveness and eternal life as you've come to receive them.

- You would agree with God and His other disciples that while (fill in their name here) may not be receptive and responsive to God's free gift yet, they deserve every opportunity to receive it as you have received them.

- You would agree with God and His other disciples that as you pray and make yourself available to (fill in their name here), you would not let anything in your control stand in the way of their receiving God's free gift, even as you've come to receive God's free gift.

From this point forward, you will ask the Holy Spirit to keep you in humble submission before God on their behalf.

RM: *Consider praying this prayer: "O Lord, I know how much You desire to place (fill in their name here) on your shoulders, returning them to God's fold! Use me, when-ever and where-ever and how-ever, to allow Your saving work to be done in them. Take away any obstacle I or the devil would place in this relationship. Enable the Holy Spirit free course for the saving knowledge of Jesus to enter their mind and change their heart. I commit myself and (fill in their name here) into Your saving hands, for Jesus' sake! Amen."*

Won't you pray that prayer or one similar a couple of times a day? How about three times a day, pray? Morning, Noon, and Night you'll be reminded to pray this prayer for them? What a start that would be!

What more will be helpful? What's the next step? Spending some prayer-filled time recalling how unique they are within the relationship you've come to know them! Find a means to record, recall, and update information as you come to know it. I like index cards, more durable than a piece of paper, and less likely to get misplaced or lost!

Think of your Lost person as being a house with windows and doors. We understand that Jesus is their searching Good Shepherd, having left the 99 sheep safe and secure. Jesus will direct all His efforts towards finding your Lost person as that one sheep He's looking for. We recall Jesus' words in Revelation 3:20, " 'I stand at the door and knock. If anyone hears my voice and opens the door, I will come in and eat with him, and he with me.'" Do you see and hear Jesus knocking at the front door of your Lost person's life?

What's their response to Jesus? Do they even go to the door to see who's knocking? Do they ignore the knocking, believing it will go away? Do they go to the door in response to Jesus knocking but only look through the peephole? Are they receptive and ready to open the door to Jesus, their Good Shepherd, ready to carry them on His shoulders and rejoice? Are they ready to receive salvation, forgiveness, and eternal life that this same Jesus died on the cross and rose again to give them?

What about the windows in their life? As the Holy Spirit would come to speak to them, perhaps through you or others, what's their response? Are their windows closed tight? Are their windows slightly opened? Are their windows wide open so that the Holy Spirit can enter in and speak to them? How receptive are they to the Holy Spirit's voice through you or others? Were their windows open at one time, but now have been shut in response to something or someone in their life?

Would those windows be so stained and dirty by sin that no one can look outside themselves? How is it a real challenge for the light of Christ's love, mercy, and grace to shine through and into the windows of their soul and heart? How receptive are they to the exposing light of Christ?

Remind yourself of the description Jesus gives regarding those in darkness from John 3:19-20: "Light has come into the world, but men loved darkness instead of light because their deeds were evil. Everyone who does evil hates the light, and will not come into the light for fear that his deeds will be exposed."

As you prayerfully consider these analogies, you can begin an accountability record that addresses the reception through the doors and windows of your Lost person. You will update it as regularly as you speak with them. As your write these responses and recollections out, leave yourself enough room after each phone call or in-person encounter for any updates. Create and use a prayer log noting what and when you interceded for them. Leave a space following your intercession to record God's answer. Utilize this prayer log as a source of prayer requests made to other prayer partners on their behalf.

Just as a reminder, Whose plan is it? Who will bring them? Keep these encouraging words highlighted from Isaiah 55:6-7, where you can be reminded: " 'Seek the Lord while he may be found; call on him while he is near. Let the wicked forsake his way and the evil man his thoughts. Let him turn to the Lord, and he will have mercy on him, and to our God, for he will freely pardon. Who would know them better? Call upon God's knowledge and depend upon God to do all He can!

Randy Michael Wendt

Remember the desire of the devil in contrast to Jesus? Jesus says, " 'I am the gate; whoever enters through me will be saved. He will come in and go out, and find pasture. The thief comes only to steal and kill and destroy; I have come that they may have life, and have it to the full." (John 10:9-10) The devil would steal God's gift from every person, even before they received it! How would he do so? How will we know the devil's attempts? We need to be on the alert within our conversations with them. Know the devil will be "turning up the heat" of rejecting God's gift. Especially as the Holy Spirit gets closer to their accepting God's gift! The power of persistent prayer can't be overlooked or undermined here, can it?

Jesus also describes His commitment to them as their shepherd. " 'I am the good shepherd; I know my sheep and my sheep know me--just as the Father knows me and I know the Father--and I lay down my life for the sheep. I have other sheep that are not of this sheep pen. I must bring them also. They too will listen to my voice, and there shall be one flock and one shepherd.' " (John 10:14-16) God doesn't say, "You, My disciple, must bring them into the fold." We can't...but He CAN! How will He use us to such an end?

Ever wonder why God has chosen you? What's God's desire as He would use you? Why are you God's channel of His good news and gracious gift? It's all about your abiding IN Jesus! Remember from Jesus' teaching in John 15, we are the branch connected to Him, the vine?

What's our relationship with Him? What would be His result? " 'Remain in me, and I will remain in you. No branch can bear fruit by itself; it must remain in the vine. Neither can you bear

252

fruit unless you remain in me.' " (John 15:4) Jesus takes the burden of bearing fruit upon Himself. Through our baptism, we are clothed with Jesus. We experience His death in order to receive His resurrected life. As we remain in Him, we find ourselves vitally joined to Him. We would die apart from Jesus, wouldn't we? So important is the life line Jesus established with us through His death and our baptism. We would never sever it!

What's my role? What's my responsibility? " 'I am the vine; you are the branches. If a man remains in me and I in him, he will bear much fruit; apart from me you can do nothing.' " (John 15:5) Why not me? We're not the ones who've created or purchased the gift God offers. We're only the recipients. We could do nothing to earn or receive it!

Let God's fruit in your life bear witness to the love and mercy of God that's instore for them, as well!

What help is available? How would God use me? " 'You did not choose me, but I chose you and appointed you to go and bear fruit--fruit that will last. Then the Father will give you whatever you ask in my name." (John 15:16) Whatever we pray on behalf of this person, God would grant according to His will because He knows the outcome! Note Jesus doesn't say "instantly." We have to allow God's own Holy Spirit the space to work. (We'll say more on levels of receptivity in Chapter Sixteen.)

Why ought we to trust, obey, and hang in there? "The one who sows to please his sinful nature, from that nature will reap destruction; the one who sows to please the Spirit, from the Spirit will reap eternal life. Let us not become weary in doing good, for at the proper time we will reap a harvest if we do not give up. Therefore, as we have opportunity, let us do good to all people, especially to those who belong to the family of believers." (Galatians 6:8-10)

> RM: *Highlight a couple of words here, mentally or otherwise: "let us not become weary" means there will be times you'll want to give up! When? When you don't see the results you would expect? By now? After repeated rejection? Depending upon who they are and the heart they maintain, it may take a season or two of softening! That's where the power of persistent praying needs to be employed by you and others. What's the application to your circumstances? How would you be challenged to become weary? What would you recognize as the remedy for weariness?*

We would be praying for that "proper time we will reap a harvest if we do not give up." Remember, GOD is at work here! His good works bear fruit when they are connected to Jesus by faith in Him, a faith that doesn't give up! The Holy Spirit will give us opportunities.

> RM: *How will we take the opportunities and allow the Holy Spirit to work through us? Think through a couple of realistic opportunities within the context of your Lost person. Describe what could likely happen and how you would "hang in there!"*

What IS the promise of the Holy Spirit at work? " 'As the rain and the snow come down from heaven, and do not return to it without watering the earth and making it bud and flourish, so that it yields seed for the sower and bread for the eater, so is my word that goes out from my mouth: It will not return to me empty, but will accomplish what I desire and achieve the purpose for which I sent it." (Isaiah 55:10-11) HE will succeed. We must have the faith to believe our Lost person will receive God's gift. So, we ought to PRAY and ACT accordingly.

> RM: *What would be some signs we would want to be looking for? How might we be encouraged as this person gets closer to receiving God's free gift for them? How would our prayers change? Would they lose their frequency or fervency?*

I don't know about you, but I'm totally overwhelmed by the power of God and His purpose through us. As we experience an ever deepening daily discipleship with Jesus, we will have a life testimony that demonstrates God's power and purpose at work in our lives. He will have shown both to us and through us the Holy Spirit's ability to sanctify us.

Sanctifying is not just making us holy. Sanctifying is also setting us apart for God's will and work, isn't it? When God has full access to every inch of our will and ways, we will see the results. Our testimony will clearly be He will bear such abiding fruit in our lives. We then, like Peter and John, cannot help but talk about what we have seen and heard in our own lives. Our life and words truly become a sign that reads "Disciple Under Construction...God IS at Work!"

> RM: *For starters, come up with one paragraph or so of testimony pointing to your discipleship under*

construction. Describe briefly and simply how God has been at work in your life. Share it with a prayer partner and ask them for their testimony as well. Celebrate with each other God's love and mercy in action in your lives!

We would be reminded of John's testimony found in 1 John 4:13-16 and his instructions to us on being used by God. "We know that we live in him and he in us, because he has given us of his Spirit. And we have seen and testify that the Father has sent his Son to be the Savior of the world. If anyone acknowledges that Jesus is the Son of God, God lives in him and he in God. And so we know and rely on the love God has for us."

He has given us the Holy Spirit. We know well by now ALL He can accomplish don't we? We have seen and testify of ALL He can and does accomplish, don't we? We acknowledge ALL He can and does accomplish through others as well. There's nothing special about us. The Holy Spirit stands ready to bear good fruit through anyone vitally connected to Jesus, the Vine!

We KNOW therefore that God lives in us and remains with us! We KNOW and can rely upon God's love to be the life-changing and life-giving power it has become for countless millions, ourselves, and awaits to be at work in their life!

Enough said? Well then, let's get out to the field God has already been preparing. Let's join our prayers together with others, who would daily pray for the world and all in it, so that as many as can will accept His good and gracious gift before it's too late!

Let's pray: Father God, You are in some stage of preparation or actively bringing together everything and everyone necessary for our Lost person's acceptance of your free gift of salvation. We thank You that You have chosen to use us and others for such a purpose. We pray, keep us fixed and focused on our Lost person's need for You. Help us not to become weary as You are at work through us. Remind us of the joy there will be in Heaven when Your Lost son or daughter has been found! Help us to encourage and be encouraged as we join fellow disciples in sowing Your seeds. May they fall upon good soil and spring up to souls destined for eternal life. In Jesus' Name, we ask this! Amen.

Chapter Fourteen

Praying and preparing their soil

Prayer becomes many things to the daily disciple of Jesus as we addressed it earlier in Part One of this book. As Jesus' TALKing disciples, we would move the focus of our prayers upon a person and their needs. We would also pray for the Holy Spirit to extend an invitation for God to be at work through us and others. Prayer also becomes the opportunity to gauge the receptiveness of God's gift. How are they responding to God's free gift of forgiveness and eternal life? We would also pray that God would enlist others, who will be used in God's work of disciple making.

How can prayer prepare their soil (and soul)? It begins with our understanding the power of prayer even as it relates to sharing our faith with others. What good is prayer for others, whether they be LOST or Dechurched? "I urge, then, first of all, that requests, prayers, intercession and thanksgiving be made for everyone....This is good, and pleases God our Savior, who wants all men to be saved and to come to a knowledge of the truth." (1 Timothy 2:1, 3-4) Paul points out four aspects of prayer that we ought to be aware of. What are these? How are they different? How are they necessary? In looking at other

English versions, I've found the word, "supplications" used in place of the NIV's "requests." For this instance, I prefer looking at the word "supplications."

Supplications: When I take apart that word, I found the word, "supply" or "supple". I come to understand that as we pray for our Lost person, we want to call upon God's able supply of strength. We understand through His Word He accomplishes what He desires and sets out to do! Within the heart of each person, God's word is able to convince them of their circumstances and need for Him. If it were not so, who of us would have a chance? Would any of us be exempt or removed from the opportunity to receive God's free gift? NO, not if it is truly free and available to all the world!

> RM: *Write out a simple four sentence prayer that would be an example of a prayer focusing on supplications. Please make the focus applicable to the Lost person in your life you would be praying for.*

Prayers: Going beyond words within our prayers, we would find ourselves submitting our weak wills to God's strong and saving will for each Lost person we would pray for. God seeks permission from those who would receive His gift. We can choose not to accept His gift, and sadly, many have. They won't truly know the outcome until Judgment Day. If they had any doubt until then, sadly their fate will become reality before their eyes for the rest of eternity. We WANT and NEED to be IN prayer for each Lost one!

> RM: *Write out another simple four sentence prayer that would be an example of a prayer focusing on submitting our will to God's will. Again, please make*

> *the focus applicable to the Lost person in your life*
> *you would be praying for.*

Intercessions: Where we know specifics in their lives through our conversations, we want to pray specifics in our prayers for them. Knowing the specifics of the person tells us many help-full and hope-full things, doesn't it? We would know what's preventing them from receiving God's gift. We would know what remains as an obstacle to be removed by God. We would know how helpful it would be to pray for God to provide another person who could become their friend and God's additional voice. As we go before Jesus on their behalf, we want to be specific and persistent in our interceding for them!

> RM: *Write out another simple four sentence prayer to*
> *be prayed in the manner of an intercession, keeping*
> *some of the same descriptive characteristics as a*
> *part of your prayer. Please make sure your requests*
> *are as specific as you received them on behalf of your*
> *Lost person.*

Thanksgivings: We would all be thank-full to God for many things on their behalf and ours! We would give thanks for the free gift of God through Jesus. Someone in our life extended such a prayer on our behalf, and now we are giving the same extended focus in our prayer for our Lost person. We would be giving thanks for the many opportunities the Holy Spirit gives us. We would be giving thanks for the patience of God as He (and we) eagerly wait. We would be giving thanks for His love that covers any and every sin and obstacle they would place before Him.

RM: *Can you think of some others? Give thanks for them, too, by writing a simple four sentence prayer to be prayed in the manner of thanksgivings, keeping some of the same descriptive characteristics as a part of your prayer. Please make sure your requests are as specific as you received them on behalf of your Lost person.*

For the WALKing disciple, the Holy Spirit helps us identify and focus our prayers on the Lost or De-churched person God has placed in our lives. As we see them appearing on our radar screen, we would be praying intercessorily from a distinct position or location or receptivity we would find them in now. We would be watchfully praying that they would move closer and closer to receiving God's free gift...and our prayer focus would intercede accordingly.

We would be aware to follow their movement in quite a disciplined way! Jesus wants us to be such a laborer in Harvest. He invites us to share His need with other daily disciples in our midst and fellowship. He wants us to join them in their prayers for their Lost persons and vice versa as we wait for a harvest!

"When he saw the crowds, he had compassion on them, because they were harassed and helpless, like sheep without a shepherd. Then he said to his disciples, 'The harvest is plentiful but the workers are few. Ask the Lord of the harvest, therefore, to send out workers into his harvest field.' " (Matthew 9:36-38)

RM: *Think about the fellow daily disciples at your church or fellowship. How do they appear to you to be sent out by God into His harvest field? What*

*kinds of conversations or shared prayers have you
had with them for your mutually Lost persons?
What might you focus on that will intensify the holy
heartburn God would have you bearing for the Lost?*

For the TALKing disciple, do you recognize how the Holy Spirit guides our conversations? The results would impact upon our prayers. We can be current and specific with intercessions on their behalf. When you let the Holy Spirit speak His words through you, you will stand amazed at what He will say through you!

What about those times when we're literally at a loss for words. We don't know where to begin to pray? We're puzzled and unsure how responsive our Lost person is to the Holy Spirit at work? We can depend upon Jesus promise that the Holy Spirit will help us to pray even when we would not know what to pray for.

Turn with me to God's Word for both these promises fulfilled! "...do not worry about what to say and how to say it. At that time you will be given what to say, for it will not be you speaking, but the Spirit of your Father speaking through you." (Matthew 10:19b-20) "In the same way, the Spirit helps us in our weakness. We do not know what we ought to pray for, but the Spirit himself intercedes for us with groans that words cannot express. And he who searches our hearts knows the mind of the Spirit, because the Spirit intercedes for the saints in accordance with God's will." (Romans 8:26-27)

How will the Spirit help us? He, the Holy Spirit, will pray through us, even when we don't know what we would be praying for on their behalf. We can expect the Holy Spirit would pray specifically, wouldn't He? He would pray that God's will would be accomplished so that the Lost would be found, so that the De-churched would be Re-churched!

Our times of conversation with our Lost or De-churched person PUTS US IN TOUCH with what's on their mind and WHAT WE SHOULD PRAY FOR! How nearer are they to receiving God's gift and a daily relationship with God in their lives? Remember, we want to find the "current position" on our radar screen of them. If radar is too old a concept for you, you're free to utilize Global Positioning Systems, also known as GPS! In this case, you might want to engage in "recalculating" to make sure you're on the right road! You would "recalculate" when you recognize they're not at the same place of receptiveness they were the last time...or where you expected them still to be!

What's happening within and without their ability to influence or control the outcome in their life? That's a basic question to ask yourself as you're trying to determine their receptiveness to God's offer. How can the Holy Spirit help us know what they're thinking? Two verses would point us to God's answer, which we would know to be true!

- " 'No eye has seen, no ear has heard, no mind has conceived what God has prepared for those who love him'—but God has revealed it to us by his Spirit. The Spirit searches all things, even the deep things of God. For who among men knows the thoughts of a man except the man's spirit within him? In the same way no one knows the thoughts of God except the Spirit of God." (1 Corinthians 2:9-11)

- "For God is greater than our hearts, and he knows everything." (1 John 3:20)

God does not operate blindly or without knowledge of the person's receptivity. That's why we want that radar on or that GPS updated so that we can be praying, "Holy Spirit, provide everything and everyone necessary that You would accomplish Your will and work in (fill in their name here)."

How does God want to use our conversations as we think about them? "So what shall I do? I will pray with my spirit, but I will also pray with my mind; I will sing with my spirit, but I will also sing with my mind." (1 Corinthians 14:15) God would have us balance our activity of prayer as we reposition or recalculate where they are in receiving His gift. We can be intelligent and responsive. By praying with the Holy Spirit and our mind, we would come to ask further questions to reveal more of their willingness to receive God's gift NOW. There's a lot to be said about having head and heart in sync with each other, isn't there? We would pray that the Holy Spirit will give us insight as they come nearer to receiving His gift of salvation.

Who should we also be praying for and to what end? "And pray in the Spirit on all occasions with all kinds of prayers and requests. With this in mind, be alert and always keep on praying for all the saints." (Ephesians 6:18-20) God would have us know that no one and nothing would be left out of our prayers. This verse and command tie in well with the 1 Timothy 2:1, 3-4 passage I shared with you earlier in this chapter. We focus all our prayers and supplications (God's supply of strength and power to change) upon the Lost and De-churched, upon ourselves and our partners in the Gospel or co-harvesters in the ripe fields!

Why are we not on our own? What also should be the subject of our intercessory prayers? "I thank my God every time I remember you. In all my prayers for all of you, I always pray with joy because of your partnership in the gospel from the first day until now, being confident of this, that he who began a good work in you will carry it on to completion until the day of Christ Jesus." (Philippians 1:3-6) Jesus wants us not to be without encouragement or partners in His Gospel work! Remember, Jesus always sent disciples out in two's. Would one be speaking while the other would be praying? Do you see the tie-in between this verse and the Ephesians passage in the paragraph above?

As we are Jesus' TALKing disciples, what is God's will for you concerning your prayers? "Be joyful always; pray continually; give thanks in all circumstances, for this is God's will for you in Christ Jesus." (1 Thessalonians 5:16-18) Think about the circumstances as you are used by God to be a TALKing disciple. Why rejoice, give thanks, be patient, be constant, be persistent in PRAYER? So that, you would KNOW "all things are possible with God" ... even THIS person's salvation, no matter how far away or hard their heart!

How will our prayers work? "The prayer of a righteous man is powerful and effective." (James 5:16b) As holy as God is, He yields His "YES"-based will through our prayers. As Jesus instructed Paul, " 'My grace is sufficient for you, for my power is made perfect in weakness.' " (2 Corinthians 12:9) How else would we see His power except through our weakness?

> RM: *Think about those words of Jesus to Paul! We know Paul confessed himself as not having any*

*power within himself, that it was all from God, which
we read previously in 1 Corinthians 2:1-5. How have
you seen God at work through your weakness? In
what ways has this impacted upon your Lost person?*

How can prayer build US up in our faith as we pray for the Lost and De-churched? "But you, dear friends, build yourselves up in your most holy faith and pray in the Holy Spirit. Keep yourselves in God's love as you wait for the mercy of our Lord Jesus Christ to bring you to eternal life." (Jude 20-21) Jude exhorts us to be praying in the Holy Spirit as we would be built up in our holy faith. We are building ourselves up as we get closer to the power and perfect will of God, not our own weak inability. Prayer becomes that exercise which builds up our spiritual bodies, doesn't it? We can gauge our muscular strength through prayer in a sense if you agree with my analogy!

When do we give up praying? Never? Never! Our prayer chain has links that connect us to God and each other. They were cast previously in 1 Thessalonians 5, and now in this verse, "Be joyful in hope, patient in affliction, faithful in prayer." (Romans 12:12) When do we give up praying? As I've said before, we would stop praying when we stop breathing. Just as we need to breathe to live physically, we need to pray to live spiritually. So, depending upon their response, we can expect times and seasons when they would become more and more receptive of God's gift of grace. We would find times of hope, for which we would rejoice! As well, we would find times of doubt and tribulation, when they would refuse God's gift. Nevertheless, we would be patient IN prayer. We don't skip a few days...we remain breathing constantly IN prayer for our Lost or Dechurched person!

What can we share in addition to praying with our Lost and De-Churched person? "[We have a] God of all comfort, who comforts us in all our troubles, so that we can comfort those in any trouble with the comfort we ourselves have received from God. For just as the sufferings of Christ flow over into our lives, so also through Christ our comfort overflows." (2 Corinthians 1:3b-5) Our experiencing God's comfort through God and each other becomes the testimonies the Holy Spirit can use to speak to the Lost and De-Churched...through us! They will see through our lives (WALK) and hear through our words (TALK) the very comfort of God!

We ought to depend upon God's demonstrated love for the world and all those in it, Lost and Found! It's what keeps Him from bringing an end to the world until as many as can be found are found. "The Lord is not slow in keeping his promise, as some understand slowness. He is patient with you, not wanting anyone to perish, but everyone to come to repentance." (2 Peter 3:9)

Guess what obstacle the devil loves to put before people? Can you hear the devil saying, "God is a God of judgment. God set up the Ten Commandments and His Law because God KNEW we wouldn't be able to meet them!"

WRONG! God is a Holy God and doesn't need to apologize for His holiness.

KNOWING that, God would have holy expectations of us. God also is the God who made it possible for His Son to take our place with His death on the cross, "the righteous for the unrighteous, to bring you to God." (1 Peter 3:18b) And, so we are as we accept His gift of love and grace on our behalf!

No one can be so sinful that God's love would exclude them from His mercy and forgiveness in Jesus. As we read in John 3:17, "For God did not send his Son into the world to condemn the world, but to save the world through him." As Jesus also reminds us, " 'In the same way your Father in heaven is not willing that any of these little ones should be lost." (Matthew 18:14)

We ought to respond accordingly to the Holy Spirit's work in and through us! God DOES CARE that we pray and allow faith to play a role in our prayers! How small does our faith have to be in order for God to be at work? " '...I tell you the truth, if you have faith as small as a mustard seed, you can say to this mountain, 'Move from here to there' and it will move. Nothing will be impossible for you.' " (Matthew 17:20-21)

> RM: *God wants to encourage us, doesn't He? If our faith were as large as a speck, mountains would be moved in His name according to His will! We then would ask ourselves, "What obstacles does God need to move in our lives, like the mountains we can't move?" How will such stories and testimonies be used by God and the Holy Spirit for the Lost and De-Churched? How will they impact upon accepting God's free gift of forgiveness and eternal life?*

Not meaning to command or predict HOW the Holy Spirit will work, here are some possible areas where His patience and ours will need to be in place!

REALIZE our Lost person is not seeking God or recognizes a need for God in their lives. Paul speaks from much experience before the Lost when he describes his experience, " 'There is no one who understands, no one who seeks God. All have turned away, they have together become worthless; there is no one who does good, not even one.' " (Romans 3:11-12)

Look within your own experience to see or hear a Lost person's response to be just like the one Paul recalls in 1 Corinthians 2:14, "The man without the Spirit does not accept the things that come from the Spirit of God, for they are foolishness to him, and he cannot understand them, because they are spiritually discerned." As we read previously about those in darkness not seeking the light, we can conclude with Paul that forgiveness and salvation are not on the minds of the Lost. We have come to understand spiritual things because of the spiritual life we live. We have come to the understanding that KNOWING they are dead in their sins, they can't save themselves. Either they can only receive God's gift, which can save them by faith, or refuse it! Isn't it sad when people fail to see this gift of God wrapped with a name tag bearing their name written on it? Perhaps it doesn't help either that this is a GIFT. How many people feel they don't deserve a gift or that they must give something back in return (or in exchange)? And so, the value of the gift from a grace perspective is diminished completely because they lack the faith to recognize and receive this grace-given gift of God.

"For it is by grace you have been saved, through faith—and this not from yourselves, it is the gift of God—not by works, so than no one can boast." (Ephesians 2:8-9)

THIS is the ground of grace necessary for the seed of God's Word to fall upon them and take root. Depending upon where they are at in their life with God, the type of soil and the germination of faith in their soul will be determined. Their receptivity to the Gospel can be a changing soil condition for the Holy Spirit to do His specific work at that time. We would be IN prayer for such a time and work. We would need to know what season it is in their lives? Is it a time of preparing? Planting? Watering? Cultivating? Harvesting?

We also would want to assess and reassess their location on radar or GPS and its' impact on their soil and soul quite regularly. Hear again the words of Jesus in the Parable of the Sower and see where your person might be at!

The PATH: " 'When anyone hears the message about the kingdom and does not understand it, the evil one comes and snatches away what was sown in his heart.' " (Matthew 13:19) Are they here, just really not interested and not caring to listen? Are they politely shutting you off without much care or concern for their soil or soul?

ROCKY GROUND: " 'The one who received the seed that fell on rocky places is the man who hears the word and at once receives it with joy. But since he had no root, he lasts only a short time. When trouble or persecution comes because of the word, he quickly falls away.' " (Matthew 13:20-21) Have they moved towards greater receptivity? How have they shown some interest, maybe attended a worship service? But once it seems like all is breaking loose, they're not interested in anything but their problems?

The THORNS: " 'The one who received the seed that fell among the thorns is the man who hears the word, but the worries of this life and the deceitfulness of wealth choke it, making it unfruitful.' " (Matthew 13:22) Are they here finding the stuff of life? Do they determine that what they can see and taste and gather up NOW is far more important and valued? They definitely aren't interested in some insurance policy for the future that THEY can't benefit from now or ever?

The GOOD SOIL: " 'But the one who received the seed that fell on good soil is the man who hears the word and understands it. He produces a crop, yielding a hundred, sixty or thirty times what was sown.' " (Matthew 13:23) THIS is the goal, isn't it? They're in the arms of God for now and eternity! They KNOW in whom they have believed. They DON'T want any more empty promises of the devil. They have been transformed, and there is no going back! They have tasted and seen that the Lord is good! They know they're going to have difficulties and problems. They also know they have God who will love and care for them for eternity!

Can you sense the excitement in the air? Has your holy heartburn turned up a notch or two since you've realized God desires to be at work in your Lost and De-Churched person's life? Have you been further heart-burdened for them? Are you committed with the help of God to allow the Holy Spirit to speak and work through you and others He will gather?

If NO, go back to God IN prayer and ask Him to place such a burden and burn upon and within your heart. Without such a commitment to Him, He will not work through you. Don't try anything on your own. You will fail because it is not your responsibility or ability. But, it is the commission from God for you, as His redeemed child! Note, co-mission, because God is always in and working through you, and He even invites others to join as partners with you in the harvest fields!

If YES, you're ready to move on to the next chapter.

Chapter Fifteen

Discovering the way the Holy Spirit works

How many means and methods have you been exposed to concerning witnessing? Have any of them ever encouraged you to share your faith once you mastered them? IF you mastered them? We would always PRAY for OPPORTUNITIES rather than lean upon our own ability to learn and enlist witnessing tools! Wouldn't you agree? Some disciples push memorizing outlines. They would suggest that the faithful delivery of an outline, perhaps even verbatim, is what the Holy Spirit will use to bring someone to faith. They go on to say that until we have it committed to memory and rehearsed often, we ought not venture out and witness!

The approach God's own Holy Spirit has led me to understand may be quite different than what you've seen or heard before. I hope so! I want to encourage you, not discourage you! I want to show you that there's no burden or baggage you should be carrying when it comes to sharing your faith! Quite the opposite! I would respond to those above, "Look less upon yourself and more upon God, who would be at work in and through you!" As we would come to know that "It's NOT me, but HE!" referring to the Holy Spirit!

Recall what Solomon prayed for and God granted? Let's look into that God-inspired wisdom, within God's Word, for a confirmation of our approach in sharing our faith! "Trust in the Lord with all your heart and lean not on your own understanding; in all your ways acknowledge him, and he will make your paths straight. Do not be wise in your own eyes; fear the Lord and shun evil." (Proverbs 3:5-7)

> RM: *Is this easy or difficult for you to believe and practice? Who challenges you to think it's up to you and how well you're prepared to witness? What would it take to convert you over to God's way of thinking and behaving?*

When you witnessed to someone did you do so with forgetfulness or fear? Were you challenged to recall the steps on an outline or the Bible references? Did it seem as if the path you were taking your hearer became crooked? God would take upon His own shoulders ALL the burden of sharing His gift with the Lost. We don't have to become fearful or frustrated leaning upon our own weak selves! Why not be joyful and confident as we hear God's own Holy Spirit speak through us? That's what He wants to do, you know? If we would acknowledge HIS desire and ability "with all our heart" and "head," what can't He accomplish through us?

Remember, once more for reinforcement: Look less upon yourself and your ability, which is your weakness! Look more upon God and His ability, which is His strength! Let His Word work through your daily discipleship experiences shared. Your WALK with Jesus becomes His TALK through you!

As we look at Matthew 10, discover with me the value and necessity Jesus saw of disciples being used to make disciples. Note that in verse one, Jesus gives them authority to do a variety of things. Jesus recognizes that people's inclinations are to look at who we are and what we do. What does it appear we represent first and foremost? For this time, Jesus equips them with the authority "to drive out evil spirits and to heal every disease and sickness." (Matthew 10:1) Nothing is lacking for the disciples because they have God's authority in place and working through them.

Jesus sends them out with instructions which complete the remaining 41 verses of this chapter. What would Jesus hope they would accomplish? I would point back to Proverbs 3:5-7. They would need to learn from experience that they couldn't do any of these things without the power and authority of God, wouldn't they? Where would they put their faith and confidence? In God, who would accomplish all these things? Or in themselves, who would accomplish nothing? Remember Jesus says in John 15:5, "...apart from me you can do nothing"?

Within Matthew 10:5-10, Jesus instructs them by their actions to show or prove they have the faith to believe in the authority given to them by God to accomplish His work. Within verses 11-16, Jesus would instruct them to recognize different responses due to the season and receptivity they would find among hearers. Also, be aware of the activity of the devil, who would thwart such efforts! Jesus doesn't underestimate the opposition the devil will cast before them, like so many obstacles in such spiritual warfare.

Within verses 17-18, Jesus alerts them to the opportunities they will have before authorities, whether civil or religious, on Jesus' account! Jesus tells it like it is, doesn't He? Can you imagine being flogged in the synagogues? Within verses 19-20, Jesus reminds them "God is at Work!" and the Holy Spirit will step in to do His part. So, " '...do not worry about what to say or how to say it. At that time you will be given what to say, for it will not be you speaking, but the Spirit of your Father speaking through you.' " (Matthew 10:19-20)

WRITE those words out, daily TALKing disciple of Jesus! Carry them as your business card! Be bold and confident! The Holy Spirit stands ready, willing, and overwhelmingly ABLE to speak God's Word through you. His is the power that will change a person's heart and mind! So, let's discover in more detail the way the Holy Spirit can choose to work.

There are four working pre-suppositions the Holy Spirit can choose to use, according to His unique plan for each unique person. These are not guarantees, mind you, but options. What opportunities will the Holy Spirit choose to use? It's up to Him! He knows each person and where they are at in their receptivity for God's free gift.

The fundamental first understanding is this: GOD is able to DO His work! He invites us to be a channel through which His words of Law and Gospel can be shared.

Remember, the Law shows us we're sinners in need of forgiveness. The Gospel shows us we have a Savior who earned forgiveness for us. Together we hear the whole reason why God hasn't given up on us. We come to know God wants to give us the gift only His Son could give us!

RM: *Read and respond to the following verses from God's Word serving as the "proof texts" for this first pre-supposition.*

"For it is God who works in you to will and to act according to his good purpose." (Philippians 2:13) Describe an opportunity where you have clearly seen God working in you to accomplish His good purpose.

"Therefore I tell you that no one who is speaking by the Spirit of God says, 'Jesus be cursed,' and no one can say, 'Jesus is Lord,' except by the Holy Spirit." (1 Corinthians 12:3) Verbalize how you know this is so based upon what you've read thus far.

"There are different kinds of gifts, but the same Spirit. There are different kinds of service, but the same Lord. There are different kinds of working, but the same God works all of them in all men." (1 Corinthians 12:4-6) Describe the different gifts and service God has empowered in you to accomplish His work.

"[May God]...equip you with everything good for doing his will, and may he work in us what is pleasing to him, through Jesus Christ...." (Hebrews 13:21). Recall how you have depended upon God's equipping you for His work in you through Jesus.

"But by the grace of God I am what I am, and his grace to me was not without effect. No, I worked harder than all of them—yet not I, but the grace of God that was with me."

(1 Corinthians 15:10) Paul wants to be clear how hard God's grace worked through him. Describe how you know this is so within your daily WALK and TALK as Jesus disciple.

God USES His Word to bring faith into the minds and hearts of believers. Knowing his Word assists us in HIS Work, I would neither encourage or discourage memorizing Scripture for the purpose of faith sharing or witnessing, especially if memorizing verbatim is a real challenge for you. A great Bible is a resource-full Bible. I lean heavily on the Word of God that's equipped with tools, like a thorough concordance. At the back of your version of God's Word, make sure there's an ample listing of words and their Scriptural locations. (Always go and read in its' entirety the reference cited in the concordance. Don't depend upon any fragment as conveying the entire meaning or application you're looking for!)

Another useful tool in God's Word is a center cross-reference. Believe me, you can enhance your time in God's Word many times over by looking up and prospecting through the additional citations scholars have found for you. This lets Scripture interpret Scripture. You will find so many more nuggets of God's gold and silver or His precious gems laden within the caverns of God's mine, the Bible. Just as you wouldn't enter a mine with just your bare hands, a center cross-reference can be the best pick axe the Holy Spirit would equip you with.

Finally, you would benefit from the scholarship of reputable and learned Biblical scholars. Their insights can be found within your Bible in the form of study notes. They know and apply the use of the original languages God chose to communicate

His Word through. You can depend upon their sound teaching to enhance your understanding. Unlike English, the Biblical Hebrew of the Old Testament and the Biblical Greek of the New Testament are quite specific languages that are full blown, vivid high definition color rather than black and white English! They become the enhanced seasoning of what would otherwise be a bland reading.

So, own and use the Bible equipped with tools to find ALL God would have you learn and take with you from His precious Word!

Turning to that very Word of God, here are two proof texts worth chewing and digesting:

- "But as for you, continue in what you have learned and have become convinced of, because you know those from whom you learned it, and how from infancy you have known the holy Scriptures, which are able to make you wise for salvation through faith in Christ Jesus." (2 Timothy 3:14-15)

I saw first hand the influence of my Grandma Wendt's faithful and public reading of God's Word as part of her devotional life. She never hid her time with God. It was out there for anyone to see. Her devotional habits had their influence upon me.

> RM: *Describe your own childhood acquaintance with God's Word, whether it be a parent, grandparent, or a Sunday School teacher who was used by God in such a way.*

- "All Scripture is God-breathed and is useful for teaching, rebuking, correcting and training in righteousness, so that the man of God may be thoroughly equipped for every good work." (2 Timothy 3:16-17)

RM: *Recall how God's Word has been used in your life, causing you to become competent and equipped. How was it taught to you to be used to reprove, correct, and/or train you in righteousness?*

You are a little Christ, a disciple of our Lord Jesus. ACT like Him. Take a stand IN JESUS' love! What would you consider being the testimony of man in contrast to the testimony of God? John brings up this matter of discussion from the point of view of considering how much our WALK impacts upon our TALK. Consider the weight of what we say arising out of what we do. Now compare the difference between a sinful, human being's actions and those of a righteous, holy God at work. Which would you more likely accept and depend upon?

John brings up this argument in 1 John 5:9-12, "We accept man's testimony, but God's testimony is greater because it is the testimony of God, which he has given about his Son. Anyone who believes in the Son of God has this testimony in his heart. Anyone who does not believe God has made him out to be a liar, because he has not believed the testimony God has given about his Son. And this is the testimony: God has given us eternal life, and this life is in his Son. He who has the Son has life; he who does not have the Son of God does not have life."

Know that your testimony has its useful place. Don't neglect sharing it as the Spirit prompts you. The Holy Spirit helped John to recall what Jesus spoke of originally in John 5:31-47. It is the job of the Holy Spirit to provide the assistance we need.

As Jesus points out, "But the Counselor, the Holy Spirit, whom the Father will send in my name, will teach you all things and will remind you of everything I have said to you." (John 14:26)

Jesus challenges His hearers, including us readers, to look to all that God demonstrates through His Word within the lives of people, namely His daily disciples.

Just because we see the activities and hear the testimonies of men, does that confirm and convey the power and purpose of God at work? No, that would not be enough. We would need to see how God's Word itself points back to, and thus testifies or bears witness, of God at work in and through us. We would need a relationship based upon the unconditional love of God. Such a relationship allows God to perform unconditional acts of love towards us. Our testimony would include conversation about how God's unconditional love was at work in and through us during these specific and verifiable circumstances.

The following proof text demonstrates this best: "To this you were called, because Christ suffered for you, leaving you an example, that you should follow in his steps. 'He committed no sin, and no deceit was found in his mouth.' When they hurled their insults at him, he did not retaliate; when he suffered, he made no threats. Instead, he entrusted himself to him who judges justly." (1 Peter 2:21-23)

One need only look at the life witness and example Jesus left for us within the Scriptures. Wouldn't we see how the testimony of God is in sync with all the Scriptures prophesied and fulfilled through Jesus? Don't they confirm Jesus was sent by God and completed all God expected of Him?

> RM: *Peter even shares some specifics here, doesn't*
> *he? Recall some of the aspects of your WALK that*
> *will TALK for you. As you may have heard it said,*
> *"Sometimes we are the ONLY Bible a person will*
> *read." Describe how you are that testimony of God*
> *through living His Word.*

Realize Christ's message will not always be received in the manner to which it is given. Don't take it personally! Understand that they are not rejecting you, but the Christ IN you and ultimately God the Father. Jesus tells us, "He who listens to you listens to me; he who rejects you rejects me; but he who rejects me rejects him who sent me." (Luke 10:16)

How has the Holy Spirit been at work? We would look to the fruit, wouldn't we? We don't have to pull up the roots of a plant to see if there's life through connectivity. The same with us, as we are rooted and grow through our connection with Jesus! It will be evident through the fruit the Holy Spirit bears in our life.

Remember the message of Jesus through us, laden with prophesies and promises made and kept, can either be received or rejected. It has nothing to do with us. It has all to do with God and His offer through His word of gift giving.

If a person is situated in life as the rocky or thorny ground we spoke of earlier, then who will they tend to listen to and respond accordingly? No doubt, the world and the things of this world through the devil. We, who are IN Jesus, born of water and the Spirit through baptism have the Spirit in us. We would hear and believe the things of the Spirit, wouldn't we?

Hear how John describes the challenge we face WALKing and TALKing about the Jesus IN us! "You, dear children, are from God and have overcome them, because the one who is in you is greater than the one who is in the world. They are from the world and therefore speak from the viewpoint of the world, and the world listens to them. We are from God, and whoever knows God listens to us; but whoever is not from God does not listen to us. This is how we recognize the Spirit of truth and the spirit of falsehood." (1 John 4:4-6)

The reception Peter and John received in Acts 4 before the religious leaders was a result of their testimony of the things they had seen and heard. As such their testimony fell on the ears of those in the world, not being influenced by the Spirit of God. It's no doubt as John would say from the previous paragraph, that he writes recalling his own experience going back to Acts 4!

Jesus had predicted back in Matthew 10:15-17, " 'I tell you the truth, it will be more bearable for Sodom and Gomorrah on the day of judgment than for that town. I am sending you out like sheep among wolves. Therefore be as shrewd as snakes and as innocent as doves. Be on your guard against men; they will hand you over to the local councils and flog you in their synagogues.' "

Now, hear the words of the other guy there that day in Acts 4, Peter! He would recognize how often those, not of God would refuse to listen, choosing to respond with persecution, "Who is going to harm you if you are eager to do good? But even if you should suffer for what is right, you are blessed. 'Do not fear what they fear; do not be frightened.' " (1 Peter 3:13-14)

> RM: *Where is the blessing Peter speaks about? How*
> *is this the same blessing Jesus spoke about in His*
> *teaching of the Be-attitudes? " 'Blessed are you when*
> *people insult you, persecute you and falsely say all*
> *kinds of evil against you because of me. Rejoice and*
> *be glad, because great is your reward in heaven, for*
> *in the same way they persecuted the prophets who*
> *were before you.' " (Matthew 5:11-12)*

Peter and John LIVED the experience, gained the blessing, and prayed for MORE! Be encouraged as I am with the following testimony after this first go-around in Acts 4! "On their release, Peter and John went back to their own people and reported all that the chief priests and elders had said to them. When they heard this, they raised their voices together in prayer to God." (Acts 4:23-24) Their prayer, continuing with verse 25, became the testimony of God through the very acts of God: from creation and the fall into sin through to the death and salvation given to us as God's free gift through Jesus.

Unlike the time when the disciples were locked behind closed doors the first day of the week following Jesus' crucifixion "for fear of the Jews" (John 20:19b), hear how they recognized they lived and spoke the testimony of God at work as we read further in Acts 4:28-30: " 'They did what your power and will had decided beforehand should happen. Now, Lord, consider their threats and enable your servants to speak your word with great boldness. Stretch out your hand to heal and perform miraculous signs and wonders through the name of your holy servant Jesus.' "

How did God answer their prayer? "After they prayed, the place where they were meeting was shaken. And they were all filled with the Holy Spirit and spoke the word of God boldly." (Acts 4:31) I wonder if that's where the saying arose, "Be careful what you pray for!"?

> RM: *Would you pray a similar prayer? How would your expectation of God's answer confirm the Holy Spirit was working in and through you? How would you consider this be-attitude necessary if the Holy Spirit is to be working in and through you?*

The testimony of God at work continued in response to that prayer. Peter and the other apostles again were brought before the Sanhedrin in Acts 5 for a time of further testimony and rebuke. Having been flogged and ordered "not to speak in the name of Jesus...the apostles left the Sanhedrin, rejoicing because they had been counted worthy of suffering disgrace for the Name." (Acts 5:40b-41)

The outcome of their testimony is what we need to experience now in our corner of the world! "Day after day, in the temple courts and from house to house, they never stopped teaching and proclaiming the good news that Jesus is the Christ." (Acts 5:42) Are we seeing that growth today because we would not be afraid to LIVE and GIVE the testimony of God at work?

Would we put to rest the devil's "fear-filled" whispering, "What would people think if I spoke about Jesus?" What if we truly let God have His way in and through each of us to reach the Lost before time runs out? Doesn't it get back to, "Less of ME, more of THEE"?

Let's conclude this chapter with a few more powerful proof texts that would point to the same conclusion in the previous paragraph. Do you recall how Peter spoke from experience here? "But in your hearts set apart Christ as Lord. Always be prepared to give an answer to everyone who asks you to give the reason for the hope that you have. But do this with gentleness and respect" (1 Peter 3:15).

> RM: *Consider whether you have had such an opportunity. Why ought you pray daily, asking the Holy Spirit to keep your "opportunity eyes" open for such a time of testimony?*

"Keeping a clear conscience, so that those who speak maliciously against your good behavior in Christ may be ashamed of their slander. It is better, if it is God's will, to suffer for doing good than for doing evil." (1 Peter 3:16-17)

> RM: *If this has happened in your daily discipleship, how was your Lost person getting closer or farther away from accepting God's gift, based upon their response to the Spirit speaking through you?*

"If you are insulted because of the name of Christ, you are blessed, for the Spirit of glory and of God rests on you." (1 Peter 4:14) As it was said of Peter and John, how can people testify that you have been with Jesus (Acts 4:13)? How does it become a fruit-bearing opportunity (Acts 4:29)?

"Be self-controlled and alert. Your enemy the devil prowls around like a roaring lion looking for someone to devour. Resist him, standing firm in the faith, because you know that your brothers throughout the world are undergoing the same kind of sufferings." (1 Peter 5:8-9) Until Jesus returns, the devil persists as God would expect and permit...and respond!

Persecution continues in our day around the world. The attitude and testimony of men hasn't changed since the time of Acts 4 and 5 as we reviewed previously.

God continues to work through the devil's obstacles, and we would pray as these daily disciples did in response! " 'Now, Lord, consider their threats and enable your servants to speak your word with great boldness.' " (Acts 4:29)

> RM: *What obstacles apparently stand between you and your Lost person? What have you been able to identify so far or over time through your prayer-filled conversations with them? How have you been praying for this enabling boldness to let the Holy Spirit speak through you?*

While I've held off trying to insist the Holy Spirit work the way I believe He ought, or provide you with some tried and true plan that includes outlines to memorize and exercise, I will suggest one way you can prayerfully seek God's direction and guidance in the next chapter. I want to say beforehand, that as we have read and heard both in Part One and Part Two of this book, we have to let GOD be God! Do not expect our thoughts and methods to jive with His...or happen according to OUR timetable instead of HIS, as Isaiah 55 and other Scriptures point out!

We have to face and overcome with God's help the obstacle the devil would roll out into our path. The devil would discourage us when we don't see things happening as we think they should and when they should! Yes, how often have you been influenced and held off allowing the Holy Spirit to respond through you during those times? Recognize it for the obstacle it is from the devil. Get on with letting GOD work through you.

Chapter Sixteen

How would the Holy Spirit enable a ladder for His work?

We have read Jesus' desire to leave the 99 sheep safely in the fold while going out to find that one lost sheep. (Matthew 18:10-14) Yes, even for that ONE Jesus came and died for! YES, that UNIQUE one, unlike any other! That's why we have to persistently pray for that ONE based upon the unique needs and soil they have and are! Our relationship with Jack is not the same as with Joe, even though we remain the common denominator in both. Does that make sense?

That's how specific and "honed in" I have to become in my WALKing and TALKing Jesus to them. The more I am used by God to reach those He places in my life, the more I will see these uniquenesses and allow God's Holy Spirit to respond accordingly.

With that in mind, let me cautiously propose an illustration for your prayer-filled consideration. Please let the Holy Spirit do HIS work and have HIS way in response, however! Consider

how we may find different people at a different point on a
ladder as we encounter and move with them as well!

The FIRST Rung
Identification of My Lost Person
WHO? The ONE person in my circle of family, friends, and
associates I will focus my prayers and invite God's performance
upon.

You may have had this person in mind for a long time. Why
did you select this book? Do you want to be used by God to
reach them, but don't know how? LET the praying begin, dear
daily disciple of Jesus! Pray to know or confirm WHO God will
focus His efforts through you and others! Consider re-reading
Chapters Twelve and Thirteen in Part Two of this book so that
you can move to the next rung on the ladder.

The SECOND Rung
Understanding My Lost Person
WHAT? What makes them uniquely Lost?

I want to recall their history, their previous life experiences
within the baggage they carry it in. What condition is their soil
in? What time is it within the season of preparing, planting,
or cultivating before the harvest? That's a lot to unpack, isn't
it? I would suggest keeping some confidential notes because
I believe it helps to see things in print and be able to refer to.
No, you don't have to run out and find a diary with a locking
mechanism! (I don't think they even make those any more,
do you?) I like note cards or loose leaf paper. Both are very
portable and can be stashed away rather than a binder or

notebook. You want to keep a record you can pray over. (More on that in a minute!)

So, as I mentioned previously, have conversations with them that have been prepared in prayer and conducted with prayer. You're on fact and feeling-finding missions, not dominating a conversation or regurgitating their remarks back to them. More listening, less talking! In fact, let your pen be the response shared only with the note card or paper. No, I'm not suggesting you become a stone or wood object, but don't be so quick to answer their questions for them. Try to understand why they're asking their questions.

The THIRD Rung

Praying for My Lost Person

WHERE? Intentional petitions that can be prayed by me and others.

What I have discovered on the Second Rung will be brought up to the Third Rung. I would expect you will be going between these two rungs often in God's use of you! God is a SPECIFIC God! He's a DETAIL oriented God, isn't He? He sees you and your Lost person as unique. As you've heard it said that no two snowflakes are alike, are they?

It's time to get personal and persistent with prayers in response! It's also time to become confidential and maintain confidences, especially in your partnering with others. DON'T invite people you know who can't maintain confidentiality. DO invite people who have a heart for the Lost. They don't have to be outgoing, vocal pray-ERS as long as they've got the Holy Heartburn and will respond accordingly.

The Fourth Rung

Communicating with My Lost Person

SEEING? Following these upward steps as the Holy Spirit provides the opportunities He enables you to see.

As you listen, you want to confirm and move through the conversations into a relationship that grows closer to Jesus and each other. To that end, move as the Holy Spirit moves and opens doors of further discussion. Become both Mary, the sister of Martha and Mary, the mother of Jesus: Sit and listen while pondering what you hear in your heart!

The Fifth Rung

Openness for God Talk

RECEPTIVE? Listening for their interest and questions about their relationship with God.

Without judgment or condemnation, be reminded to be prepared to "give an answer to everyone who asks you to give the reason for the hope that you have. But do this with gentleness and respect..." as we read previously from 1 Peter 3:15b-16a. Follow the Holy Spirit's lead, remembering it is ALL His work. He will provide both the opportunity and the words as we allow Him to! Sometimes tearing items from the daily news is a great starting point for such conversation. "What do you think about....?" Let them start, and you finish with a God-centered reply that takes God's stand without a bullhorn on a soapbox on a street corner!

The Sixth Rung

Gospel Reading and Discussion

HEARING GOD SPEAK?

Invite them to read with you the Gospel According to MARK or JOHN and have a chapter-by-chapter discussion. Get them in God's Word so that they can hear what God has to say to them. "How, then, can they call on the one they have not believed in? And how can they believe in the one of whom they have not heard? And how can they hear without someone preaching to them? And how can they preach unless they are sent? As it is written, 'How beautiful are the feet of those who bring good news!' " (Romans 10:14-15)

You don't have to write a sermon and deliver it. You can converse as you read together God's Word, can't you? Won't that become an opportunity for them to hear God's Word? Recall the power and promise of God's Word, as you read previously in Romans 1:16, as being the power of God and in Isaiah 55: 11, as God's Word achieving the purpose for which it goes forth and is sent.

How will God send you then, in response? You can be sent, like Philip, to explain the good news and gift of God as he did with the Ethiopian eunuch in Acts 8:26-39. Prayerfully consider the who, what, where, and when of doing so. Who will you invite to join your study? What Gospel will you study and will you use an easy to understand version? Where will you hold your study? When will you study and how often?

The Seventh Rung

Fellowship with Other Disciples

PARTNERS? Planned opportunities where my Lost person can do things with other church-based disciples.

I always like to tell people that Christianity is not a religion, but a relationship. Who can I be led by God to invite into this extending relationship with my Lost person? You might be led to look at similarities or shared interests to draw fellow daily disciples into God's service. You might be led to discover unmet needs that could be met by another daily disciple in your fellowship. Activities are opportunities that shouldn't be challenging or putting them "on the spot!" Remember "gentleness and respect"!

Prayerfully consider asking them to come to some activity at church or with church members. Seasonal times when "everybody's doing it" are often potentially receptive in response and participation. Again, KNOW your unique person and gauge their response as you invite them.

As you discuss and pray with your fellow disciple, see if they may have some Spirit-led opportunities. Don't neglect your partner's being inspired and led by the Holy Spirit!

The Eighth Rung

Worship and Bible Class Participation Bears Fruit

INTERACTING WITHIN THE BODY OF CHRIST? Inviting and accompanying your Lost person during Worship and Bible Class opportunities.

Ask the Holy Spirit and your Lost person if it's time to join you for worship and/or Bible class. Knowing their baggage and receptivity, you'll either get a yes or no. Rest assured the research shows upwards of 80% of people are waiting to be invited to a worship service, and WOULD participate if asked! Here, again is why persistent prayer is so necessary, as you move forward by the Holy Spirit and their receptiveness in response! Again, it might be more responsive to invite them for Christmas or Easter services...or the meal-before-the-midweek-service in either or both seasons! Meals can melt those awkward obstacles of not knowing anyone or being the focus as a guest at church!

Regarding Bible Class invitations, ask your Lost person what "they" would be interested in studying. Don't assume a topic is too tough or not very stimulating. Let them decide! ALWAYS accompany them! If you've had them meet others, make sure they link up with them during the same opportunity to help reinforce efforts!

Be in "prayer overtime" after the invitation is accepted, encouraging your fellow PRAY-ers to ask the Holy Spirit for an extra measure of His anointing upon the opportunity.

The Ninth Rung

Faith Achieved...Growing to Go!

HARVEST TIME? Baptism, Catechetical Adult Instruction, and Membership Reception as a result of faith being created by the Holy Spirit through Baptism and God's use of His daily disciples.

Depending upon your own church's means of receiving newborn Christians, you will want to assist where and when ever possible for the connecting of your once Lost person with the Body of Christ.

As they now have become a disciple of Jesus, you would want to encourage them by your own life example to allow God's Holy

Spirit to shape them into a daily disciple. You would also be IN prayer as you invite them to discuss and pray with you and yours about someone God has placed in their life who needs to know Jesus.

NO person, as Lost as they may be, stands so far away from a Father God, whose outstretched arms are waiting to receive them. He stands with forgiveness and an outpouring of unconditional love, just as He did for us! We find this picture in the parable of the Lost Son in Luke 15:11-32.

While you may be familiar with this parable and the other "losts" of sheep and coin, it's this one that most folks can identify with. Whether or not we would admit it, "We all, like sheep, have gone astray, each of us has turned to his own way," as Isaiah confesses (Isaiah 53:6). It's within that entire chapter that God declares the prophecy to be fulfilled through His Son Jesus. Jesus has taken upon us wayward sheep the role of a faithful Shepherd as also prophesied in Ezekiel 34. Both chapters are well worth your prayerful study in light of your WALKing and TALKing as Jesus' discipler!

Not seeing the results WE would expect (i.e. a person coming into a faith relationship with God), we may give up on them and stop praying for them...or even stop thinking about their spiritual needs. This is both tragic and unnecessary! We should be constant in prayer and weekly in conversation with our Lost person. You do not know from day to day or week to week how much closer your Lost person is nearing receptivity to the gift God's Gospel offers. By checking in with them regularly, you let the Holy Spirit's gentle persistence and persuasion show them God (and you and others) CARE through your actions (WALK) and reactions (TALK).

As I've said previously, let the Holy Spirit become your compass or GPS! Know there may be times to "recalculate" by updating your note card or loose leaf sheet. So, don't forget how important it is to listen and make notes in response to what they are telling you...and what you'll be refreshing and refocusing your (and others) prayers for them. Don't become complacent! Keep your trust in the Lord, the Lord's words on your lips, and them in God's hands. God will bless His efforts through you.

Do you believe God will accomplish His will and work through you and others? To what extent? How much proof or confidence do you need? Recall these words to heart and mind and see where they can reveal God's will for you in sharing your faith with them: "The Lord is not slow in keeping his promise, as some understand slowness. He is patient with you, not wanting anyone to perish, but everyone to come to repentance." (2 Peter 3:9)

When there may be times your invitation is rejected, don't take it personally. Jesus encourages each of His daily disciples, "'Whoever acknowledges me before men, I will also acknowledge him before my Father in heaven.'" (Matthew 10:32) Jesus goes on to say, "'He who receives you receives me, and he who receives me receives the one who sent me.'" (Matthew 10:40) Pray inviting the Holy Spirit to keep on offering that cup of cold water in Jesus name, by letting Him do His good works through you! (Matthew 10:42) Truly, the Holy Spirit will enable your WALK and TALK to be IN sync with our Savior Jesus!

Chapter Seventeen

How do disciples help other disciples to disciple?

While serving a congregation as their Outreach and Assimilation Coordinator in a part time capacity for five years, I wrote and spoke and encouraged and invited disciples to join me in discipleship. It was not as nearly as fruitful as I desired. Only a small handful of the same people would respond. The demand was greater than the response.

Why didn't people eagerly respond to the call to go out and visit new neighbors? We purchased the names and addresses of recent move-ins in several surrounding zip codes. We sent letters of information and invitation. We prepared welcome bags. We prepared maps with driving instructions from our church. We advertised and encouraged members to take a few bags and make a few visits on their way home from Sunday service. With an average of over 200 homes per month, we probably only visited and contacted 10%. With such an effort being conducted by less than 12 persons for about one year, we had one elderly couple come and join our church in response. Thank the Lord for the fruit He bore through that endeavor.

Why not more volunteers and more new members in response? I think a lot of it can be "chalked up" to the "we" instead of "Thee" approach.

What? I believe as the dust has settled, the emphasis was not bathed in prayer and dependent upon God or the Holy Spirit. I, myself, as the part time paid staff member shouldered a lot of responsibility. I sought "to prepare God's people for works of service, so that the body of Christ may be built up" (Ephesians 4:12). But did I commit myself and others TO PRAY? Did I expect GOD to accomplish the work He would set out to do? No.

Why? I didn't fully recognize how this was GOD's work and not mine! By that I mean, I depended more upon myself and others and less upon the Holy Spirit. I didn't recognize how much a role prayer plays. Prayer that is specific and persistent. Prayer that acknowledges this IS God's work. Prayer that offers up oneself to God's service and God's working.

The other understanding I came to recognize is this, simply put, "It's hard to expect someone to be out making disciples if they aren't a disciple!" As I said in Part One of this book, there is a real challenge present in Christian circles for daily discipleship, for daily WALKing with Jesus in contrast to Sunday walking!

Sunday walkers will not respond to the invitation to become God's disciple makers. They see no need and have no desire. They even would lack any "nagging guilt" about not responding. "That's somebody else's job! Don't we have Pastor or the Evangelism Board or what about the staff member we pay to do Evangelism and visits?"

No, that's the devil's obstacle. He's the one talking, isn't he? Did you ever come to realize that every response, every excuse for not being the witness Jesus calls as His disciple, is another obstacle set up and maintained by the devil? He does not want to further God's work through individual disciples of Jesus. It's that plain and simple.

What our response ought to be is, "Here am I, Lord! Send me, send me!" What our response ought to be is, "I've got a spiritual heartburn for the Lost that won't be put out!" What our response ought to be is, "Less of me, Lord! More of Thee!"

As we find ourselves becoming more intentional, by identifying Lost people in our daily relationships, the devil will become more intentional in putting up obstacles. What have you seen him doing? How effective has he been? What ought our response to be? Who is greater, the devil or the Holy Spirit at work through the daily disciple of Jesus?

As I mentioned previously, we have the testimony of John, who stood with Peter before the religious leaders and the Sanhedrin in Acts 4 and 5, who speaks from his own experience with this testimony in 1 John 4:4, "You, dear children, are from God and have overcome them, because the one who is in you is greater than the one who is in the world."

Jesus told John and us, " 'In this world you will have trouble. But take heart! I have overcome the world.' " (John 16:33b) John goes on in chapter 17 to write, "After Jesus said this, he looked toward heaven and prayed...." (John 17:1) Have you read John 17? Jesus prayer is filled with petition and promise for His disciples. See how many petitions and promises you can find within this chapter.

RM: *How has God answered those petitions and fulfilled those promises within His discipleship work of you and through you to others?*

Jesus knows the need we disciples have for mentoring, accountability, fellowship, and partnership in His vital and life changing work! That's why He asked the Father for the Holy Spirit's power and presence as we have been sent into the world to carry out His work. He asked the Father that we might " 'have the full measure of my joy within them.' " (John 17:13b)

This full measure of Jesus' joy within us can be seen in our willing response to the Holy Spirit working through us! Jesus prays knowing the world will hate us because we " 'are not of the world any more than' " Jesus is of the world. (John 17:14b) The joy of the world and the joy of heaven can't mix just like the devil and God, sin and holiness, are diametrically opposed to each other.

Jesus knows and Jesus prays, " 'Sanctify them by the truth; your word is truth.' " (John 17:17) The power of the Word of God can also be seen in the sanctifying work God's Word can perform in our daily discipleship. Dining daily on the Bread of Life is vitally necessary, isn't it? We need to be studying and hearing God's Word, whether it be in worship or Bible study. "Consequently, faith comes from hearing the message, and the message is heard through the word of Christ." (Romans 10:17)

Jesus knows, and Jesus prays, " 'My prayer is not that you take them out of the world but that you protect them from the evil one.' " (John 17:15) Doesn't Jesus ask us to pray this petition as often as we pray? " 'And lead us not into temptation, but deliver us from the evil one' " (Matthew 6:13)? Yes, the devil IS real and IS really out to oppose and out to set obstacles before the daily WALKing and TALKing disciples!

God is equally real and is ready to eliminate or transform the devil's obstacles into God's opportunities. James 4:7 gives us the Holy Spirit's mindset and practice we need to be engaged in when the devil's obstacles sit before us! "Submit yourselves, then, to God. Resist the devil, and he will flee from you." As I've heard it said, and try to put into practice, "When the devil comes knocking at your door, send Jesus to answer the door!"

We also have each other, as fellow daily disciples of Jesus, for such a purpose as can be found in 1 Corinthians 7:5, "Do not deprive each other except by mutual consent and for a time, so that you may devote yourselves to prayer. Then come together again so that Satan will not tempt you because of your lack of self-control."

> RM: *How would we benefit by being in partnership AND prayer that the devil's work would be destroyed? Consider how you would share this with another daily disciple not as experienced as you.*

We are not an army of one! We have each other within the Body of Christ. We would look to each other for God's help, and assistance as He gives it to us through our fellow soldiers. "Endure hardship with us like a good soldier of Christ Jesus." (2 Timothy 2:3) We will face hardships. We will face tribulations. We will feel weak and weary. We will need to look to each other, and the strength Jesus can give us.

"Let us not become weary in doing good, for at the proper time we will reap a harvest if we do not give up." (Galatians 6:9)

Do you notice Paul says "we"? Yes, thank God, we're in this together... God, ourselves, and each other! "Therefore, my dear brothers, stand firm. Let nothing move you. Always give yourselves fully to the work of the Lord, because you know that your labor in the Lord is not in vain." (1 Corinthians 15:58)

> RM: *How might the devil cause you to think your work with your Lost person was in vain? How would you respond with such a promise as this one?*

Aren't you encouraged by Paul's recognition of this? God accomplishes His mighty will and work through our partnership together. God tells us that in His Word so that we can read and remind ourselves, "We ought always to thank God for you, brothers, and rightly so, because your faith is growing more and more, and the love every one of you has for each other is increasing. Therefore, among God's churches we boast about your perseverance and faith in all the persecutions and trials you are enduring." (2 Thessalonians 1:3-4) Expect this saying to be true: Where God is at work, the devil is working even harder!"

I would share with you these other Godly directives for our life together, as Jesus daily WALKing and TALKing disciples:

- "Be devoted to one another in brotherly love. Honor one another above yourselves." (Romans 12:10)

- "Now that you have purified yourselves by obeying the truth so that you have sincere love for your brothers, love one another deeply, from the heart." (1 Peter 1:22)

- "But you, dear friends, build yourselves up in your most holy faith and pray in the Holy Spirit. Keep yourselves in God's love as you wait for the mercy of our Lord Jesus Christ to bring you to eternal life." (Jude 20-22)

> RM: *Which of these three would encourage you in your daily discipleship with Jesus? Which one would you find helpful enough to commit to memory to recall?*

As we stand firm together, being built up in our faith, the Holy Spirit is at work in and through each of us. We receive His love, grace, and eternal encouragement SO THAT our hearts would be encouraged and strengthened "in every good deed and word." (2 Thessalonians 2:17) I would encourage you to share these words with the peace of Christ as you encourage others WALKing and TALKing as Jesus daily disciples, "May the Lord direct your hearts into God's love and Christ's perseverance." (2 Thessalonians 3:5)

Despite the devil's obstacles, we would recognize that disciples can help other disciples to disciple! Sharing and recalling the testimonies of God at work in and through us is something we come together to give thanks. Wouldn't we pray with and for each other, as Paul says, "I thank my God every time I remember you. In all my prayers for all of you, I always pray with joy because of your partnership in the gospel from the first time until now" (Philippians 1:3-5)?

> RM: *What blessings have you benefited from the ongoing prayer and support of your partners? What haven't you been sharing and why?*

Within this partnership, the Holy Spirit will join and maintain partnerships with a fulfilling purpose and fruit-full outcome, "being confident of this, that he who began a good work in you will carry it on to completion until the day of Christ Jesus." (Philippians 1:6) The elderly may ask, "Why does God keep my tent up?" The elderly can be encouraged, "Why wouldn't God want you to be used by Him according to His will, not your own?"

Two verses from Psalm 71 are a testimony of God's use of senior adults: "Since my youth, O God, you have taught me, and to this day, I declare your marvelous deeds. Even when I am old and gray, do not forsake me, O God, till I declare your power to the next generation, your might to all who are to come." (Psalm 71:17-18)

Until the day God folds our tent or Jesus returns, He has begun His good work in us and wants to see it finished. Only HE knows what that is...we need to trust Him that He truly knows what's best for us and the Kingdom!

We can be blessed by helping each other grow through the disciple-making process. The Holy Spirit continues His sanctifying work within us. The fruit that Jesus bears through us testifies to the glory of God. Jesus tells us, "This is to my Father's glory, that you bear much fruit, showing yourselves to be my disciples." (John 15:8) It is to the glory of GOD, not to ourselves. We don't take credit for what God does, even through us!

"And this is my prayer: that your love may abound more and more in knowledge and depth of insight, so that you may be able to discern what is best and may be pure and blameless until the day of Christ, filled with the fruit of righteousness that comes through Jesus Christ—to the glory and praise of God." (Philippians 1:9-11) What a prayer is this, packed with so many petitions and intercessions ? Can't you sense the joyful experience that awaits you within the fellowship Jesus puts together and maintains?

"Whatever happens, conduct yourselves in a manner worthy of the gospel of Christ. Then, whether I come and see you or only hear about you in my absence, I will know that you stand firm in one spirit, contending as one man for the faith of the gospel" (Philippians 1:27).

> RM: *How are you working side by side with others for such a purpose? How do you recognize and give thanks for Jesus' strength made perfect through the fellowship of other daily disciples in your WALK and TALK?*

Look to see who God has placed in your life to partner with you. Along with Jesus, who can further the Gospel's work in your Lost person? For that matter, see if God wouldn't bless you with a team of people! Wouldn't this be God pleasing, to truly be in a prayerful partnership with each other? Wouldn't God want to hear and answer such a prayer and any other petitions or intercessions according to His perfect will?

Of course! So, we need to remind each other OF each other, and the common confidence we can have through Jesus IN each other! "This is the confidence we have in approaching God: that if we ask anything according to his will, he hears us. And if we know that he hears us—whatever we ask—we know that we have what we asked of him." (1 John 5:14-15)

I spoke earlier about five years of work as a part time Outreach/ Assimilation coordinator for a church...and how I tried to make MY plan work based on MY thinking and doing, involving whomever would help. It was surely without confidence and surely without asking God for HIS will and work to be done. I'm so glad I recognized that and let God tear down that obstacle of the devil.

That became the turning point for me to realize I had to stop trying to do it on my own, including feeling guilty when the results weren't abundant and apparent. John 21:1-6 was a revelation to me! Peter, the skilled and experienced and passionate fisherman, hadn't caught any fish having been out at work all night. How do you think he felt? (Remember Jesus called him to put down his nets because He was calling him to become a fisher of men in Luke 5:10b?)

If Peter was to become the fisher of men that Jesus called him to be, and then spent nearly three years teaching him, when would he learn he couldn't do it on his own, with his own experience and wisdom dictating his actions?

By acknowledging WHO truly had the ability to catch fish (and men), Peter would realize that only God could find them and catch them. God desired to catch men through Peter. Look at the results when Peter stopped trying and let God start trying? How about 3000 on the day of Pentecost, as Peter let the Holy Spirit speak through him? (Acts 2:41)

> RM: *What can the Holy Spirit accomplish through you and others partnering with you? Who can the Holy Spirit seek and save? How about (insert your Lost person's name here)?*

It all starts with God and allowing Him to cast the net with your hands off the right side of the boat. (Rather than right as opposed to left, right in terms of correct!)

Consider the following questions as you come before God and each other, seeking God's power and work in the life of your Lost person:

- Would you pray for confidence in the Holy Spirit's ability to work God's will for your Lost person?

- Why would you pray for confidence that He will hear and answer your prayers... as you pray His will be done in your Lost person's life?

- Who could God place in your life as a prayer and accountability partner?

- Who would have similar interests or background among the daily disciples you know?

- Who has the holy heartburn evident in their life? Who has a shared burden for the Lost? Who has seen the light of John 21:1-6 and would recognize and call upon the Holy Spirit to do the fishing through you and them?

- What would you prayerfully propose to your pastor or evangelism board in order to receive and interact with your Lost person? Would you need to establish a Gospel of Mark or John study that would be convenient to convene? What resources could your church prepare or provide that would assist the Holy Spirit's efforts through you?

Speaking of prayer, why don't you join with me as we would pray for those TALKing the TALK?

Father God, You stand at the door of our hearts, Your prodigal children and see us not so far off. Your heart goes out to us faster than our arms can reach You. Ever since our first parents fell into sin and separated themselves from You, You prepared a plan that You carried out at the perfect time in our sinful history on Earth. When Your Son said, "It is finished!"...it was! Now, time is running out, but not Your love or desire to bring every created human being back into the fold. Use us, as You see fit, and partner us with others to reach out in whatever way You choose.

Lord Jesus, You are the Good Shepherd, out and about looking to bring those sheep not in Your fold back home. You have given us so much this day that we can focus on. It can be overwhelming. But, nothing is impossible with You. For when we are weak, we are strong. Apart from You, we can do nothing. We have the promise of Your Holy Spirit, so make room in our lives for Him to be at work in and through us!

Holy Spirit, You are the ONLY One who can bring a person into a faith-filled, grace laden life with God through Jesus Christ. Keep our eyes and minds open and ready to channel Your words through our mouths to those ready to hear and receive them. Help us to remember, it's not ME or WE...it's THEE! Keep us faithful and confident in our prayers for the Lost person You have placed in our lives. Create in us faith even as small as a mustard seed. Such a seed will not be planted or germinate or take root on any soil or soul of a person's life except for those ready to receive Your gift of forgiveness and eternal life.

O, Father, Son, and Holy Spirit, be about Your work through our lives and our partners, as only You can enable us to WALK the Walk and TALK the Talk. For Jesus' sake and their soul's salvation, AMEN!

Chapter Eighteen

WILLing to witness?

I invite you to join me in the Holy Spirit's class with the topic, "WILLing to witness?" In case you've not noticed by now, there are two writing stylisms I love to employ: one is alliteration! It doesn't seem to be a difficult thing for me to find words I wish to convey that start with the same letter. Amazing! The other is emphasizing the root of a word by capitalizing it. I want to emphasize the power found within it, or I want to animate its power by offsetting key letters with capitals! (Does it work for you? Am I getting across my intended meaning?)

Just as, I am WILLing to wake up (see, there's the alliteration at work)when God calls class in session, my WILLing witness must be grounded in God's WILL and desire to use me as His voice. It's a conscious commitment to WALK and TALK the words, "Less of me...more of Thee!"

> RM: *What are some things you are more than WILLing to do? If you're living in a multi-person home, do you do your share of the household chores? What would they include or not include? What's your*

attitude about doing them? Do you do them "when you get around to it"? Do you do them when they need to be done? Do you do them with a thankful heart that you can do your part for your household?

BEattitudes are the necessary fuel to generate the power to move a WILLing witness! Jesus' teaching early in His earthly ministry covered tenets He would challenge His daily disciples to BE aware of and BE about doing! These are recorded with some similarities and differences in both Matthew 5:3-11 and Luke 6:20-22. Matthew's account goes into more references to the BEhaviors that would follow our BEattititudes.

I'd like to allow the Holy Spirit to unleash the power of these important words of Jesus. So, instead of making you go and hunt in your Bible to remind yourself at this juncture, just what those BEattitudes are, allow me the opportunity to present them before you now, from Matthew's account.

" 'Blessed are the poor in spirit, for theirs is the kingdom of heaven.

Blessed are those who mourn, for they will be comforted.

Blessed are the meek, for they will inherit the earth.

Blessed are those who hunger and thirst for righteousness, for they will be filled.

Blessed are the merciful, for they will be shown mercy.

Blessed are the pure in heart, for they will see God.

Blessed are the peacemakers, for they will be called sons of God.

Blessed are those who are persecuted because of righteousness, for theirs is the kingdom of heaven.

Blessed are you when people insult you, persecute you and falsely say all kinds of evil against you because of me.

(Matthew 5:3-11)

Have you ever wondered why in these BEattitudes Jesus starts each one with "blessed"? Why is that? For starters, who wouldn't want God's blessings? Who wouldn't want God to smile down upon and shine and shower all His blessings upon us? I can see myself standing outside under the sky, arms extended above my head, and shout to God, "I'm ready, Father! Give me all You've got!" Can't you see yourself in the same way?

Yes, it helps to have a mindset that we would WANT God's blessings. We would WANT them in abundance, as much as we could handle, wouldn't we? I understand Jesus recognizes that in each of us. It's His desire that we receive ALL God has to bless His children with, don't you agree? Let those not just be my words, but another promise from God you can depend upon. Back to the Sermon on the Mount in Matthew's Gospel for just such a promise from God that He keeps!

"If you, then, though you are evil, know how to give good gifts to your children, how much more will your Father in heaven give good gifts to those who ask him!" (Matthew 7:11) James goes on to describe, "Every good and perfect gift is from above, coming down from the Father of the heavenly lights, who does not change like shifting shadows." (James 1:17)

> RM: *Recall some of those good gifts you've received from God. Did you earn them or did God give them to you by His grace and mercy? Which ones did you feel confident asking for?*

Who are we again? Who have we BEcome? Through our baptism, God's Holy Spirit has worked through water, and the very Word of God. He created the new life in each of us that Jesus came and died to give us. As we're reminded in Titus 3:5-7, "he saved us, not because of righteous things we had done, but because of his mercy. He saved us through the washing of rebirth and renewal by the Holy Spirit, whom he poured out on us generously through Jesus Christ our Savior, so that, having been justified by his grace, we might become heirs having the hope of eternal life."

John tells us, "Yet to all who received him, to those who believed in his name, he gave the right to become children of God—children born not of natural descent, nor of human decision or a husband's will, but born of God." (John 1:12-13) Consider your relationship with God as His son or daughter. What aspect of His love for you has God failed to reveal or remind you of? Remember, God has taken us over completely; we are no longer our own. We have been bought with the price of the blood of Jesus Christ, His Son! (1 Corinthians 6:19-20)

We would understand and confess, " We're reborn. We, who were once dead in our sins have been made alive in Jesus!" Remember Romans 6:3, 5? "Or don't you know that all of us who were baptized into Christ Jesus were baptized into his death?... If we have been united with him like this in his death, we will certainly also be united with him in his resurrection." We're renewed as Paul reminds us in Romans 12:2, "Do not conform any longer to the pattern of this world, but be transformed by the renewing of your mind."

The Holy Spirit daily makes us new in our thinking and living. He is enabled with a WILLingness from us for Him to do so because our WILL is no longer ours, but Jesus will! We have a new attitude, which only God's Holy Spirit can give us, "to be made new in the attitude of your minds; and to put on the new self, created to be like God in true righteousness and holiness." (Ephesians 4:23-24) Do you see that in your own life?

Again, because of the daily effects of our baptism, "All of you who were baptized into Christ have clothed yourselves with Christ." (Galatians 3:27) Our wardrobe has changed! The old stuff just doesn't fit any more. No point in holding on to it... throw it out rather than pass it along to someone else! We would give up the clothing of slavery to sin and wear our new WILL and walk our new WAY every day. But, it requires a WILLingness to let the Holy Spirit perform such a work daily in us. "For we know that our old self was crucified with him so that the body of sin might be done away with, that we should no longer be slaves to sin" (Romans 6:6).

Another concept in this verse is from Titus: we have this WILLfullness in abundance without any desire to hold back. That's what I understand when I read Paul's words, "whom He poured out on us generously" (Titus 3:6)! Again I'm reminded that it's not me...but all HE when Paul recognizes how each of us has "been justified by His grace" (Titus 3:7), nothing we have done nor deserved.

What can be challenging sometimes to our understanding and willingness to WALK with Jesus are those times of testing. As we spoke previously in this book, God never tempts! God often tests, however. We've spoken of the value and the outcome of

God's testing us. Such an outcome that after a while, we would prayerfully welcome all God would seek to do in our lives, including testing!

I'm reminded of this verse in the light of God's testing and renewal. It's a testimony from Paul of God at work in his life, and those other daily disciples Paul prayed with. "Therefore we do not lose heart. Though outwardly we are wasting away, yet inwardly we are being renewed day by day." (2 Corinthians 4:16) Do you wonder what caused Paul to think that way about himself and others? Those who were obviously WALKing and TALKing daily disciples of Jesus? You could see it in their lives, on their bodies, within their bodies. Of course, Paul would conclude, tents that are used will get worn out! (Remember, he calls these temporary dwellings from God for us "earthly tents" in 2 Corinthians 5:1-4)

Paul brings up the renewal going on inside of us day by day. "For our light and momentary troubles are achieving for us an eternal glory that far outweighs them all." (2 Corinthians 4:17) Can't you look into the eyes of those first century martyrs, whose tents were going to be ripped to shreds, and know they were just seconds away from obtaining "an eternal glory that far outweighs" all trials, troubles, and testing?

Paul concludes this passage with a directive, an attitude, a perspective we should cast our vision through! "So we fix our eyes not on what is seen, but on what is unseen. For what is seen is temporary, but what is unseen is eternal." (2 Corinthians 4:18). Doesn't that speak to the very contrasting nature of God Our Father? The Lost would see only the temporary as mattering. That's why they would build up their earthly wealth upon themselves. Death will cause them to leave it all behind. After all, isn't it so temporary?

We have come to know the Truth in our Savior and Lord Jesus. We have passports ready for entry into the Kingdom of God and Heaven. Jesus didn't remain dead on the cross, to be taken down, and placed in a tomb. No, death would not withhold that gift God would extend to us through the blood of Jesus. He truly has given us a new self, transformed by Jesus for His purpose!

Paul tells us in Ephesians 4:24, "Put on the new self, created to be like God in true righteousness and holiness." We must BE allowing His Will to work out His Ways, in and through us. His light fills our darkness so that Jesus can be seen through us. The world can see this new self by the fruit we allow Him to bear in and through us!

Back to the BEattitudes

As we take a look at some of these BEattitudes cited within Matthew 5:3-11, consider how they would require a necessary change in your thinking and living, WALKing and TALKing.

BEing poor in spirit towards the things of this world so as to be rich in the things of God's kingdom. " 'But seek first his kingdom and his righteousness, and all these things will be given to you as well.' " (Matthew 6:33) " 'For where your treasure is, there your heart will be also.' " (Matthew 6:21) Both of these verses speak for themselves, don't they, in light of this BEatttitude. They describe the necessary and fundamental change in our WILL becoming God's! We can't become so focused and driven for the things of this world that will perish.

RM: *In light of this BEattitude, are there any aspects of your life and discipleship that you find potential or real struggles? Ask the Holy Spirit to reveal them to you as you speak with a trusted fellow disciple. Once you recognize this, confess this before the Lord and ask for His continual grace and mercy!*

BEing hungry and thirsty for righteousness is a sign of the Holy Spirit's working presence in you. Your diet changes from the things of the flesh to the things of God found within the Word of God. You desire and feed upon the Bread of Life for your spiritual body and soul. As Jesus reminded the devil, " 'Man does not live on bread alone, but on every word that comes from the mouth of God.' " (Matthew 4:4)

Peter describe the young in faith, who would have an appetite, "like newborn babies crave pure spiritual milk, so that by it you may grow up in your salvation." (1 Peter 2:2)

The writer to the Hebrews describes the mature Christian's diet: "solid food is for the mature, who by constant use have trained themselves to distinguish good from evil." (Hebrews 6:14)

RM: *In light of this BEattitude, do you find yourself starving for the milk or meat of God's Word? Ask the Holy Spirit to reveal what has held you back from His milk or meat. Pray and invite regular opportunities for God to feed you and satisfy your spiritual hunger.*

BEing pure in heart enables us to be in the presence of God where we will see Him. I was astonished when I saw the multitude of references to the word "heart" in my concordance.

I can't begin to quote them all. I encourage you to prospect through some of them in order to hear what God has to say about a heart that's been made right by the blood of Jesus! The mind is always tied to the heart as we've come to recognize the heart is often the seat of our emotions.

Love itself is recognized with a heart. Can you imagine the unconditional love that flows from the heart of God? Can't you see God's heart demonstrated by His will at work in our daily discipleship? I would encourage you to prospect and study 1 Corinthians 2:6-16 in light of this BEattitude. " 'No eye has seen, no ear has heard, no mind has conceived what God has prepared for those who love him' – but God has revealed it to us by his Spirit." (1 Corinthians 2:9-10)

> RM: *In light of this BEattitude, do you find yourself, not living and loving the way God desires? Ask the Holy Spirit to reveal what obstacles of the devil stand between you and the heart of God being channeled through you. Pray and ask the Holy Spirit to guard your heart and mind in Jesus.*

Has this discussion of the BEattitudes BEgun a change in your way of thinking and BEing? How would you respond with such a change in your thinking? Would you offer a willing and ready heart and will for God to use? In whatever way He would know best? Do you recognize what you were in your past before Jesus saving work in your life? Do you recognize what you are in your present life as the Holy Spirit has begun His sanctifying work in your life?

Our will and ways are weak. God's will and ways are strong. When it comes to WALKing and TALKing as Jesus' daily disciple, we can't do it! Not just because Jesus tells us, but also because we've experienced it for ourselves, haven't we?

ALL that we have received from God through our baptism is not just our start, but our continuation. The opportunities God shares with us each day are not only amazing; they're exciting! Look at all those earthly possessions we must simply have, like little children during Christmas.

Wouldn't it be better for me (and you?) if I could scale it all away so that my home and heart and hands would be empty of any obstacle between me and God? Recall Jesus' teaching in Matthew 6:19-24 about the true treasures in heaven. Contrast what the world believes are the things of this life worth worrying over with how we can rejoice and be glad in all the Lord has given us for this day as you read Matthew 6:25-34!

Couldn't it be an answer to prayer, "Less of me, more of Thee!" if I had more room for God in my life? For all I've journeyed through with God, I've come to see the blessing in the BEattitudes simplify my life so that I welcome HIS intended blessings for me! The kinds of blessings He truly knows are not of this world. The kinds of blessings that last for eternity.

All that we know is that we have today! (We may not even have all of today!) The blessed child of God, empowered by God to live His BEattitudes, takes such an inventory and prays for answers to the following questions:

- What will the Lord accomplish today through me?

- How will the Lord direct and guide my footsteps as we WALK together?

- What opportunities will the Holy Spirit open before me so that He can speak just the right message for just the right receiving person?

- What more motivation do I need to let the Holy Spirit loose in my life?

- What more must I see or hear to convince me that Jesus is real and really wants to bear the fruit of the Holy Spirit's words through me?

Having God's Word, reading God's Word, applying God's Word with the Holy Spirit's daily discipleship of me is so necessary, so vital! Not only is God's Word the spiritual food my soul seeks, it is the means by which my will can be more fully transformed into God's will. I have come to know who Jesus really is and why He is obedient to Our Father. I have come to know through His example why I am to be obedient to Our Father.

Consider ALL that God tells us about His wonderful work in the lives of those saints who have gone on before us. It's so encouraging to recognize He's the same God who wants to accomplish His wonderful work through me! Will I let Him? Will I let His will become mine? Will I let the Holy Spirit set my compass or GPS according to God's position or destination?

My will can so easily become God's will when I read and respond to His Word in my Bible.

I wasn't an eye witness. But I have received the blessing Jesus speaks about when He says to Thomas, "Blessed are those who have not seen and yet have believed." (John 20:29b) I didn't see any of the "many other miraculous signs" which Jesus did "in the presence of his disciples, which are not recorded" in God's Word (John 20:30). But as I've come to read and reflect upon them, the Holy Spirit responds with an ever growing faith and confidence in Jesus. I learn of this same Jesus through His Word, "But these are written that you may believe that Jesus is the Christ, the Son of God, and that by believing you may have life in his name." (John 20:31)

I didn't walk down the road to Emmaus that Easter afternoon to discover the resurrected Jesus explaining "what was said in all the Scriptures concerning himself." (Luke 24:27b) I didn't sit in His company at the table with them when "he took bread, gave thanks, broke it, and began to give it to them." (Luke 24:30) But as I received Jesus' very body and blood in, with, and under the bread and wine in His Holy Communion, I can testify that I, too, have the Holy Heartburn those two daily disciples of Jesus had! I can ask with them, "Were not our hearts burning within us while he talked with us on the road and opened the Scriptures to us?" (Luke 24:32)

I didn't stand with Peter and John as they met the crippled beggar at the temple gate Beautiful. I didn't hear them say, " 'Silver or gold I do not have, but what I have I give you. In the name of Jesus Christ of Nazareth, walk." (Acts 3:6) But I can read within the Word of God and testify "with wonder and amazement at what had happened to him." (Acts 3:10b)

Nor did I stand with Peter and John before the crowd of believers and non-believers after the crippled beggar was healed. Like Peter and John, I would consider myself as one with them, "unschooled, ordinary men." (Acts 4:13) Having read God's Word and the testimony of God at work, I would be led by God's Holy Spirit to confess with them, "For we cannot help speaking about what we have seen and heard." (Acts 4:20) I find as God enables me, I, too, can speak with joy and boldness about all the things I have seen and heard God do in my life.

It truly is something when you experience God's purpose fulfilled by His power in and through your life. I have tasted and seen that the Lord is good! I have been a recipient of God's enduring love. I may not always know God's thoughts and ways, and I'm fine with that. After all, He IS God, you know? Don't I have to let Him BE Who He is so that I can speak from my heart these words from Psalm 117?

"Praise the Lord, all you nations; extol him, all you peoples. For great is his love toward us, and the faithfulness of the Lord endures forever. Praise the Lord." (Psalm 117)

It remains my prayer for you: BE in the WORD of GOD DAILY, dear WALKing and TALKing disciple. As you study His Word, "Do your best to present yourself to God as one approved, a workman who does not need to be ashamed and who correctly handles the word of truth." (2 Timothy 2:15)

You will see for yourself if you haven't already, "we are God's workmanship, created in Christ Jesus to do good works, which God prepared in advance for us to do." (Ephesians 2:10)

We may not always know the how, what, where, when or why! But, BE confident in knowing He DOES! Just let Jesus' will and willingness become yours. Through the fruit He will bear in your life, those once Lost will be found!

Chapter Nineteen

In the end, what more can be said?
Perhaps I ought to pray instead?

You have read so much within both the WALK and the TALK of a Disciple, two parts contained in this one book. Are you experiencing a brain freeze or information overload? Have you had the opportunity to put this book down several times just to squeeze the sponge free of all that you absorbed in order to absorb more?

Can any more be said or done on the topic of this book? I don't believe so. I believe you've been given plenty by God's own Holy Spirit. Through His Word, I pray God will convince you to BE actively asking for everything you need from God to GROW and GO as His daily disciple.

What I can say is that we never pray enough! Would you agree? As I've suggested previously, our will and way of praying ought to be priority number 1! We ought to pray as a first fruits response within our relationship with God, Father, Son, and Holy Spirit...and NOT offer our prayertime to God as lousy leftovers, just so that we can be getting on with other things!

So, I'd like to take the lead by example, and offer up to you some heartfelt, head-processed prayers you may choose to employ as you daily WALK and TALK with and for Jesus.

Let these words percolate in the coffee pot of your prayer life. Put them in your slow cooker and ponder them. See if you can't find a single line that would serve as a prayer point you would persistently ponder. Then, when you've chewed and savored all the flavor out of it, move on to the next bite!

As I wrote these words on the evening of Ascension Day entering the early morning hours, I believe these words from Hebrews 4:14-16 are an appropriate dedication to the following prayers. "Therefore, since we have a great high priest who has gone through the heavens, Jesus the Son of God, let us hold firmly to the faith we profess. For we do not have a high priest who is unable to sympathize with our weaknesses, but we have one who has been tempted in every way, just as we are—yet was without sin. Let us then approach the throne of grace with confidence, so that we may receive mercy and find grace to help us in our time of need." (Hebrews 4:14-16)

May you recognize Jesus' kneeling presence in your life. Recall that Jesus not only kneels to wash your feet, but lifts up your heart felt prayers to Our Father. As our great high priest, Jesus knows our needs and brings them before Our Father faithfully.

Prayers for and by WALKing Daily Disciples of Jesus

Starting the Day in His Way

Heavenly Father, I am so thankful You have granted me another day's journey with You. As I begin with You, I ask for Your mercy and grace upon my way today. You have such fruit-filled plans for me. Cause my will to disappear into Yours as You would lead me and guide me. Keep my opportunity eyes open, Holy Spirit! May I always welcome Your use of my tongue to speak Your words. By the end of this day, may I have travelled one day closer to my eternal home, which You have prepared for me, dear Jesus, because of Your love for me. In Your Name, I ask this. Amen.

Before the Word

I give You thanks, Our Father, for Your sweet words I would find and feed upon today in my Bible. You have placed before me all the truths that would lead me and guide me along life's way. Would You bless me, Father God, with a glimpse of Your presence in my life today? Would you lead me, Holy Spirit, to the lesson You have prepared just for me to learn this day? Would You show me, dear Savior Jesus, how I might do unto others what I would do for You? Speak through Your Word that I might GROW and GO forth in Your light and love this day. In Jesus Name, Amen.

As I Pray

Dear Savior Jesus, Who having ascended to Our Father, now lives to make intercession for us. Keep my thoughts fixed and focused on You alone! Cause me not to drift away from Your will with self-centered prayers and petitions! Turn my heart and mind to see the needs of others before my very own. As You love to hear and answer our prayers, may I pray for Your will to be done, as I come before You now. May the supplications I bring before You be answered with Your ample strength. May You supply all our needs IN Christ Jesus, to whom I call upon and pray. Amen.

When I Doubt or Question

Do I have Your permission, O God, to doubt or question what captivates my mind for the moment? "Why?" keeps relentlessly whispering in my ears. I can't seem to dismiss it! While I know You are God, whose ways and thoughts are ever higher than mine, arrest this restless spirit with Your strong arms of love and mercy. Help me, dear Savior, to hear Your voice! Once in human flesh and confronted by all manner of doubt and temptation, You understand my questioning the circumstances confronting me. Give me the patience of Your love to recognize ALL You can accomplish in response to this opportunity. May I give You all thanks and praise now for this blessing You alone would bestow. For Jesus' sake, I ask this, Amen.

Prayers for and by TALKing Daily Disciples of Jesus

Speak, O Holy Spirit, Speak!

I am so grateful and thankful, Holy Spirit, that You would choose to use me to speak Your words of mercy, forgiveness, and grace. Keep my eyes and ears open and responsive to the opportunities You will create this day. Let not my head or my heart cause me to go to the right or to the left of the person You would place in front of me! As the devil is walking about, seeking to place an obstacle in front of me, roll away any stone the devil would put between me and Thee! Help me experience the boldness and power of the Gospel at work in and through me. May my WALK with Jesus enable Your words, O Holy Spirit, to speak volumes! In Jesus Name, I ask all these things! Amen.

Fill me with Your Spirit

I stand before You as Your temple, Holy Spirit. While You would never leave me or forsake me, I always need Your renewing power and presence. Renew my heart and refresh Your Spirit within me. Proclaim Your love and forgiveness through Your words of testimony shared with others. May Your Spirit cast the light of Christ upon God's ongoing work in me. May my days be filled with songs of thankfulness and praise. Sing Your songs through me, Holy Spirit, that they would be a sweet melody heard by all, for Jesus' sake, Amen!

When I can't speak or pray

Holy Spirit, there are times when I find myself unable to speak or pray. The devil would throw obstacles of fear before me. The devil would desire my heart not to feel a burden for the Lost person, who just doesn't seem to be responding to You. Not only would I no longer wish to speak or pray for them, I'm at the point of giving up! Arrest my weak will, Holy Spirit. Disable the devil's desire to derail Your work through me! Remind me... "Less of me, more of Thee!" Help me not to grow weary so that, according to Your will, I might reap the harvest You would desire to produce in this Lost person. In Jesus' Name, I pray! Amen.

Less Talking, More Listening, Lord!

Dear Jesus, my heart-felt desire is to be used by You! I so much want to be your WALKing and TALKing daily disciple. Re-ignite the humble, holy heartburn You show to me in Your Word! Help me, Holy Spirit, not to speak when I should listen. Help me, Holy Spirit, not to dominate the discussion You would welcome with the Lost person You have placed in my life. Help me, Holy Spirit, to sense Your timing and see Your opening to speak. Let me learn from listening what I can be praying for. Let me learn from listening how receptive their soul's soil has begun in response to Your Word planted. Let me learn from listening what more I or others need to be ready to respond. Thank You for Your guidance and direction for Jesus' sake, Amen.

Our time in God's Word can be Prayer-Filled, too!

Take to heart these words, as you would see opportunities through God's WALK to become God's TALK through you!

" I seek you with all my heart; do not let me stray from your commands. I have hidden your word in my heart that I might not sin against you. Praise be to you, O Lord; teach me your decrees. With my lips I recount all the laws that come from your mouth. I rejoice in following your statutes as one rejoices in great riches. I meditate on your precepts and consider your ways. I delight in your decrees; I will not neglect your word." (Psalm 119:10-16)

As I prospected and pondered the richness within this Word of God, prayers flowed through me in response. I'm including them as a testimony of the work of God to instruct and inspire you. May He instruct and inspire you as He would generate prayers for WALKing and TALKing daily disciples like you and me!

I open up my heart, my mind, and my will to You, O Lord!
ALL thanks and praise, glory and honor, to You, O Lord! Amen.

Pour Your water upon me, O Holy Spirit,
and flush out all the impurities of a self
centered in sin! Amen.

Take, Holy Spirit,
the shortness of my breath
and extend it to touch the soul of another! Amen.

Fall fresh upon me, Holy Spirit,
that I might write and recite
Your heart's desire for me and Thee. Amen.

Suspend upon this soul of mine
Your wisdom, Spirit,
Your joy Divine. Amen.

With a cross in my pocket,
let His love shine through my heart.
May my feet never walk so heavy
lest from Thee, dear Lord, depart! Amen.

Singing songs of thanks and praise
from the stillness of my heart
causes joy to spring eternal
through His love He deigns to impart. Amen.

Rhyming rhythms of my soul
His Spirit speaks to me.
Cleansing thoughts that would be Heavenward
brings me back, O Lord, to Thee! Amen.

Jingle, jangle, jingle, jangle,
gone the chains! I've been set free!
Cause me now, O Holy Spirit,
Sing Your new song sung by Thee!
Sing Your new song sung through me! Amen.

With a sigh,
I hear my heart cry:
Less of me, Lord!
More of Thee! Amen.

Will you come to know my Jesus?
He stands before you to forgive!
Each and every sin you carry
Give to Him, be no more grim!
For He knows the weight you carry,
Need no longer in sin tarry!
Give it all, dear child, to Him! Amen.

Speak, O Lord, to one so weak,
blessed promises You keep!
Strengthen arms and strengthen feet.
Cause me walk, Thy mercy greet! Amen.

Blessed Holy Trinity,
Be my all in all for Thee!
Capture now my heart's desire,
Set my will ablaze on fire!

May my will no longer be!
Strengthened, nourished
alone by Thee! Amen!

Let me rest, Lord. Linger near!
Speak Your words,
O Spirit dear!
From Your heart, dear Father, BE
all the blessings You grant to me! Amen.

Father, Son and Holy Ghost
Only Thee, I adore the most! Amen.

May I praise Thee ever more,
Father, Savior, Spirit SOAR!
Within my heart, Your chamber be
Kept aglow by love from Thee, Amen!

Blessed fellowship with me
grant Your child, blessed Trinity.
Father, Son and Spirit, adore!
Make my home forever more, Amen.

As I've read and prayed these prayers over again, I've sensed
the Spirit's presence and desire to produce such abundant
good fruit within each of us. How about you? I know as I read
God's promises in His Word, these aren't just words! They are
promises He keeps as He fulfills them throughout our daily
discipleship.

What words of Scripture or prayer has God placed on your
heart, within your hearing? Don't keep them to yourself! Won't
you share them with others? "Where?" You may ask? Talk to

your church secretary, who is always looking for input from members for the church newsletter or worship folder. Perhaps your pastor is looking for some prayers from the people of God for the people of God? You can also share them with me via email at randy@WALKingandTALKingMinistries.com

I look forward to praying with you across the miles and months! Truly, God's RICHEST blessings be lavished upon You because He truly loves you, dear daily WALKing and TALKing disciple!

Chapter Twenty

Final thoughts and a prayer

Have we arrived here already, the last chapter? I pray you've been able to hear God's voice. He alone has provided these words to instruct and inspire you along your daily discipleship with Jesus!

Did you grow up having the opportunity I had when you went to the dentist? After everything was done, no matter how good or bad you had been in your dental care, did the dental assistant re-enter the room after the dentist said, "See you next time"? Did she have clutched in her hands the reason why you endured that seemingly endless time ? Did she present to you a treasure chest filled with all kinds of little toys?

Sure, I know some of you grown ups would think, "How can a toy that probably cost the dentist about a quarter at the most be so rewarding?" But, for this six year old, they were treasures indeed! It was worth the pain and torture as I squirmed in the chair! Just so that I could dig into that treasure chest! How about you?

With that recollection in mind, let me ask, "Have you found all the daily treasure God wants you to find in your Bible?"

"My son, if you accept my words and store up my commands within you, turning your ear to wisdom and applying your heart to understanding, and if you call out for insight and cry aloud for understanding; and if you look for it as silver and search for it as hidden treasure, then you will understand the fear of the Lord and find the knowledge of God." (Proverbs 2:1-5)

I've informed, instructed, and inspired you to prospect through God's Word. Be looking for the gold or silver nuggets or the precious gems or jewels God wants you to find for your very own!

- "And the words of the Lord are flawless, like silver refined in a furnace of clay, purified seven times." (Psalm 12:6)

- "He tunnels through the rock; his eyes see all its treasures. He searches the sources of the rivers and brings hidden things to light. But where can wisdom be found? Where does understanding dwell? Man does not comprehend its worth; it cannot be found in the land of the living." (Job 28:10-13)

- "Blessed is the man who finds wisdom, the man who gains understanding, for she is more profitable than silver and yields better return than gold. She is more precious than rubies; nothing you desire can compare with her." (Proverbs 3:13-16)

- "The ordinances of the Lord are sure and altogether righteous. They are more precious than gold, than much pure gold." (Psalm 19:9-10)

It's my prayer throughout both parts of this book, you've come to find some new nuggets or gems from God's Word. Perhaps you've even reclaimed treasures you once found yourself!

It's fitting that these be the closing thoughts for you, daily disciple of Jesus. As you are enabled by the Holy Spirit, may you be blessed as Jesus leads you on the journey. It's a journey He leads you to the home He has prepared for you with our Heavenly Father.

Hear then and marvel at the beauty and luster of God's words of encouragement, direction and power for both your WALK and TALK with and for Him! Don't keep them to yourself. Don't hide them from others the Holy Spirit would desire you to share with them.

- "Therefore, brothers, since we have confidence to enter the Most Holy Place by the blood of Jesus, by a new and living way opened for us through the curtain, that is, his body, and since we have a great priest over the house of God, let us draw near to God with a sincere heart in full assurance of faith, having our hearts sprinkled to cleanse us from a guilty conscience and having our bodies washed with pure water. Let us hold unswervingly to the hope we profess, for he who promised is faithful. And let us consider how we may spur one another on toward love and good deeds. Let us not give up meeting together, as some are in the habit of doing, but let us encourage one another—and all the more as you see the Day approaching." (Hebrews 10:19-25)

- "Finally, brothers, we instructed you how to live in order to please God, as in fact you are living. Now we ask you and urge you in the Lord Jesus to do this more and more. For you know what instructions we gave you by the authority of the Lord Jesus. It is God's will that you should be sanctified..." (1 Thessalonians 4:1-3a)

- "May God himself, the God of peace, sanctify you through and through. May your whole spirit, soul and body be kept blameless at the coming of our Lord Jesus Christ. The one who calls you is faithful and he will do it." (1 Thessalonians 5:23-24)

- "I want to know Christ and the power of his resurrection and the fellowship of sharing in his sufferings, becoming like him in his death, and so, somehow, to attain to the resurrection of the dead. Not that I have already obtained all this, or have already been made perfect, but I press on to take hold of that for which Christ Jesus took hold of me. Brothers, I do not consider myself yet to have taken hold of it. But one thing I do: Forgetting what is behind and straining toward what is ahead, I press on toward the goal to win the prize for which God has called me heavenward in Christ Jesus." (Philippians 3:10-14)

- "But Zion said, 'The Lord has forsaken me, the Lord has forgotten me.' 'Can a mother forget the baby at her breast and have no compassion on the child she has borne? Though she may forget, I will not forget you! See, I have engraved you on the palms of my hands; your walls are ever before me.' " (Isaiah 49:14-16)

• "But now, this is what the Lord says—he who created you, O Jacob, he who formed you, O Israel: 'Fear not, for I have redeemed you; I have summoned you by name; you are mine. When you pass through the waters, I will be with you; and when you pass through the rivers, they will not sweep over you. When you walk through the fire, you will not be burned; the flames will not set you ablaze. For I am the Lord, your God, the Holy One of Israel, your Savior' " (Isaiah 43:1-3a).

• "This is what God the Lord says—he who created the heavens and stretched them out, who spread out the earth and all that comes out of it, who gives breath to its people, and life to those who walk on it: 'I, the Lord, have called you in righteousness; I will take hold of your hand. I will keep you and will make you to be a covenant for the people and a light for the Gentiles, to open the eyes that are blind, to free captives from prison and to release from the dungeon those who sit in darkness.' " (Isaiah 42:5-7)

• "Therefore, since we have been justified through faith, we have peace with God through our Lord Jesus Christ, through whom we have gained access by faith into this grace in which we now stand. And we rejoice in the hope of the glory of God. Not only so, but we also rejoice in our sufferings, because we know that suffering produces perseverance; perseverance, character; and character, hope. And hope does not disappoint us, because God has poured out his love into our hearts by the Holy Spirit, whom he has given us." (Romans 5:1-5)

- "Therefore, if anyone is in Christ, he is a new creation; the old has gone, the new has come! All this is from God, who reconciled us to himself through Christ and gave us the ministry of reconciliation: that God was reconciling the world to himself in Christ, not counting men's sins against them. And he has committed to us the message of reconciliation. We are therefore Christ's ambassadors, as though God were making his appeal through us. We implore you on Christ's behalf: Be reconciled to God. God made him who had no sin to be sin for us, so that in him we might become the righteousness of God." (2 Corinthians 5:17-21)

- "Do not be anxious about anything, but in everything, by prayer and petition, with thanksgiving, present your requests to God. And the peace of God, which transcends all understanding, will guard your hearts and your minds in Christ Jesus." (Philippians 4:6-7)

- "Let the word of Christ dwell in you richly as you teach and admonish one another with all wisdom, and as you sing psalms, hymns and spiritual songs with gratitude in your hearts to God. And whatever you do, whether in word or deed, do it all in the name of the Lord Jesus, giving thanks to God the Father through him." (Colossians 3:16-17)

- "But join with me in suffering for the gospel, by the power of God, who has saved us and called us to a holy life—not because of anything we have done but because of his own purpose and grace." (2 Timothy 1:8b-9)

- "I always thank my God as I remember you in my prayers, because I hear about your faith in the Lord Jesus and your love for all the saints. I pray that you may be active in sharing your faith, so that you will have a full understanding of every good thing we have in Christ. Your love has given me great joy and encouragement, because you, brother, have refreshed the hearts of the saints." (Philemon 4-7)

Let's PRAY!

It continues to be a blessing, Lord Jesus, to be on the journey You lead us daily through our baptism. These Scriptures we have prospected out of the wealth of Your Word are treasures indeed! As we savor them, read and re-read them over and over, may our hearts and minds be renewed daily as Your disciples. May we remain fully rooted and cultivated as a living branch to you, our living Vine. May we remain faithful as You prune us in order that You would be able to produce even more abundant good fruit through us!

Holy Spirit, keep Your holy heartburn ablaze in our spiritual lives and bodies. May You have full access through us to the Lost and De-Churched You continue to seek within our relationships with them. Keep our bodies in a responsive posture of persistent prayer. Keep our eyes open to the opportunities only You can provide. Keep our ears attentive to all conversation You would enable. Keep our mouths responsive with Your words spoken according to Your perfect will and timing.

Father God, we can't thank You enough for being Our Faithful Father! We love You because You first loved us. You tell us You love us. You show us You love us. You invite us to be Your redeemed children through the blood of Jesus. You invite us to be used by Your Holy Spirit to seek and save the Lost! Thank You for daily continuing to provide opportunities for transforming or replacing all the obstacles our enemy, the devil, would seek to place before our WALKing and TALKing for you!

Keep us ever faithful and ever fruitful until You fold our tents and bring us into our heavenly reward!

In Jesus' Name, we ask all these things!

Amen!

A Word about WALKing and TALKing Ministries (WTM)

As I am writing this, God has been at work for seven months opening an opportunity to teach my three main courses in Myanmar at The Lutheran Bible Training Institute for hungry, Burmese daily disciples of our Savior and Lord Jesus. Who would have ever thought WTM would have an opportunity to literally go into all the world as Jesus asks us in Matthew 28:19-20? Isn't that the fruit that Jesus can bear through us if we remain abiding and obedient IN Him?

Who knows what the next opportunity will be opened by God by the time this book "hits the stands"?

While preparing the WALK/TALK Cross for the cover, over the course of several days, God's own Holy Spirit inspired me to further utilize an ancient symbol known as the Jerusalem Cross as both a personal cross for each of us to carry as well as the logo for WTM.

Truly, the WTM logoed Jerusalem Cross speaks of the directing Holy Spirit revealing His desire to use WTM and me to fulfill His expectations for me, Randy Michael Wendt, in response to Matthew 28:19-20. I'm inserting a rendition done by a dear brother IN Christ, Paul E. Opel, whose father and my father were both confirmed in the Lutheran Christian faith in Detroit in 1944. (Small world, isn't it?)

As it was given to me, the name of Jesus Christ appears on the arms of the Cross, as would His very arms. It is the work and message of Jesus' sacrifice on the Cross that we are engaged in the WALK and TALK, as you see them intersecting in the center of the cross.

At the bottom, the Latin word "Formatio" referring to the Holy Spirit forming us like sanctifying clay into the vessel He will pour Himself into daily, inviting Him and remembering His indwelling power

At the top, the Latin word "Missio" refers to why the Holy Spirit does His work in and through us. We are being sent daily into our world on His mission to be used by Him to make disciples.

The four crosses, for me, represent the places where God continues to open doors of opportunity for WTM , whether presently in the Americas and Asia, then Africa and Europe. To each of those continents God has been at work claiming the lost sheep. The harvests continue to be carried out. There remains an abundance of open opportunities for obedient daily disciples to be used by God in harvesting!

Won't you consider taking the next step upon finishing this book? What that would be only God knows! You will come to know it as you faithfully follow Jesus' words in Matthew 7:7, quoted throughout this book, and summarized by me again, "Ask and keep on asking God how He might use you! Seek and keep on seeking for the open opportunities He alone can provide for you! Knock and keep on knocking through emails, phone calls, face to face meetings with those on the other side of the door, literally the other side of your world, who wish to know about discipleship and disciplemaking as you've come to know and experience them.

I also invite you to check out the ever evolving WALKing and TALKing Ministries website.

www.WALKingandTALKingMinistries.com
Don't worry, you can keep the address all lower case letters! Don't you know my style by now?

Be on the prayerfull look out for more books as the Holy Spirit inspires me to write His words and teachings. I anticipate a second book to be forthcoming, also published by WestBow Press. It is with the gracious financial support of my dear brother and sister in Christ, Brian and Kim, that have made this book and that book possible!

I also invite the Spiritual Body Builders who've emerged from their gyms to write and tell me how their training is going, what they've found helpful to share with others, and how I can come alongside to pray and encourage you. Please address your email to randy@walkingandtalkingministries.com

Blessings as you remain obedient to His daily opportunities, BEcoming HIS daily WALKing and TALKing disciple for Jesus' sake!

Randy Michael Wendt, Director

WALKing and TALKing Ministries

John 15:16